# MOSES
## *MAN OF GOD*

LOREN VANGALDER

SPIRITUAL FATHER PUBLICATIONS

All scripture quotations, unless otherwise indicated, are taken from the *Holy Bible*, New International Version®, NIV®. Copyright ©1973, 1978, 1984, 2011 by Biblica, Inc.™All rights reserved worldwide. The "NIV" and "New International Version" are trademarks registered in the United States Patent and Trademark Office by Biblica, Inc.™

Copyright © 2017 by Loren VanGalder. All rights reserved.

ISBN-10: 0-9982798-8-9

ISBN-13: 978-0-9982798-8-6

# TABLE OF CONTENTS

INTRODUCTION...1

PART ONE: THE MISSION BEGINS: FROM THE BURNING BUSH TO PHARAOH'S COURT...3

1 WATCH OUT FOR THE BURNING BUSH! (IT COULD CHANGE YOUR LIFE!) *(EXODUS 3:1–12)*...5

2 SIX STEPS TO GET THE MISSION MOVING *(EXODUS 4:27–5:21)*...15

3 WHY, LORD? *(EXODUS 5:22–23)*...23

4 GOD'S ANSWER TO "WHY?": KEEP GOING! *(EXODUS 6:1)*...29

5 HOW TO MOVE FORWARD WITH CONFIDENCE *(EXODUS 6:2–12 & 6:28–7:13)*...33

6 THE PLAGUE OF DARKNESS *(EXODUS 10:21–29)*...41

PART TWO: INTO THE WILDERNESS: THE FIRST DAYS OF FREEDOM...47

7 DELIVERANCE! *(EXODUS 12:31–41)*...49

8 READY FOR BATTLE? *(EXODUS 13:17–22)*...53

9 BETWEEN A ROCK AND A HARD PLACE *(EXODUS 14)*...59

10 WORSHIP! *(EXODUS 15:1–21)*...71

PART THREE: TESTING AND TEACHING IN THE WILDERNESS...81

11 RELIEF IS JUST AHEAD! *(EXODUS 15:22–27)*...83

12 THE DESERT OF SIN *(EXODUS 16:1–12)*...93

13 HOW WELL DO YOU FOLLOW DIRECTIONS? *(EXODUS 16:13–35)*...103

14 DEALING WITH THE DRY PLACES *(EXODUS 17:1–7)*...113

15 THE FIRST BATTLE *(EXODUS 17:8–16)*...121

16 MOSES THE FAMILY MAN *(EXODUS 18:1–12)*...129

17 SOMEONE TO LOOK OUT FOR YOU *(EXODUS 18:13–27)*...135

PART FOUR: MOUNT SINAI: MEETING GOD...143

**18** THE PROPOSAL: GOD'S INVITATION TO COVENANT RELATIONSHIP *(EXODUS 19:1-9)*...145

**19** THE WEDDING: SEALING THE COVENANT *(EXODUS 19:10-25; 20:18-21)*...151

**20** HOW TO DEFEAT YOUR ENEMIES *(EXODUS 23:20-33)*...159

**21** ARE YOU READY TO MEET GOD? *(EXODUS 24)*...169

**22** A GOLDEN CALF EMERGES FROM THE FIRE *(EXODUS 32)*...177

**23** THE HEART OF A MAN OF GOD *(EXODUS 32)*...185

**24** I WON'T GO WITHOUT GOD'S PRESENCE *(EXODUS 33)*...197

**25** THE END OF THE CRISIS *(EXODUS 34)*...209

**26** GIFTS OF CRAFTSMANSHIP *(EXODUS 35:30-36:7)*...219

PART FIVE: AUTHORITY AND REBELLION...225

**27** WILL YOU ENTER THE KINGDOM? *(NUMBERS 9:15-23)*...227

**28** REBELLION: COMPLAINTS AND DISCONTENT *(NUMBERS 11:1-34)*...241

**29** THE DANGER OF UNDERMINING GOD'S LEADERS *(NUMBERS 12)*...255

**30** INVITATION TO REBELLION *(NUMBERS 13)*...263

**31** ALL-OUT REBELLION *(NUMBERS 14:1-19)*...269

**32** THE DEVASTATING FRUIT OF REBELLION *(NUMBERS 14:20-45)*...279

**33** STRANGE FIRE *(LEVITICUS 10)*...289

**34** KORAH'S REBELLION *(NUMBERS 16)*...297

**35** MOSES' COSTLY MISTAKE *(NUMBERS 20)*...309

**36** SALVATION THROUGH A SNAKE *(NUMBERS 21)*...319

**37** SEX AS A WEAPON *(NUMBERS 25 AND 31)*...325

PART SIX: MOSES REFLECTS ON HIS 40 YEARS LEADING ISRAEL...335

**38** HIGHLIGHTS OF THE JOURNEY *(DEUTERONOMY 2 & 3)*...337

**39** OUT OF THE IRON-SMELTING FURNACE *(DEUTERONOMY 4:1-40)*..**345**

**40** THE SHEMA – HEART OF THE JEWISH RELIGION *(DEUTERONOMY 6:4-19)*..**357**

**41** WHEN...NOT IF *(DEUTERONOMY 7)*..**367**

**42** THE DANGER OF PROSPERITY *(DEUTERONOMY 8)*..**379**

**43** WHY WOULD GOD COMMAND YOU TO KILL "THE WIFE WHOM YOU LOVE"? *(DEUTERONOMY 13 & 18)*..**389**

**PART SEVEN: THE END OF THE ROAD...401**

**44** I WILL NEVER LEAVE YOU OR FORSAKE YOU *(DEUTERONOMY 31)*..**403**

**45** MOSES' SONG *(DEUTERONOMY 32)*..**417**

**46** MOSES' DEATH *(DEUTERONOMY 34)*..**433**

**47** MOSES IN THE REST OF THE BIBLE...**439**

# Introduction

It is time we rediscover Moses.

Who else:

Divided the Red Sea?

Struck a rock to provide water for thousands?

Brought the most powerful nation on earth to its knees?

Guided a multitude of ex-slaves through a brutal wilderness and prepared them to be a nation?

Probably performed more miracles than anyone but Jesus?

Obviously, God was the miracle worker. But it took a very special man to do all that – and still be called the most humble man on earth. He is the most significant figure in Judaism and near the top for both Christians and Muslims.

Moses would have to be included among the ten greatest men of all time, so I went to several web sites to find out what others thought. Who did they choose? Most of them thankfully place Jesus at the top of the list. But nowhere did I find Moses. Wikipedia included people like Thomas Jefferson and William Shakespeare among the top ten. Really? William Shakespeare greater than Moses? *Ranker.com* placed him at number sixteen of the fifty most influential men of all time. I couldn't believe that *Time Magazine* found no place for him among the "One Hundred Most Significant Figures in History."

Yes, it is time to rediscover Moses. I believe you will find his life has tremendous lessons for you.

## 2  MOSES: MAN OF GOD

This is not a commentary on the Pentateuch. Most of us would never make our way through all the technical questions and endless laws. Nor is it a biography of Moses reconstructed from what we know about him. It is an exegetical study of his "autobiography," designed to help you apply the Scriptures to your life and make Moses come alive. It offers particular riches to leaders, both inside and outside the church.

Ladies, in no way do I intend to exclude you from leadership, but this book is written for men. I was a prison chaplain for 21 years and have ministered mainly to men. I believe there is a great need to men to rise up as effective leaders today, and I believe Moses has much to offer them. But if you can excuse the occasional references to fathers or husbands, you will find many treasures in God's Word.

# PART ONE

*THE MISSION BEGINS:
FROM THE BURNING BUSH TO PHARAOH'S
COURT*

# 1

# WATCH OUT FOR THE BURNING BUSH! (IT COULD CHANGE YOUR LIFE!)

### *EXODUS 3:1–12*

*¹Now Moses was tending the flock of Jethro his father-in-law, the priest of Midian, and he led the flock to the far side of the wilderness and came to Horeb, the mountain of God. ² There the angel of the Lord appeared to him in flames of fire from within a bush. Moses saw that though the bush was on fire it did not burn up. ³ So Moses thought, "I will go over and see this strange sight— why the bush does not burn up."*

*⁴ When the Lord saw that he had gone over to look, God called to him from within the bush, "Moses! Moses!"*

*And Moses said, "Here I am."*

Would you like a burning bush experience? I would love the clarity of knowing exactly what God wants me to do. I believe I am following his call, but it wouldn't hurt to have that verbal confirmation. On the other hand, am I ready to handle everything God might say? Moses might have wished he had never checked out his burning bush! He would have had a much easier life herding sheep. He didn't know it that day, but he would spend the next forty years wandering around the wilderness with thousands of rebellious ex-slaves. Are you sure you're ready for something new and dramatic from the Lord? What do you want in this life? Could you deal with a diet of manna, fasting for weeks at a time, and sleeping without your wife? Yet Moses also had the great privilege of intimate communion with God, leading his people to freedom, and receiving tablets of the law written by the very finger of God.

## Do you need to go to the mountain?
We don't know why Moses went to the mountain of God that day. Maybe he sensed an urgency to seek the Lord. Maybe God put a hunger in his heart to go to the mountain that was the subject of so many legends. Maybe he went there regularly. It seems he purposely went to a place where he could hear God's voice. If he had listened to the enemy and ignored the gentle urgings of the Spirit, he might have ended up in the tents of the women who serviced travelers on that route through Sinai. It would have been easier than pushing on through the barren wilderness to Horeb (also known more commonly as Mount Sinai). But he would have missed out on this encounter with God and might never have learned of God's plans for him. Are you in a place where you can hear God's voice? Or have you been distracted by the pleasures of this world? Is your world so full of other things that you would barely pay attention to a burning bush? Is it time to get away and go to the mountain of God?

## How did Moses get to that point?
Few would disagree that Moses was one of the greatest leaders in history, although it certainly wasn't evident that day on the far side of the wilderness. Sure, he had a charmed youth. His mother's ingenuity saved him from Pharaoh's edict to kill all male babies. After the king's daughter just "happened" to find him (or was guided by a God she didn't even know), she allowed his own mother to nurse him – and teach him about the God of Israel.

Later he returned to the palace and learned the language and ways of the Egyptians, which would be useful later on. He may have been the only Hebrew who learned how to write, which prepared him to give us the first five books of the Bible. What a start!

But all that came to a screaming halt in a moment of angry impulsiveness, when he killed an Egyptian taskmaster who was abusing a fellow Hebrew. Now a fugitive facing a death sentence himself, he spent the next forty years in the wilderness. Aside from raising a family and tending sheep, little is known about those years, but undoubtedly God was doing some intensive character formation. I'm sure there were many times when Moses cried out to the Lord: "How long? Will I never see my mother again? I thought you had something special planned for me, but I feel like you have forgotten me."

## HAVE YOU DERAILED OFF THE FAST TRACK?
Perhaps you can identify with elements of Moses' story. You may have been on the fast track to success in ministry, politics, or business. Maybe you still are; amazed at the way God has blessed you. It certainly isn't inevitable that you will derail, but it seems part of the preparation of many of God's servants. We need to get off the world's track, or our own ego-driven track, and get on track with God. God needed to get Moses away from the temptations of Pharaoh's palace to a place where he could shape his character.

We usually don't derail on purpose. Certainly there are easier ways. There are always the "would haves," "should haves," and "could haves." If only Moses hadn't killed that Egyptian, maybe he could have advocated for his people from within the palace. Maybe he could have witnessed to Pharaoh, who would get saved, and they would all live as one big happy family. But that wasn't in God's plan. In the end, God writes the story of your life, much as you may try to prepare the script and revise it yourself.

The derailment is often quick and totally unexpected. So many things can happen:

- A moral indiscretion.
- Financial need that leads to cheating on taxes or "borrowing" from your job.
- Divorce.
- Illness or accident.
- Layoff from work.

Some might see it coming. If Moses had confidants in the palace, they might have sensed some simmering anger about the slaves' treatment and gnawing questions about his identity. Those who are closest to you may know your weaknesses. Do you have any idea what they might be? Is there a scenario that has haunted you? Have you already derailed? Have you done something foolish in a moment of impulsive anger?

God doesn't want you living in fear of what might happen, or with regrets of what could have happened. Wherever you are at on your journey, draw close to Jesus, walk with him, and trust that he has a plan for your life. You may get off track for a while, but in all your mistakes God works for your good. As Moses was fleeing into the desert, he never dreamed he would return forty years later as a deliverer. As the years stretched on he probably thought he would never do anything more than herd sheep. He didn't try to make anything happen. When God was ready he made sure Moses got the message. He will do the same with you. This was the only burning bush recorded in the Bible, so if you are waiting for a burning bush you may have a long wait. But keep your eyes open for something unusual, out of the ordinary. Pay attention to it. It was only when Moses went to find out what the burning bush was all about that God spoke to him. Could it be that there are burning bushes around us, but we are too busy to bother checking them out? And we miss out on what God wants to say to us? He will go out of his way to get our attention, but if we are too caught up with other things he may just go looking for someone who is ready to listen.

*5 "Do not come any closer," God said. "Take off your sandals, for the place where you are standing is holy ground." 6 Then he said, "I am the God of your father, the God of Abraham, the God of Isaac and the God of Jacob." At this, Moses hid his face, because he was afraid to look at God.*

What has happened to a healthy fear and reverence for God? True, Jesus is a great friend and older brother, and God is Abba Father. But some churches feel more like a circus than holy ground. Maybe it's time to take off our sandals and think about who it is we are worshipping and talking with.

## GOD KNOWS YOUR SUFFERING
*7 The Lord said, "I have indeed seen the misery of my people in Egypt. I have heard them crying out because of their slave drivers, and I am concerned about their suffering.*

There are three things here that God has done:

- He has seen his peoples' misery. God has seen all your afflictions, and everything happening with his church throughout the world.
- He heard the cries of those slaves. God has heard your cry. He has heard your prayers. The slaves would have been surprised to know that. They hadn't seen any change. But God hears your cries.
- He is *concerned* about their suffering, but the literal meaning is far deeper than simple concern: literally it

says he *knows* their suffering. He has felt it; he has shared in their suffering. Way beyond just seeing your struggles and hearing your prayers, he has entered into your pain and knows what you are going through.

That is great, but it wasn't of much help to the slaves in Egypt. They endured hundreds of years of slavery. They had cried out to God countless times for relief. And it seemed like he turned a deaf ear. Sometimes it's like that. I'm not sure where we have gotten the idea that we deserve a great marriage, model children, success at work, and beautiful homes and cars. Supposedly, if we only have enough faith, we will prosper and live the good life. But after describing the great heroes of the faith, Hebrews 11 closes by saying: *These were all commended for their faith, yet none of them received what had been promised.* Of course, in his grace and mercy, God can bless us with a good marriage, but it is not the result of our great faith. True faith keeps believing what God has said despite devastating circumstances. It keeps crying out to God even when it seems he doesn't hear. The first verse of Hebrews 11 says: *Now faith is confidence in what we hope for and assurance about what we do not see.* If we already have all those blessings, we don't need much faith. The test of faith comes when year after year you continue in slavery to pharaoh – but keep trusting in God's promise that someday he will take you to the Promised Land.

It is not for us to "declare" when God has to act; we have to wait for God's time. And, for those slaves in Egypt, that time had come. Because now God is not only going to see, hear, and be concerned about their plight. He is ready to act.

## GOD CAME DOWN
[8] *So I have come down to rescue them from the hand of the Egyptians and to bring them up out of that land into a good and*

# Watch out for the burning bush! (It could change your life!)

*spacious land, a land flowing with milk and honey—the home of the Canaanites, Hittites, Amorites, Perizzites, Hivites and Jebusites* ⁹*And now the cry of the Israelites has reached me, and I have seen the way the Egyptians are oppressing them.*

God has come down to rescue them from Egypt. Moses is the first to see him, but their deliverance has begun. Just as Jesus came down as a baby in Bethlehem, and only a few people had any idea of what had started in that humble manger. But God had seen our struggles, had heard the cries of many faithful saints for a Messiah, and now would know firsthand what it was like to be a man. Jesus came down to rescue us from Satan's oppression and our slavery to sin. He brings us up from the depths to his heavenly kingdom where we will reign with him.

Unfortunately, none of those slaves would make it to the land flowing with milk and honey; only Caleb and Joshua would be spared death because of the peoples' rebellion. Not even Moses would make it in! What seemed like a minor slipup would keep him out; he could only see it from afar. God has come down and done everything necessary for our salvation, but we must continue walking in faith and obedience to him.

This must have seemed like great news to Moses. He probably expected to stay with his family and sheep in Midian; maybe one day he could travel to the Promised Land to see his relatives. It is easy for us to intercede for the needs of a hurting world in the comfort of our homes, asking God to touch our leaders and send someone to preach to relatives who need the Lord. But God had a surprise for Moses, and sometimes he has a surprise for us as well.

## Me? Who am I?
¹⁰ *So now, go. I am sending you to Pharaoh to bring my people the Israelites out of Egypt."*

"What? *I* am going back to Egypt?" Yes, Moses was the chosen man for the task. And it just may be that you are God's chosen vessel whom he will use to answer your prayers and bring help to hurting people. This isn't a job offer; God doesn't give Moses a chance to decide whether he wants to go or not. This is a call. Moses can obey, or rebel and suffer the consequences.

*¹¹ But Moses said to God, "Who am I that I should go to Pharaoh and bring the Israelites out of Egypt?"*

Have you ever thought the same thing? Who am I? You may not have the education, experience, or talent that it seems you need, but that doesn't matter. What matters is that God calls you, and God knows what he is doing. God doesn't need overly confident men who think they are God's man for the hour. It is hard for God to use a prideful man. But a man who says "Who am I?" is very useful in God's hands.

## I WILL BE WITH YOU

*¹² And God said, "I will be with you. And this will be the sign to you that it is I who have sent you: When you have brought the people out of Egypt, you will worship God on this mountain."*

God never responded to Moses' question; he simply assures Moses that he will be with him. If you know you are in God's will and walking in obedience to God's call, you can be confident that God is with you. And if God is for you, who can be against you? He will fight the battles and do everything necessary to complete his plans. The only sign offered Moses will come long after he confronts Pharaoh and brings the people out: he will return to that same mountain to worship God.

Moses will find out that God had been right there in the midst of all his suffering. God had a plan for his life even before he was conceived, and he would use all his experiences in this new calling. This book might be your burning bush, which God would use to open your eyes and reveal his call on your life. When he calls, hopefully you will respond without hesitation: "Here I am." You just may need to take your sandals off, because the place you're at has become holy ground.

# 2

## Six Steps to Get the Mission Moving
### *Exodus 4:27–5:21*

Moses reluctantly agreed to obey God and go back to Egypt to liberate the Hebrews. What is your mission? These are the first steps Moses followed as he began his. Could they apply to yours as well?

*²⁷ The Lord said to Aaron, "Go into the wilderness to meet Moses." So he met Moses at the mountain of God and kissed him. ²⁸ Then Moses told Aaron everything the Lord had sent him to say, and also about all the signs he had commanded him to perform.*

### First step: Gather the leadership team

The slaves had no idea that their deliverance was at hand, but God was already putting the pieces together. He had been working on Moses for years, and now he moves Aaron into position to stand with his brother and be his mouthpiece. That's right: Just two men undertook one of the most difficult missions in history. Alone, the pressure would be almost unbearable, but when two are one in spirit, Jesus said anything would be possible (Matthew 18:18-20).

- Do you have someone to stand with you? Someone whose heart beats with yours – and the Lord's? Maybe your wife?

- Are you an Aaron who needs to offer your support to a Moses?

- Perhaps you have a team you're working with. You are blessed! They are a treasure! Be sure to treat them accordingly!

[29] *Moses and Aaron brought together all the elders of the Israelites,* [30] *and Aaron told them everything the Lord had said to Moses. He also performed the signs before the people,* [31] *and they believed. And when they heard that the Lord was concerned about them and had seen their misery, they bowed down and worshiped.*

## SECOND STEP: SPEAK TO THE CHURCH

Your first stop needs to be the church. It might seem easier to bypass it. The church is not always the glorious body it should be, but God has chosen to work through it.

How do you communicate a vision to oppressed, desperate people?

- Start with the established leadership. You are not in competition with them. Humbly share what God has sent you to do. They may be skeptical. Don't let that deter you from God's call.

- Make sure the word you share is from the Lord – and then proclaim it in boldness and faith. Be careful not to embellish it or try to make it more appealing.

- Trust God for signs and wonders to confirm the word.

- You are on a mission from God. Preach his word. Be obedient and trust the Spirit to manifest himself in miraculous confirmation. If you do, they should respond in faith. But don't be surprised if that faith is shaky, especially when things don't happen as fast as they expect. Don't let their doubts discourage you. You are the one who needs to stand firm in your faith.

- Don't get so caught up in great visions that you neglect to minister God's love to the people. Each person was important to Jesus. Don't forget about the little guy just because you are on some great mission. God may need to remind you right now that he is concerned about you and knows about everything going on in your life. Just as he sent Moses with that word, maybe he sent me with this word just to let you know that you are truly important to him.

- The natural response to such an obvious move of God should be worship. There is no indication that Moses pumped them up to worship, or had experience in worship leadership. You don't need a worship band or great sound system. When you sense the people are ready to worship, stop your program, encourage them, and join in. That worship is essential.

- Etch this tremendous time in your memory. Write it down in your journal. Make a video of the service if you can. You are going to need the encouragement in the days to come. They may be brief, but God provides these faith-building moments to assure you that he is with you. It may be a while before the next one, though, so hold onto them and treasure them.

⁵:¹*Afterward Moses and Aaron went to Pharaoh and said, "This is what the Lord, the God of Israel, says: 'Let my people go, so that they may hold a festival to me in the wilderness.'"*

² *Pharaoh said, "Who is the Lord, that I should obey him and let Israel go? I do not know the Lord and I will not let Israel go."*

³ *Then they said, "The God of the Hebrews has met with us. Now let us take a three-day journey into the wilderness to offer sacrifices to the Lord our God, or he may strike us with plagues or with the sword."*

## STEP THREE: MOVE INTO THE WORLD TO CONFRONT THE ENEMY WITH GOD'S WORD

A lot of men wimp out right here. They have a calling, assemble a ministry team, and get the church hyped up. But confrontation is hard. Especially going to Pharaoh! And especially when there had been a price on your head for murder! Suddenly that "festival in the wilderness" sounds silly. The threat of plagues or sword from a God that Pharaoh doesn't acknowledge probably won't move him. This is where real faith begins. It is one thing to preach with anointing in the church; another to go with that anointing to government officials and make a request you know won't be well received.

What's important here is Moses' obedience. Pharaoh is God's problem. As long as Moses carefully follows what he is told to do, God will take care of him. But if he disobeys, he will have God to deal with.

⁴ *But the king of Egypt said, "Moses and Aaron, why are you taking the people away from their labor? Get back to your work!"* ⁵ *Then Pharaoh said, "Look, the people of the land are now numerous, and you are stopping them from working."*

⁶ *That same day Pharaoh gave this order to the slave drivers and overseers in charge of the people:* ⁷ *"You are no longer to supply the people with straw for making bricks; let them go and gather their own straw.* ⁸ *But require them to make the same number of bricks as before; don't reduce the quota. They are lazy; that is why they are crying out, 'Let us go and sacrifice to our God.'* ⁹ *Make the work harder for the people so that they keep working and pay no attention to lies."*

¹⁰ *Then the slave drivers and the overseers went out and said to the people, "This is what Pharaoh says: 'I will not give you any more straw.* ¹¹ *Go and get your own straw wherever you can find it, but your work will not be reduced at all.'"* ¹² *So the people scattered all over Egypt to gather stubble to use for straw.* ¹³ *The slave drivers kept pressing them, saying, "Complete the work required of you for each day, just as when you had straw."*

## STEP FOUR: BE PREPARED FOR SETBACKS IN THE BATTLE

There's a great book about marriage called *What Did You Expect*? That title could probably apply to Moses. He wasn't prepared for Pharaoh's response. Maybe he expected him to agree to everything they asked. But there no deliverance. Instead, things got much worse. And that is what often happens when we get serious about confronting the powers of darkness. It is enough to make many people give up and go back to the safety of singing worship choruses and hearing feel-good preaching in church.

Whether you are trying to address injustice, or help your family or church, the enemy may attack them and turn them against you. Their burden may seem so unbearable they prefer serving the enemy and staying in bondage to doing the hard work to get free.

*14 And Pharaoh's slave drivers beat the Israelite overseers they had appointed, demanding, "Why haven't you met your quota of bricks yesterday or today, as before?"*

*15 Then the Israelite overseers went and appealed to Pharaoh: "Why have you treated your servants this way? 16 Your servants are given no straw, yet we are told, 'Make bricks!' Your servants are being beaten, but the fault is with your own people."*

## STEP FIVE: WATCH FOR ATTACKS ON PEOPLE WHOSE SUPPORT YOU NEED

In prison they are sometimes called trustees: inmates the administration relies on to get information and help the institution run smoothly. They are in a tough position because they have to please both the administration and the inmates, or they can be in big trouble with both. The Israelite overseers were getting beaten for something they are powerless to perform. But they did have access to Pharaoh himself, which tells me the Hebrew slave labor was very important to him!

The overseers' help would be critical in encouraging the people to follow Moses. Without their support, his job will be much harder - if not impossible. But the beatings aren't helping his cause!

*17 Pharaoh said, "Lazy, that's what you are—lazy! That is why you keep saying, 'Let us go and sacrifice to the Lord.' 18 Now get to work. You will not be given any straw, yet you must produce your full quota of bricks."*

*19 The Israelite overseers realized they were in trouble when they were told, "You are not to reduce the number of bricks required of you for each day." 20 When they left Pharaoh, they found Moses and Aaron waiting to meet them, 21 and they said, "May the Lord look on you and judge you! You have made us obnoxious* to Pharaoh and his officials and have put a sword in their hand to kill us."

## STEP SIX: PERSONAL HARDSHIP BLINDS PEOPLE TO GOD'S GREATER PURPOSES

Moses and Aaron were waiting to meet the overseers, maybe hoping to encourage them or somehow salvage the mission, but the liberators have become enemy #1. How would you feel if your key people were asking God to judge you? It's normal for personal comfort and well-being to take priority, so when an already horrendous situation becomes even worse, it is unlikely they will be excited about God's great plan of deliverance. Suffering people have a hard time thinking about great spiritual truth. They just need help to make it through the day! Moses' words about God's concern for them seem like a fantasy now. They are certainly not about to bow down in worship!

## STAND FIRM!

At this point everyone is against Moses: Pharaoh, the Hebrew elders and overseers, and the people, who are being pressured far beyond their ability to endure. This isn't just discouraging, most people would give up and get out of town!

But most people don't get involved in such critical battles. They are too busy thinking about their own comfort and happiness - and they're not stupid. Especially with all the information we have today, they know how things are stacked against the Kingdom of light. Maybe you are one of the few who has dared to believe God is able to move as powerfully now as he did then. Maybe you have encountered some of what Moses did as you took the first steps. You might be seriously discouraged and ready to give up right now. I wish I could tell you that God is going to take care of everything and make it easy, but that would be a lie. He could - but it just doesn't seem to happen that way. The best I can offer you right now is the encouragement that Moses went through the same thing. The whole project seemed like a disaster, and it didn't get any better once they got out of Egypt. But you know what? They did end up in the Promised Land! God was true to his word! Don't give up! If God has called you and given you a message, keep pressing on! Don't be discouraged by attacks from the church or the enemy. Study Moses' first steps in the development of his mission and see if they relate to your situation. Keep your eyes on Jesus and be faithful to what he has called you to do. Stand firm – God is counting on you!

# 3

## WHY, LORD?
### EXODUS 5:22-23

*²² Moses returned to the Lord and said, "Why, Lord, why have you brought trouble on this people? Is this why you sent me? ²³ Ever since I went to Pharaoh to speak in your name, he has brought trouble on this people, and you have not rescued your people at all."*

Poor Moses. He was doing just fine herding sheep and enjoying his family back in Midian. He didn't ask for this. He wasn't looking for fame or fortune. As we are all prone to do, Moses probably underestimated the difficulty of the task, and also suffered from a short (or selective) memory.

God clearly told him that Pharaoh's heart would be hardened (4:21), yet somehow I suspect Moses thought they would waltz into the palace and Pharaoh would send them on their way with his blessing. Moses certainly wasn't expecting trouble from his own people. Instead of being grateful for his help, they are ready to send him back to Midian! And with good reason! Agonizing as it was, they were used to slavery, and could manage it. The Israelite overseers developed good relationships with the Egyptians. But Moses meddled with the system, and now they are faced with an impossible burden! His own people are angry with him. He was a joke to Pharaoh, and even his wife wasn't happy with him (4:23).

## CHALLENGING THE SYSTEM

Things haven't changed much in thousands of years. We still think God should do miracles, change hearts, and make our lives easy. That is the gospel we have been sold all too often: health, wealth, and happiness. Unfortunately, it's not reality. Only after a long, hard, journey, and many battles, would these slaves be safely settled in the land flowing with milk and honey (and not even them – they all died in the wilderness!). Things often get worse before they get better. The devil takes full advantage of that to make us reconsider leaving our slavery to sin. What is familiar can have a powerful hold on us. Making huge changes and challenging the powers that be can seem overwhelming. That is why inmates sometimes purposely mess up shortly before release. The security of prison seems safer than all the unknowns of the free world, and they are absolutely right. "Three hots and a cot," with no major responsibilities, can be very appealing, if you don't mind very limited freedom and doing without certain things, like women. But God designed you for something far better than prison life, slavery to Pharaoh, or whatever bondage you might have. Yet when you challenge the status quo, all hell may break loose. It happens in government, the workplace, and even church. And it happens when you take the first steps to changing your own life or marriage. Be ready for it. Expect backlash, accusations, misunderstanding, and some very tough days.

## WHERE CAN YOU GO?

Moses did the only thing he could do: run to the Lord. That's a good choice. Where else could he go? Even his wife probably didn't want to hear about it, and Aaron may not have been too happy about being pressed into this whole venture.

Moses' prayer certainly is not an example of great faith. It could more appropriately be called a prayer of complaint. But do you know something? God can handle it! He didn't even get down on Moses! Do you feel that freedom to express anger or frustration to God?

## Why?

Do you have any "why" questions for God? Everybody does. Many times we never really get an answer to our "why's" – which can sound all too much like "whyning." But often we are asking the wrong person. Was it God who increased the burden on the Hebrews? Of course not! It was Pharaoh! God sent them a deliverer! And many times when we ask God why, if we really think about it, it is Satan or sinful man who caused the problem. Of course God is sovereign, and we somehow think that makes him responsible, but he has also given us free will, and that is how we got into this whole mess.

God sent another deliverer, far greater than Moses: His own Son. If Moses thought he had it bad, Jesus had it far worse! They crucified him!

## Questioning Your Calling

The second thing Moses questions is his calling. He underestimated its difficulty: *"Is this why you sent me?"* Just to cause trouble and turn his own people against him? To make their lives harder? If you are a pastor, maybe you have felt that way. You believed God was sending you to a city to raise up a powerful church of committed believers. So far, it just hasn't turned out that way. You preach the Word and some key people leave. Giving is down. Other pastors in town misunderstand you and think you are arrogant or uppity because you are challenging the way church has been done for years.

We can ask this "why" question on a variety of levels. "Is this why you gave me that wife?" You thought marriage would be about companionship and sexual satisfaction. Maybe even helping you achieve a better standard of living. Or, if you are a traditionalist, good cooking and housekeeping. You may have been in for a big surprise.

## THE ROOT OF OUR "WHY" QUESTIONS

Both these questions often betray a severe self-centeredness and shallowness. We see only the surface, and how our life could be easier. We want everything done now. God is looking at things from the perspective of eternity, and usually he is not in a particular hurry. His agenda goes far deeper than ours. He is concerned about his own glory, bringing deep, lasting change, and forming the character of someone who is going to reign in his kingdom.

## WHY AREN'T YOU DOING YOUR PART, LORD?

Moses' final complaint essentially is: I followed your rules, did what I was supposed to do, and you haven't done anything.

It is so easy to think God is obligated to bless us and give us whatever we are asking for, if only we pray in faith, make a positive confession, go to church, and live right. Especially if you are in God's will. Here it clearly is his will is to rescue and deliver his people. There may be things you are waiting on God for that are clearly his will - yet he may not answer how or when you think he should. If Moses stopped to think about it, God did tell him this would take a while.

The temptation usually is to just give up.

- "What else is Pharaoh going to do if we go back to him again?"
- "Will I just make things even worse for the people? Will they really turn against me?"

- "Maybe I should just shut up and forget about proclaiming God's Word and boldly stepping forth in faith."

It's a test of faith, isn't it?

- Was God honest when he told Moses about his mission?
- Is God capable of moving Pharaoh's heart?
- If Moses continues to follow God's program, will deliverance actually happen?

Or would it be better for Moses to take things into his own hands? Organize a union? Assassinate Pharaoh? Incite an armed uprising – kind of like he tried to do forty years before?

Do you ever question if God really knows what he is doing? Are you ever tempted to give up on God's way, and do things your own way – or the world's way? What "why" questions do you have for God? How do you think he would answer them?

# 4

# GOD'S ANSWER TO "WHY?": KEEP GOING!
## *EXODUS 6:1*

So far, Moses' great mission to rescue his people from slavery in Egypt seems like a disaster.

- Initial Hebrew enthusiasm quickly turned to anger and despair as Pharaoh made their lives impossible.
- He got nowhere with Pharaoh.
- His wife and brother are unsure about the wisdom of this whole venture.

So what is Moses to do? Go to the One who got him into this mess! "Why, God? Why aren't you doing anything?" Perhaps you have your own complaint or "why?" for the Lord. How does God respond to complaints? How does he answer Moses' "why" questions and deal with his discouragement?

*¹Then the Lord said to Moses, "Now you will see what I will do to Pharaoh. Because of my mighty hand he will let them go; because of my mighty hand he will drive them out of his country."*

## GOD MAY IGNORE YOUR "WHY"
It's a basic principle of human relations: If you want someone to respect you and work for you, listen to their concerns and give them honest answers. Take them seriously. Try to make things

better for them. Make them feel that you truly empathize with them. Is God deaf? Didn't he catch the frustration, anger, and pain in Moses' prayer? Doesn't he care about him and his feelings? God totally disregards what Moses prayed!

Apparently God missed the class on human relations. He totally brushed aside Moses' concerns, and simply restates what he previously told him. No mid-course correction based on these new developments. Because they weren't new to God. He knew all along what would happen. Everything is going as planned. The problem is, Moses didn't fully comprehend that plan. He applied his own expectations to what God was going to do, and got frustrated when things didn't work out according to his plan.

Are you baffled at what is going on in your life right now? Are things turning out different than you planned? Did you have a nice idea of how God was supposed to work? Are you frustrated because he seems to be turning a deaf ear to your complaints?

It is easy to wallow in self-pity, but God is not into coddling us. He remains on message, steadily pursuing what he originally planned. Despite the appearances, he wants to strengthen Moses' faith that he will do what he said he would do. And in spite of how things may look in your life right now, God's call and purposes haven't changed. He is busy preparing a bride for his Son, and getting her ready to reign with him for eternity. Your momentary discomforts just may not be all that important to him.

What God fails to include is the time frame. He does start by saying "now." It would be easy to think that means the next couple days. Not so. It is all future tense – which would mean weeks and multiple rejections and battles. There is no question that it is going to happen. Three times God says it "will." We just don't know when. So often it is the timing that trips us up. We usually expect things to happen faster than what God actually has planned, and get impatient when they don't. God's purposes for you haven't changed. Hang in there. He knows what he is doing. The wait just builds perseverance and character. It may seem like he is ignoring your prayer, but as we will see shortly, he has something important to tell you.

# 5

# HOW TO MOVE FORWARD WITH CONFIDENCE
## EXODUS 6:2-12 & 6:28-7:13

*² God also said to Moses, "I am the Lord. ³ I appeared to Abraham, to Isaac and to Jacob as God Almighty, but by my name the Lord I did not make myself fully known to them. ⁴ I also established my covenant with them to give them the land of Canaan, where they resided as foreigners. ⁵ Moreover, I have heard the groaning of the Israelites, whom the Egyptians are enslaving, and I have remembered my covenant.*

## A REMINDER OF WHO GOD IS

With the mission reaffirmed, God reminds Moses of who it is he is dealing with, past, present and future:

- His promises are future tense.
- His very nature is the ever-present "I AM."
- Wedged in between is the past tense reminder of God's faithfulness.

We are quick to forget God's character and past deeds. That was understandable for Moses, since he was basically alone and facing a huge task. But we have the Bible, centuries of testimonies, almost infinite opportunities for faith-affirming messages on the internet, and the loving support of the church. What is our excuse?

It is easy to focus on the immediate circumstance and forget about who we are dealing with. We are surrounded by a culture obsessed with everything but the God of the universe. Multiple distractions draw us away from the Lord and his Word, which is why it is so important to stay in fellowship and spend regular time in the Scriptures.

Moses needs to remember:

- God's Name: I AM. He revealed his Name for the first time to Moses at the burning bush. He is the Creator, the Alpha and Omega, and the only Lord.

- Moses had the privilege of a deeper revelation than the patriarchs (Abraham, Isaac & Jacob). God loves to reveal himself, whether in visions, through Jesus Christ, or in the Bible. He has probably revealed himself to you in some way. Moses is part of a progressive revelation which climaxed in the revelation of Jesus Christ.

- God is a god of covenant, which depends on the faithfulness of both parties. God is utterly faithful. Moses can be certain that God will get the people out of Egypt because he takes his promise of the land to Abraham and his descendants very seriously. You are part of the New Covenant through Jesus Christ, a covenant sealed by his blood, which you are reminded of and reaffirm every time you take the Lord's Supper. God will be absolutely faithful in finishing the good work he has begun in you, bringing you to a place of eternal fellowship with him in heaven. Are you being faithful to your part of the covenant?

- God does hear your groaning. Sometimes those groans are too deep for words (Romans 8:22, 23, 26). Whatever form it takes, let God know what is going on in your heart. It might appear he doesn't respond to Moses' groaning here, but he does! You may not see anything happening yet, but God has heard your groaning and is at work right now on your behalf.

[6] *"Therefore, say to the Israelites: 'I am the Lord, and I will bring you out from under the yoke of the Egyptians. I will free you from being slaves to them, and I will redeem you with an outstretched arm and with mighty acts of judgment.* [7] *I will take you as my own people, and I will be your God. Then you will know that I am the Lord your God, who brought you out from under the yoke of the Egyptians.* [8] *And I will bring you to the land I swore with uplifted hand to give to Abraham, to Isaac and to Jacob. I will give it to you as a possession. I am the Lord.'"*

## GOD'S PROMISES

Based on God's character and past faithfulness to this people, the final part of God's answer to Moses is all future tense. Eight times, (in the context of three repetitions of "I AM"), God says what he *will* do, and what Israel *will* experience. They are promises, and since "I AM" makes them, they are not just empty words.

How great that we have a future tense God! It is not just ancient biblical history, and great things he did for Israel back in the day. It is not just Jesus' life on this earth or the powerful moving of the Holy Spirit in the early church. We are part of God's plan for all time. He knows the future, and is not caught unaware by anything happening in your life or in the world today! Are you familiar with the Scriptural promises that apply to you? Are there promises God has specifically given you?

Look at what God promises them – and how the same promises apply to you today:

- He will free them from their yoke of slavery. Whoever or whatever has you in bondage is no match for God's power. You may not experience it immediately, but he will free you from that yoke. It is not God's will for you to be in slavery.

- He will redeem them (buy them back) with outstretched arm & mighty works of judgment. God's redemption was most powerfully demonstrated through Jesus Christ. He paid the price for your salvation with his own blood. His outstretched arm will move just as powerfully for you as it did for Israel.

- He will "take them" as his own people. God's desire from the beginning has been for a community, a people he can fellowship with, who will worship and serve him. He sets you free, pays the price for your sin, and gives you a new life. You are his. He wants to shape and form you as part of his Son's glorious bride. Do you want to be "taken" by God?

- He will be their God. What more could you ask for? The Lord of the universe wants to be your God!

- They will know he is God. As you experience his powerful work and witness his mighty deeds you will have solid assurance and knowledge that he is God.

- He will bring them to the Promised Land. Far better than a plot in the mid-east, he has an eternal dwelling prepared for you in heaven, and he will do whatever it takes to get you there.

- He will give it to them as a possession. You are a joint heir with Jesus of God's amazing provision. That means you might not have it all yet. There may be some things you need to grab hold of now; others you can eagerly look forward to, like a child's eager expectation at Christmas.

Israel may have been unaware of these promises. Like us, even if they had heard them, they need to frequently be reminded of them, along with God's plan.

Moses probably thought he had a winner of a sermon here, straight from the Lord. If you are a preacher, God may give you an anointed word. You expect a great response - but that may not necessarily be the case. Moses could use some encouragement, with his people grabbing hold of this word, but it didn't happen. What keeps people from receiving what God has for them?

*9 Moses reported this to the Israelites, but they did not listen to him because of their discouragement and harsh labor.*

## DISCOURAGEMENT AND HARD TIMES CLOSE OUR EARS

When people are barely able to make it through the day, crushed by depression and discouragement, they probably won't be able to receive God's Word. It can sound unbelievable and unrelated to their suffering. Be patient with them. Don't accuse them of unbelief or sin. You probably can't do much to relieve their hard labor, but love them, pray for them, and continue to faithfully obey what God tells you to do. Don't let their discouragement shake your confidence in God's promises.

*10 Then the Lord said to Moses, 11 "Go, tell Pharaoh king of Egypt to let the Israelites go out of his country."*

If his own people won't listen to him, how can he expect Pharaoh to listen? After his initial failure at the palace, it would have been nice to know his own people believe in him and are standing with him, but many times leaders have to go it alone. God will definitely get his people out of Egypt, and Moses has a critical part to play in it. God also has a job for you that's important in his plan.

*¹² But Moses said to the Lord, "If the Israelites will not listen to me, why would Pharaoh listen to me, since I speak with faltering lips?" ²⁸ Now when the Lord spoke to Moses in Egypt, ²⁹ he said to him, "I am the Lord. Tell Pharaoh king of Egypt everything I tell you." ³⁰ But Moses said to the Lord, "Since I speak with faltering lips, why would Pharaoh listen to me?"*

Did Moses somehow miss everything the Lord just told him? He came to God with a prayer of complaint, and God reaffirmed his character and purposes. But Moses isn't all that much stronger than the rest of his people. He is also discouraged, and when things are that hard, we tend to go back to square one and focus on our deficiencies. Is there something that is hard for you to get past? A sin, weakness, or part of your past that is a constant reminder that you are different? Or not capable? Or that you just can't do it?

*⁷:¹Then the Lord said to Moses, "See, I have made you like God to Pharaoh, and your brother Aaron will be your prophet. ² You are to say everything I command you, and your brother Aaron is to tell Pharaoh to let the Israelites go out of his country. ³ But I will harden Pharaoh's heart, and though I multiply my signs and wonders in Egypt, ⁴ he will not listen to you. Then I will lay my hand on Egypt and with mighty acts of judgment I will bring out my divisions, my people the Israelites. ⁵ And the Egyptians will know that I am the Lord when I stretch out my hand against Egypt and bring the Israelites out of it."*

## GOD'S PROVISION FOR MOSES

God is so gracious to Moses! He doesn't get down on him for struggling. Instead he takes Moses a step higher: He has made Moses like God to Pharaoh. What does that mean? Certainly not

## How to Move Forward with Confidence

that Moses was elevated to divinity! But as God's representative, it is like the Lord himself was standing before Pharaoh. It's not that different for you, when you minister in Jesus' Name. It is like Jesus himself is doing the work. And he is. He dwells in you and works through you.

God also reminds Moses of the mouthpiece he provided, elevating Aaron to the role of prophet, speaking the words that "god" Moses has for him to say. Nothing has changed. There is no mid-course correction. What is happening is no surprise to God. All Moses has to do is communicate the words God gives him. God makes clear exactly what is going to happen:

- He will harden Pharaoh's heart.
- Pharaoh won't listen to Moses. That's tough for a preacher! His own people don't listen to him, and Pharaoh doesn't listen. It is tempting to shut up. But God's Word doesn't return void! Whether anyone listens or not, our job is to proclaim the Word.
- God will multiply signs and wonders, but even miracles may not always move hardened hearts!
- He will lay his hand on Egypt. It is one thing to have God's hand of anointing on you – it is another to have his hand of judgment!
- He will bring his people out of Egypt – despite all the evidence to the contrary!
- Both Israel and Egypt will know that he is God.

*[6] Moses and Aaron did just as the Lord commanded them. [7] Moses was eighty years old and Aaron eighty-three when they spoke to Pharaoh*

*⁸ The Lord said to Moses and Aaron, ⁹ "When Pharaoh says to you, 'Perform a miracle,' then say to Aaron, 'Take your staff and throw it down before Pharaoh,' and it will become a snake."*

*¹⁰ So Moses and Aaron went to Pharaoh and did just as the Lord commanded. Aaron threw his staff down in front of Pharaoh and his officials, and it became a snake. ¹¹ Pharaoh then summoned wise men and sorcerers, and the Egyptian magicians also did the same things by their secret arts: ¹² Each one threw down his staff and it became a snake. But Aaron's staff swallowed up their staffs. ¹³ Yet Pharaoh's heart became hard and he would not listen to them, just as the Lord had said.*

Moses is doing great! He is not seeing any success at this point, but it's not stopping him! Twice we are told that Moses and Aaron did just as the Lord commanded. Whether we see results or not, that is the only way to success! That is all we have to do. God will take care of the rest!

You may be faithfully preaching God's Word. He may even be using you in signs and wonders! You are doing everything right. But nothing is happening! People aren't getting saved. The church isn't growing. Nobody is listening to you! Don't sweat it! Just keep listening for God's Word, and doing what he tells you to do!

# 6

## THE PLAGUE OF DARKNESS
### *EXODUS 10:21-29*

Day after day, week after week, God afflicted Egypt with plagues: locusts, frogs, boils - eight plagues so far. Moses thought he was supposed to deliver his people and bring hope, but it seems all he has brought is more pain. The Hebrews still aren't sure about him, and Egypt is devastated.

It is well worth your time to read Exodus 7-11 and study all the plagues. A few things stand out from those chapters:

- At first the Egyptian magicians were able to duplicate the plague. The devil and his demons definitely have power!

- In most cases Israel (and the land they lived in) was exempt from the plague – a further demonstration to Pharaoh that God was acting on behalf of his people.

- At times an outstretched hand or staff (it could be Aaron's or Moses') produced the plague. Sometimes it just happened at the time God appointed; other times Moses would toss soot or dust into the air to initiate it.

- The Egyptians were warned about the hail, and could save their slaves and livestock if they obey God's word and bring them inside. Those who scoffed at God's word suffered loss.

- Over the course of the plagues the country was increasingly devastated. God has no desire to destroy us. Generally he starts with a relatively light judgment, but they will become increasingly severe as we harden our hearts. Eventually our lives end up totally destroyed. Amazingly, many people somehow adapt to the devastation and get even more hardened, still thinking they can make it without surrendering to what God is calling them to do.
- Pharaoh's officials ended up begging him to give in, to spare the country.

Each plague followed a similar pattern:

- Moses demands Pharaoh to let the people go – and announces a plague if he refuses. Pharaoh always refuses.
- When the plague becomes unbearable, Pharaoh summons Moses, agrees to let them go, and God grants relief.
- As soon as things get better, Pharaoh's heart gets hardened again, and he doesn't let them go.

It is not that much different today:

- God speaks to us through the Scripture or a sermon about something we need to change, with very clear consequences for disobedience.
- When we start experiencing the Lord's correction we cry out to him for relief, and at least pretend to repent.

- Once God lifts the affliction and things are back to normal, we often forget the repentance and return to our sin. And the process starts all over again.

It will take the death of Pharaoh's firstborn (and, as a result of his rebellion, all the firstborn in the land) to finally bring him to his knees. But before that there is one more plague which follows the familiar pattern. It demonstrates the steps we may follow in doing God's work.

*²¹ Then the Lord said to Moses, "Stretch out your hand toward the sky so that darkness spreads over Egypt—darkness that can be felt."*

## FIRST STEP: HEAR GOD'S VOICE
In everything he did, Moses had to wait on God and be in a place to hear his word. He never went to Pharaoh unless God sent him, and he never came up with his own ideas for a plague. That sounds obvious, but there are too many out there doing their own thing, totally out of touch with God. Before you make some declaration, claim something, or deliver a prophecy, make sure you have really heard from God.

*²² So Moses stretched out his hand toward the sky, and total darkness covered all Egypt for three days. ²³ No one could see anyone else or move about for three days. Yet all the Israelites had light in the places where they lived.*

## SECOND STEP: OBEDIENCE
There were various things God commanded to initiate the plagues. As Moses was to later learn when he struck the rock instead of speaking to it, God is serious about the details. It might not seem important whether it was Moses or Aaron stretching out his staff, or if they were to just stretch out a hand. Whether it makes sense to us or not, our job is to obey, and trust God to

bring about the desired result. Just because throwing dust in the air worked one time doesn't mean you can do that whenever you want the same result. We like to box God in to doing things certain ways; he delights in changing things up to see if we are paying attention.

*²⁴ Then Pharaoh summoned Moses and said, "Go, worship the Lord. Even your women and children may go with you; only leave your flocks and herds behind."*

## Third step: Persevere. Stand firm and don't compromise

At this point, after all Moses has been through, it might be tempting to accept Pharaoh's offer. After all, he has gotten most of what he wanted. They could always rebuild their flocks later – or go vegan!

Don't settle for less than what God has promised you! Your pharaoh may give you a hard time and accuse you of being rigid or fanatical, but stand firm on God's Word!

*²⁵ But Moses said, "You must allow us to have sacrifices and burnt offerings to present to the Lord our God. ²⁶ Our livestock too must go with us; not a hoof is to be left behind. We have to use some of them in worshiping the Lord our God, and until we get there we will not know what we are to use to worship the Lord."*

## Fourth step: Keep God at the center and make worship a priority

If the goal was just to get out of Egypt, he could have accepted Pharaoh's offer. But the livestock was necessary for much more than food; they were an essential part of their worship. Even though they had not yet been given details about sacrifices and offerings, they had an elementary understanding of them. Don't skimp on your offerings to God. Make sure that in the excitement of deliverance you don't neglect worship. Pharaoh won't respect that need to worship, and the world won't understand what true worship is about. Remember, when God is moving in power, his primary desire is to glorify himself. Don't steal his glory.

*²⁷ But the Lord hardened Pharaoh's heart, and he was not willing to let them go. ²⁸ Pharaoh said to Moses, "Get out of my sight! Make sure you do not appear before me again! The day you see my face you will die."*

## FIFTH STEP: EXPECT RESISTANCE

You can do everything right and still run up against a brick wall. This time Pharaoh has reached his limit. He is sick and tired of dealing with Moses. And, indeed, the final and most devastating judgment is just around the corner.

Many have struggled with God hardening Pharaoh's heart. Why blame the king if God was the one making him resist? It's not as simple as it may first appear:

- The Hebrew slaves were invaluable to Pharaoh; he was not about to just let them walk out of the country.

- God didn't make him increase the burden on the slaves, whom he had been brutally abusing for many years.

- Just as many times as God hardened his heart, Pharaoh hardened his own heart.

He wasn't some poor innocent guy God manipulated! God was making sure he had the chance to fully display his power to awe the Egyptians and judge them for their mistreatment of the Israelites, as well as building faith in his people.

*²⁹ "Just as you say," Moses replied. "I will never appear before you again."*

### SIXTH STEP: WAIT ON GOD FOR THE PROPER RESPONSE

When the door is closed, don't push it. Wait on God for the next step. For Moses, this may have been a relief. All these appearances before Pharaoh couldn't have been too enjoyable, although I wonder if he got some pleasure out of unleashing yet another plague.

Have you been dealing with someone who is hard hearted? Or maybe the devil himself? Do you get weary of the repeated rejection and abuse? Are you waiting on God to hear what to do next, or are you tempted to take things into your own hands? Are you being pressured to compromise and cut some corners on what God has said to do? Are you giving worship its proper place? Are you serious about doing the Lord's work in the Lord's way? As you approach a task he has given you, see if these same steps apply.

# PART 2

*INTO THE WILDERNESS:
THE FIRST DAYS OF FREEDOM*

# 7

## DELIVERANCE!
### *EXODUS 12:31–41*

*³¹ During the night Pharaoh summoned Moses and Aaron and said, "Up! Leave my people, you and the Israelites! Go, worship the Lord as you have requested. ³² Take your flocks and herds, as you have said, and go. And also bless me."*

This time Pharaoh didn't wait until the next day. He didn't choose to spend one more night under God's judgment, as he did with the frogs. This time his son had died, and he finally came to the end of himself and his rebellion. Why is it that so often we have to lose everything to finally wake up and submit to God? Did Pharaoh really think he was a match for the God of the universe? Do you really think you can fight God – and win?

God prefers to deal with us gently. Do yourself a favor. If he has been trying to get your attention, listen up. If there have been small things happening that give you the uncomfortable feeling that something is wrong, seek the Lord and ask him what he is trying to say. Don't wait until you lose your son, or your family, or your life. Yes, it is that serious. I have seen it happen only too often.

As Moses stood firm, he eventually got everything God said he would get. Don't settle for less! It would have been great if revival had swept Egypt, starting with Pharaoh's household. But that wasn't to be. They had fought God too long, and were under his judgment. Soon Pharaoh and his army would die in the waters of the Red Sea, after Israel passed safely through, as Pharaoh made one last vain attempt to rise up in defiance of God Almighty. There are times we need to let God deal with someone, and get out of town to avoid his judgment. That can even be true of a church. But make sure it is the Lord guiding you to go. It can look like an easy out, but as Israel discovered, being out in the desert isn't easy either.

## BLESS ME!

There was one surprise in Pharaoh's parting words: "Bless me!" Was there a part of Pharaoh that actually believed Moses was in touch with the living God, and had the power to bless him? Had the plagues convinced him that God was real? Even in his sin and rebellion, he seems to long for God's blessing! But not enough to truly humble himself and submit to all God wanted for him. That is true for many people who know that Jesus is real. They want to continue in their sin, but want his blessing as well. It never says if Moses blessed him or not.

*³³ The Egyptians urged the people to hurry and leave the country. "For otherwise," they said, "we will all die!" ³⁴ So the people took their dough before the yeast was added, and carried it on their shoulders in kneading troughs wrapped in clothing. ³⁵ The Israelites did as Moses instructed and asked the Egyptians for articles of silver and gold and for clothing. ³⁶ The Lord had made the Egyptians favorably disposed toward the people, and they gave them what they asked for; so they plundered the Egyptians.*

## PLEASE GO!

Talk about the fear of God! I suspect the Egyptians got the message long before their king did! Too often Christians just blend in with everyone else, but here the distinction between

God's people and those under his judgment is very clear. And the Egyptians are scared to have any believers around, lest they suffer even more! We don't always bring blessing to those around us. If they are in deep sin we can be a thorn in their sides.

In this case, even as the Egyptians begged them to go, the Lord granted the Hebrews favor in their eyes. Fortunately the Hebrews obeyed what Moses commanded them! Can you imagine slaves going to their oppressors and asking for their gold and silver and clothes!? And the Egyptians giving it to them?! Talk about God turning things around! This was something new for the Israelites – to ask, and receive!

It is possible for God to favorably dispose people to you as well. Not that we are to plunder everyone around us – or covet what they have! But when God's favor is on you and he clearly instructs you to ask for things way beyond what you expect, be obedient and ask! Ask for little and you will get little. If God is leading you, ask for much, and see how God may amaze you in bringing the world's wealth into his service! Later we will see much of that silver and gold go into building the tabernacle – and the people giving cheerfully and abundantly to God's work! Unfortunately, some of that gold also went into making an idol: the golden calf. Make sure the abundance God gives you doesn't become an idol!

There was no time for bread to rise, so the people left carrying their unleavened bread, giving birth to the Passover celebration of unleavened bread, or matzah.

*37 The Israelites journeyed from Rameses to Sukkoth. There were about six hundred thousand men on foot, besides women and children. 38 Many other people went up with them, and also large droves of livestock, both flocks and herds. 39 With the dough the Israelites had brought from Egypt, they baked loaves of unleavened bread. The dough was without yeast because they* had been driven out of Egypt and did not have time to prepare food for themselves. ⁴⁰ Now the length of time the Israelite people lived in Egypt was 430 years. ⁴¹ At the end of the 430 years, to the very day, all the Lord's divisions left Egypt.

## WHEN WILL YOUR DELIVERANCE COME?
Four hundred thirty years was a long time! And despite the oppression and Pharaoh's attempts to kill male babies, the population had swelled. We don't know who the "many other people" were who went up with them, but they may have been Egyptians who "converted" and chose to walk with God's people. Apparently they were received as part of the community.

Moses' first goal has finally been met, after much struggle! Now he will have a chance to find out what these ex-slaves are really like, as he pastors them and leads them to the Promised Land. He has demonstrated faith and perseverance in the face of great opposition.

Are you up against a pharaoh, wondering if your deliverance will ever come? God may turn things around so he comes and asks for your blessing! Are you prepared to move when God says it's time? Ready to leave everything behind and grab some unleavened bread, if that is all you have time for? Are there people whom God has favorably disposed to you? Have you asked them for help – or are you willing to?

# 8

# READY FOR BATTLE?
## *EXODUS 13:17-22*

*¹⁷ When Pharaoh let the people go, God did not lead them on the road through the Philistine country, though that was shorter. For God said, "If they face war, they might change their minds and return to Egypt." ¹⁸ So God led the people around by the desert road toward the Red Sea. The Israelites went up out of Egypt ready for battle.*

It seems like a contradiction:

- The Israelites left Egypt ready for battle. I wouldn't expect slaves to have many weapons, but they may have gotten some from the Egyptians, or had some hidden away. Or maybe mentally they were prepared for battle.

- They thought they were battle-ready - but God knew they weren't. They could have all the weapons in the world, but God knows they might have second thoughts about the whole venture if they encounter battles. Amazing as it sounds, they might decide to face the consequences and go back to Egypt.

Fortunately, God was leading them. Had they followed their GPS, or gone with the crowd of traders traveling between Egypt and Canaan, they surely would have encountered stiff opposition. Yet

God's leading meant a far longer journey. The road through Philistine country would get them to Canaan in a couple weeks. Following God, it took them forty years.

## Which road are you on?
Here is where a godly leader like Moses is so important. Too many pastors are anxious for success and comfort, and want to take the quick route to a big, flashy church - without doing the necessary body-building in the desert. Moses was listening to the Lord, and took the harder road.

Which road would you take? Which road are you on? Have you arrogantly chosen the fast route, the easier one, the road everyone is taking? Do you scoff at those who go into the desert, claiming to follow God?

## Are you ready for battle?
Do you think you are ready to fight? You need to be, because there surely will be battles. But God may be shielding you from real battles at this point because he knows they could destroy your faith. If you find yourself in a serious battle right now, it may be for one of two reasons:

### 1: You're not following the Lord

If you are doing your own thing, you may be running into the very enemies he wanted you to avoid.

- You may be reconsidering serving God. You didn't expect it to be this rough, and your old life in the world is looking very attractive.

- Don't be deceived! If these Israelites were to go back to Egypt they would face almost certain death, and certainly be subjected to slavery again. They can't go back!

# Ready for Battle? 55

- You can't go back either! Once God has delivered you out of the world, returning to it denies everything Jesus did to set you free by dying on the cross. You will face death and destruction!

## 2: God knows you're ready for battle!

It is also possible that you have been faithfully following the Lord, you have had your time in the desert, and you are truly ready for battle.

- Finding yourself in a battle doesn't necessarily mean you are doing something wrong, or that God is angry with you, or that he has deserted you.
- Sooner or later they would encounter battles; the enemy was not going away. Battles were part of taking the Promised Land.
- There are plenty of enemies in the world today who are battling the Lord and his people.

You may not even need that desert training. God knows you are strong enough! Spend some time before the Lord trying to discern where you are at along the way to the Promised Land. Wherever that may be, be prepared for battle. Be assured that God is with you in the battle! Be courageous and rise up and fight in the Name of Jesus!

[19] *Moses took the bones of Joseph with him because Joseph had made the Israelites swear an oath. He had said, "God will surely come to your aid, and then you must carry my bones up with you from this place."*

## How can you honor those who have gone before you?

Moses didn't overlook little details. In the rush to leave Egypt it would be easy to think that getting Joseph's bones wasn't such a big thing. But it was Joseph who got the nation down to Egypt. He prophesied God would come to their aid and get them out of Egypt, and now he will finally get back to the land of his birth.

Be sensitive to what your forebears have requested. It would be easy to think those people are gone and won't know whether you follow their wishes or not. Would Joseph know if Moses honored his request and fulfilled the oath? Maybe, from heaven, or maybe not. But model respect for those who have gone before you, and for their work in the Lord. Wouldn't you want your wishes to be honored?

*[20] After leaving Sukkoth they camped at Etham on the edge of the desert. [21] By day the Lord went ahead of them in a pillar of cloud to guide them on their way and by night in a pillar of fire to give them light, so that they could travel by day or night. [22] Neither the pillar of cloud by day nor the pillar of fire by night left its place in front of the people.*

## The first campout!

The first of many! In the next chapter we will find out that they were in for quite a surprise! But first we get absolute assurance that it is God who brought them to this place.

## A pillar to guide them

Wouldn't you like to have that pillar of fire and cloud? What an amazing physical reminder and assurance of God's presence, protection, and guidance!

- The Lord *went ahead of them*. Do you follow the Lord - or plot your own course, and then ask him to bless it?

- It *never left its place*. No abandonment issues here! God is assuring them of his faithfulness! You may experience that strong presence during your early days walking with the Lord. Often his presence becomes less obvious as you journey on, so you can learn to walk in faith.

- They could travel *by day or night*. It sounds nice to have the pillar of fire, but it means that just when you are settling into bed the word may come to get up and follow the fiery pillar. It would be very obvious to everyone if you chose to rebel and go your own way.

- *There was only one pillar,* which required absolute unity. Can you imagine what that would look like today? Everyone seems to be claiming their own pillar, and we are all running around like crazy men with no unified direction. Is that really of the Lord?

## SOMETHING BETTER THAN THE PILLAR

So what do you think? Do you still want the pillar? Are you aware you have something much better? You have God's own Spirit dwelling inside you, and the fire of his Spirit to guide you and counsel you. He is with you day and night. He will never leave you or forsake you.

- Are you following his leading?

- Have you learned how to hear his voice?

- Do you have any idea where you are going right now? Or are you tossed about, following one teaching and then another, running after one prophet and then another apostle, without any clear direction to your life?

God wants to guide you just as clearly as he guided Israel. He doesn't want you wandering around on your own out there in the wilderness, and he hasn't forgotten about you. Make sure you are walking with God's people. Get in touch with the fire of God that dwells in you, or seek that baptism of fire if you have never had it. Israel was about to encounter some rough times. God wants you prepared for whatever may come *your* way.

# 9

# BETWEEN A ROCK AND A HARD PLACE
## *Exodus 14*

You are exhausted after an intense time of ministry, or finally experience deliverance after a major trial. Hopefully you can relax for a while. Moses may have thought the hardest part of his job was over once he left Egypt. God hadn't given him much detail about the trip to Canaan; simply the promise to reach it and possess it. But Moses was about to discover there would be many lessons along the way, and he would find his own people could be just as challenging as Pharaoh.

### ARE YOU ON A DETOUR TO THE RED SEA?
If you think that once you are saved you will waltz into heaven after a life of blessings and prosperity, you are probably in for a shock. God has much to teach you on the journey. Life is hard, and little of value comes easily. Like Israel, you may find yourself on what seems like a detour right now. It may feel like God set you up. Your problems may seem as big as Pharaoh's armies and as deep as the Red Sea. You may think there is no way out.

*Then the Lord said to Moses, <sup>2</sup> "Tell the Israelites to turn back and encamp near Pi Hahiroth, between Migdol and the sea. They are to encamp by the sea, directly opposite Baal Zephon. <sup>3</sup> Pharaoh will think, 'The Israelites are wandering around the land in confusion, hemmed in by the desert.' <sup>4</sup> And I will harden Pharaoh's heart, and he will pursue them. But I will gain glory for myself* *through Pharaoh and all his army, and the Egyptians will know that I am the Lord." So the Israelites did this.*

## WALKING WITH GOD MAY NOT MAKE SENSE

God has just spent months displaying his power to Pharaoh so the people could be set free. They are finally on their way, but he has them take the long route, so they don't encounter warfare, get discouraged, and turn back. They are already discovering that blessing doesn't come quite as easily as they had been led to believe. Walking with God often doesn't make sense to us.

But now they are at the beach; probably in a festive mood. It seems like a well-earned vacation – a few days' rest, camping by the sea. But their vacation is about to become a nightmare. It seems like they have been through enough already. They suffered through years of slavery, only to embark on a journey to a land they know nothing about. They weren't too sure about Moses – but he has finally delivered on his promise. They obediently follow his instructions.

God was leading them straight into a hopeless situation. Without divine intervention, they are finished; and Moses would probably be the first to go. Do you think that following God, knowing his will, and hearing his voice always results in an easier, more blessed life? Do you realize God may lead you right into disaster?

After Moses' hard work gaining their trust, the last thing he needs is something to put fear in their hearts and foster rebellion. But if he was wondering how he would handle thousands of angry, desperate, ex-slaves in that wilderness, it didn't stop him from doing exactly what God told him to do. He may have learned by now that even when it doesn't make sense, we need to obey God. He had seen all those plagues and miracles first hand.

Moses had the advantage of hearing God's voice, and knew enough not to argue with him. God told him what was about to happen, but he wasn't allowed to tell the people. As a leader you don't always share everything God tells you.

## ARE YOU WILLING TO BE INCONVENIENCED SO GOD CAN BE GLORIFIED?

God is putting his beloved, chosen, people through incredible stress – to accomplish his purposes. The stated goal is to make things as hard as possible so he can gain the most glory. In the process their faith will be strengthened. Does God get more glory healing you of a cold - or of terminal cancer? Are you willing to go through desperate situations so he can be glorified? Or does it feel like he is playing with you? Has he promised you a home "flowing with milk and honey" - but right now it is a dry, thorny, painful place? Do you continue to struggle with some sin? Do you feel like you are between a rock and a hard place – and there is no way out?

Sometimes our own rebellion and sin take us there. God may still be merciful, although there can be a heavy price to pay. But if you are confident you have heard God's voice and are walking in obedience, be assured God will make a way out for you. Many times during the exodus the slaves wondered if they had done the right thing leaving Egypt. They would have gone back if they could. You may be wondering if it is worth following Jesus, since it seems to get you into more trouble. The promised peace and prosperity just isn't happening. Step back and try to see God's greater purpose in your trial. How does he want to glorify himself? Is there someone he wants to show his power - or to judge?

God may be telling you to do something that will bring your people trouble. If you are thinking of doing things your way, think again. You may avoid some hardship, but you will be in sin and your church and family will suffer.

*⁵ When the king of Egypt was told that the people had fled, Pharaoh and his officials changed their minds about them and said, "What have we done? We have let the Israelites go and have lost their services!" ⁶ So he had his chariot made ready and took his army with him. ⁷ He took six hundred of the best chariots, along with all the other chariots of Egypt, with officers over all of them. ⁸ The Lord hardened the heart of Pharaoh king of Egypt, so that he pursued the Israelites, who were marching out boldly. ⁹ The Egyptians—all Pharaoh's horses and chariots, horsemen and troops—pursued the Israelites and overtook them as they camped by the sea near Pi Hahiroth, opposite Baal Zephon.*

We may struggle with God hardening Pharaoh's heart, but his decision to let them go seems more a momentary lapse than a real change of heart. He was shaken by the death of his son and wanted relief, but his real character is quickly revealed.

## GET IN LINE WITH WHAT GOD IS TRYING TO DO

Maybe you were amazed by a sudden change of heart in your boss or your wife. What had seemed so hardened suddenly became soft - and then just as quickly hardened again. There is much more going on than meets the eye! God is working behind the scenes to accomplish his purposes! They certainly don't realize it. They may feel confused and wonder, like Pharaoh, "Why did I relent and let them go"? They won't see God's hand in it. But do you believe in God's sovereignty? Do you believe he is working for good in everything that happens to those who love and follow him? When you see a sudden change of heart, pray about what God may be trying to accomplish, and get in line with his purposes. Don't fight them, even though it may mean an ugly encounter with the enemy.

These untrained, poorly equipped slaves were no match for all Pharaoh's army and chariots. Without God you are no match for what the devil will bring against you.

*10 As Pharaoh approached, the Israelites looked up, and there were the Egyptians, marching after them. They were terrified and cried out to the Lord. 11 They said to Moses, "Was it because there were no graves in Egypt that you brought us to the desert to die? What have you done to us by bringing us out of Egypt? 12 Didn't we say to you in Egypt, 'Leave us alone; let us serve the Egyptians'? It would have been better for us to serve the Egyptians than to die in the desert!"*

## How do you respond when the devil is at your heels?

Imagine the first person who looked up from sunbathing or splashing in the water. They had been blissfully unaware of what the enemy was up to, even though Moses knew. Now panic seizes them. They thought God was with them. They were finally free and on the right path. It is a shock to find your enemy right there. Maybe you thought you were done with drugs and alcohol, or had overcome some other sin, only to look up one day and there it is, laughing in your face and about to overtake you. What do you do?

The natural reaction is fear. I'm sure you have felt it. Your stomach knots up and your heart clenches. They had the right instinct, crying out to the Lord, but they didn't wait for him to answer. Their complaint to Moses betrays their lack of faith. Since God isn't there physically (and they are in no condition to hear his voice anyway), all their fear and anger gets directed at Moses.

Be careful of getting defensive or reading too much into the desperate cry of someone who is terrified. Whether it is your child, your wife, or your church, they may blame you and be totally illogical. Israel's response is typical of how we react to desperate situations:

- Rather than blame God, they blame God's representative, the one who seems responsible for the trouble. They refuse to take responsibility for their decisions.

- They lose perspective and forget about the vision of a better life and a promised land. All they can see right now is the desert – and the very real prospect of destruction.

- The former way of life, in bondage to sin and Satan, seems attractive in comparison to the uncertainty and trials associated with following the Lord. Regret is common, and they may actually abandon the faith and return to the world.

The worst thing a leader can do is get defensive and start blaming those under him – or capitulate to their demands. Here's where his real character is revealed. His response can make or break the whole mission. Fortunately, Moses did the right thing.

*13 Moses answered the people, "Do not be afraid. Stand firm and you will see the deliverance the Lord will bring you today. The Egyptians you see today you will never see again. 14 The Lord will fight for you; you need only to be still."*

## THE LORD WILL FIGHT FOR YOU

There would be times when they needed to fight. But this time they just need to sit back and enjoy the show. Often we are too quick to fight. God may be calling you to be still, rest in him, and trust him to get you out of what he got you into. It's all about God. It's not about us.

To be still, though, they must get rid of their fear. It is very hard for God to work with fearful people. Fear destroys your faith. Countless times in his Word God tells us not to be afraid - yet that is not an easy command to obey. If something is going on in your life that is filling you with fear, God's word to you is: "Fear not. I am with you. I have everything under control."

Several times in the teaching on spiritual warfare in Ephesians six we are told to stand firm. When you are under attack and full of fear one of the worst responses is running from person to person seeking advice or help, full of faith one day and ready to give up the next. Develop stability in the good times so when adversity comes you can stand firm.

Moses doesn't know the details yet, but he has seen enough of God's power to be confident that deliverance will come. If you are God's child, it may not be at all clear *how* he could deliver you, but be assured he will.

If they have that faith and can let go of their fear, the Egyptians will be dealt with once and for all. It would be great if that was true of all our enemies: After a few stressful hours, God does a great miracle and you never see them again. That can happen, although our weak, vacillating, faith, and attempts to work things out our way, may hinder it. There may be some enemies you will see again. Be confident that God can give you victory, no matter how many battles there may be. Do you believe he is able to fight for you? Why do you insist on fighting in your own strength? He can do so much better than you! Give him your battles today and see what a great warrior he is!

*[15] Then the Lord said to Moses, "Why are you crying out to me? Tell the Israelites to move on. [16] Raise your staff and stretch out your hand over the sea to divide the water so that the Israelites can go through the sea on dry ground. [17] I will harden the hearts*

*of the Egyptians so that they will go in after them. And I will gain glory through Pharaoh and all his army, through his chariots and his horsemen. ¹⁸ The Egyptians will know that I am the Lord when I gain glory through Pharaoh, his chariots and his horsemen."*

Fear paralyzes. The people wanted to go back. God tells them to move on. Could that be God's word for you right now? Are you stuck? Are you considering going back? Or have you already? Do you just need to look the enemy in the face and move on, following the path God has shown you?

## Moses' part in the deliverance

After his faith-filled words of assurance to the people, Moses went running to God with his own cry for help. God doesn't seem too compassionate with him. Did he actually expect Moses to come up with this plan of deliverance? I doubt it – but I think he did expect Moses to have more confidence that God would get them through.

What Moses doesn't do is just as important as what he does. He doesn't "declare" that Egypt's armies will turn around or that Israel will be victorious in fighting them. Either one of those could have been God's means of deliverance – but he had something much more dramatic in mind. I have serious concerns with all the "declaring" I hear, which can come dangerously close to commanding God what to do. If they came to another sea with the Philistines behind them and Moses boldly "declared" that the sea would open based on what happened here, he would have been humiliated and his people killed. We need to wait on God in each situation, discern his will, and walk in obedience to it.

Could God have sovereignly opened the sea without Moses lifting his staff? Of course! But he usually chooses to work through us, build faith in us, test our obedience, and show people under us that we are trustworthy. If Moses scoffed at God's plan and chose not to stretch out his hand, there is a good possibility all those people would be dead.

*[19]* *Then the angel of God, who had been traveling in front of Israel's army, withdrew and went behind them. The pillar of cloud also moved from in front and stood behind them, [20] coming between the armies of Egypt and Israel. Throughout the night the cloud brought darkness to the one side and light to the other side; so neither went near the other all night long.*

## THE BATTLE IS ON!
With everything in place, God puts the angel and the pillar of cloud between Israel and their enemy. They couldn't even see each other. God's people were in the light while the enemy was in darkness.

It may not be a visible cloud, but God can still cause your enemies to grope around in the darkness while you walk in the light. He can protect you, and his angel can lead you and shield you from the enemy.

*[21] Then Moses stretched out his hand over the sea, and all that night the Lord drove the sea back with a strong east wind and turned it into dry land. The waters were divided, [22] and the Israelites went through the sea on dry ground, with a wall of water on their right and on their left.*

Much has been written about exactly how this happened. There is no need for scientific explanations. God divided the water and Israel marched through on dry ground. What looked like an impossible situation with no way out suddenly became a matter of stepping into the middle of the sea on dry ground and walking through to the other side. In doing so, the enemy was left behind.

*[23] The Egyptians pursued them, and all Pharaoh's horses and chariots and horsemen followed them into the sea. [24] During the*

*last watch of the night the Lord looked down from the pillar of fire and cloud at the Egyptian army and threw it into confusion. $^{25}$ He jammed the wheels of their chariots so that they had difficulty driving. And the Egyptians said, "Let's get away from the Israelites! The Lord is fighting for them against Egypt."*

Divine intervention can become so obvious that even the most hardened sinner has to admit that God is against them. You would think Egypt might have gotten a clue when darkness descended and the pillar came between them and Israel. If they had turned back at that point they might have survived, but God was determined to definitively judge them. Often, when we are set on a sinful course, our pride won't let us quit, no matter how clear the signs. Unfortunately, by the time we realize what is happening, it may be too late.

God can "jam the wheels" of those who are coming against you. He can throw your enemies into confusion. On numerous occasions Israel's enemies self-destructed!

*$^{26}$ Then the Lord said to Moses, "Stretch out your hand over the sea so that the waters may flow back over the Egyptians and their chariots and horsemen." $^{27}$ Moses stretched out his hand over the sea, and at daybreak the sea went back to its place. The Egyptians were fleeing toward it, and the Lord swept them into the sea. $^{28}$ The water flowed back and covered the chariots and horsemen—the entire army of Pharaoh that had followed the Israelites into the sea. Not one of them survived.*

## JUDGMENT

Was this cruel? Or was it cruel to keep people in bondage for hundreds of years? Was this simply justice? Certainly there were Egyptians who had nothing to do with the slaves, and lost their lives because of Pharaoh's hard heart. When judgment comes, the innocent also suffer.

Our prideful culture is convinced it doesn't need God. They are hell-bent on doing their own thing and resisting God's plan. But just as surely as judgment finally came on Pharaoh, judgment will come. God may just be waiting for the opportunity to gain the most glory through it.

Make sure you stay tuned to hear all God has to say! Had Moses started celebrating prematurely, and ignored God's further instruction to stretch out his hand again, the enemy might have survived to come back and plague them. That is a lot of responsibility for the leader. Is there something you need to do to free your people from their enemies?

*[29] But the Israelites went through the sea on dry ground, with a wall of water on their right and on their left. [30] That day the Lord saved Israel from the hands of the Egyptians, and Israel saw the Egyptians lying dead on the shore. [31] And when the Israelites saw the mighty hand of the Lord displayed against the Egyptians, the people feared the Lord and put their trust in him and in Moses his servant.*

They endured hours of anxiety. They grumbled and betrayed their lack of faith. But by the end of the day everything was fine. They were done with the Egyptians once and for all. They had an unforgettable miracle to strengthen their faith, which is still a source of encouragement to God's people today. They learned to fear God and trust him. And their trust in Moses was strengthened as well.

## The leader's role

And Moses? He played a critical role. Without his words of faith the people would have panicked and perished. They needed his strength to lead them through the trial. Had Moses crumbled and despaired, everything would have been lost. His work wasn't hard. He just needed to hear God, tell the people what to do, and lift up his staff and hand a couple times. It wasn't physically hard - but the weight of thousands of God's people on his shoulders could be overwhelming. Moses stood firm and did exactly what God told him to do. Was he anxious at times? Probably. But he also had an amazing experience that significantly strengthened his faith. As usual, God proved absolutely faithful. If you are a pastor or leader, or a husband or father, your church and your family are depending on you. Don't fall apart when the devil shows up! Stand firm and trust that God has a way out! Listen for God's voice like your life depended on it – because it does, along with the lives of those God has entrusted to you. Walk with them through the sea and follow through to make sure the enemy is dealt with. Don't be so macho that you insist on fighting the battle yourself, if God tells you to be still.

Who is your Pharaoh? What is your Red Sea? What looks impossible to you today? Is your faith floundering? Or can you trust that God has a way through for you? Are you holding back a miraculous deliverance because you won't lift up your hand or your staff? Is it time for you to move on in faith?

# 10

## Worship!
### *Exodus 15:1-21*

When God does a miracle in your life, how do you respond? Do you take time to give him appropriate thanks and praise? Or do you tend to forget about him once things are back to normal? I saw it countless times as a prison chaplain. Don't take me wrong, there were plenty of inmates full of worship to the Lord who sustained them through the hardest trial in their lives. But there were others who vowed to serve God the rest of their lives if he would only get them out, yet when God miraculously freed them, forgot about him the minute they walked out the gates. Not that it is only in prison. It happens all the time on the street as well. And it's nothing new.

### God is seeking worshippers

When Jesus healed the ten lepers, only one came back to give him thanks. Disappointed, he asked, *"Has no one returned to give praise to God except this foreigner?"* (Luke 17:17-18) Ungratefulness and not glorifying God are a fundamental part of our sin problem:

*For although they knew God, they neither glorified him as God nor gave thanks to him, but their thinking became futile and their foolish hearts were darkened* (Romans 1:21).

When we fail to worship God our hearts and minds are affected.

God longs for true worshippers. When you do something for your family, it means a lot to hear them thank you and tell you what a great dad you are. If they act like they deserved it and never mention it to you or anyone else, you will feel less inclined to go out of your way for them again. God is no different. He longs for our worship and deserves it, in light of all he has done for us.

Israel wasn't used to having worship services. They didn't know a lot of worship songs, but Moses took the initiative and led them in a glorious time of worship after their deliverance at the Red Sea. Worship is richer if you know the words to the song. That's why hymn books were used for centuries. Most churches today project the words of the songs. If yours doesn't, please make the effort, so everyone can join in the worship.

Pastor, you should be taking the lead in drawing your congregation into God's presence. It is fine to have a worship pastor or leader, but don't assume that frees you from any responsibility of fostering true worship in your church. That is a key part of your call to ministry. Stay involved in the worship. Join the worship band for their rehearsals from time to time. Talk and pray with worship leaders about what songs will be sung. If you haven't led your people in worship for a while, surprise them by doing so one Sunday. Fully participate in the worship. Please don't use that time to talk to people, finish preparing your sermon, or be out of sight. That sends a really bad message! Be the first to join in the worship and set the tone for the service. I am alarmed at what I observe in many "worship" services, which seem more like concerts showcasing the talents of the worship band.

This passage is frequently called The Song of the Sea. It is also known as Miriam's Song, because she is mentioned in verse 20. John Wesley suggested that Moses composed it and led it for the men, while his sister Miriam led it for the women. Exactly how we don't know. Some Jewish sources speak of men and women standing in lines and echoing back what the leader sang. They certainly weren't projecting words on a screen! It couldn't have been written in advance, since Moses had not known what God was going to do. Moses doesn't often express much emotion, but here is a view of what fills his heart, and his passionate gratitude for their deliverance.

## HE IS MY GOD – AND I WILL PRAISE HIM!
*¹Then Moses and the Israelites sang this song to the Lord:*

*"I will sing to the Lord,*
 *for he is highly exalted.*
*Both horse and driver*
 *he has hurled into the sea.*

*² "The Lord is my strength and my defense;*
 *he has become my salvation.*
*He is my God, and I will praise him,*
 *my father's God, and I will exalt him.*

The beginning is intensely personal. Eight times Moses uses "I" or "my." To truly worship the Lord, he needs to be *your* God; otherwise it just becomes music. Look around in church (not to judge people!) and you get an idea of who really knows God and is excited about what he has done in their lives, and who is just there for the show.

Some people make light of worship which is based on our personal experience, like it is somehow self-centered, but most worship is born of what God has done for us. It is through that deliverance from sin and the gift of forgiveness that we come to say from the depths of our hearts: "You have become my salvation."

How is your worship doing? Is God your strength? Or are you still relying on your own limited strength? Do you trust in him to defend you? Or do you still rise up in self-defense? Has God become your salvation? That needs to happen at some point. It wasn't automatic just because Moses was born a Jew. Is he your God? It's great that Moses could say he was his father's God – but your father's faith won't get you into heaven.

## OUR MIGHTY WARRIOR!

*3 The Lord is a warrior;*
  *the Lord is his name.*
*4 Pharaoh's chariots and his army*
  *he has hurled into the sea.*
*The best of Pharaoh's officers*
  *are drowned in the Red Sea.*
*5 The deep waters have covered them;*
  *they sank to the depths like a stone.*
*6 Your right hand, Lord,*
  *was majestic in power.*
*Your right hand, Lord,*
  *shattered the enemy.*

*7 "In the greatness of your majesty*
  *you threw down those who opposed you.*
*You unleashed your burning anger;*
  *it consumed them like stubble.*
*8 By the blast of your nostrils*
  *the waters piled up.*
*The surging waters stood up like a wall;*
  *the deep waters congealed in the heart of the sea.*
*9 The enemy boasted,*
  *'I will pursue, I will overtake them.*
*I will divide the spoils;*
  *I will gorge myself on them.*

> I will draw my sword
>   and my hand will destroy them.'
> ¹⁰ But you blew with your breath,
>   and the sea covered them.
> They sank like lead
>   in the mighty waters.
> ¹¹ Who among the gods
>   is like you, Lord?
> Who is like you—
>   majestic in holiness,
> awesome in glory,
>   working wonders?
>
> ¹² "You stretch out your right hand,
>   and the earth swallows your enemies.

Does this sound like your God? Or is yours some puny deity who needs to be coaxed into action? Is he still a baby in the manger? Or hanging on a cross? Yes, Jesus talked a lot about love. But is your only image of Jesus a sentimental nice guy? Do you think of God as a kindly, grandfatherly type? Have you forgotten that God is a mighty warrior?

Look again at how he is described here:

- He *hurled* Pharaoh's chariots and armies into the sea.
- His right hand, *majestic in power*, *shattered* the enemy.
- He *threw down* those who opposed him.
- He unleashed his *burning anger*, which *consumed* his enemies like fire.
- Forget a scientific explanation – it was the blast of God's nostrils that piled up the waters in a heap!

Do you cower before the enemy? You shouldn't! Let God be your defense and your warrior. Don't be scared of his burning anger - unless you are opposing him! Ask him to unleash it! Make sure your enemies are God's enemies as well. In other words, make sure you're fighting the right enemy. Then ask in faith that God's power be displayed in shattering them!

Truly there is no other god like our God! Three wonderful phrases describe him:

- Majestic in holiness.
- Awesome in glory.
- Wonder working.

Does that describe your God? When is the last time he worked wonders for you? When did you last see his glory and bask in its splendor? Are you aware of his holiness – which means he can't tolerate sin?

## A LOVING FATHER

*13 In your unfailing love you will lead
  the people you have redeemed.
In your strength you will guide them
  to your holy dwelling.*

Thank God he is not just consuming fire and burning anger! Those qualities are good and we should embrace them in our lives, but they are balanced with unfailing love. As a Father, he wants us living with him. He will lead you with unfailing love. He will guide you in his strength. He will do what it takes to get you through your own Red Sea, victorious over your Pharaoh, and bring you into his presence for eternity. He has redeemed you with the blood of his own Son! He is not about to let you perish!

## THE NATIONS WILL HEAR

*<sup>14</sup> The nations will hear and tremble;*
  *anguish will grip the people of Philistia.*
*<sup>15</sup> The chiefs of Edom will be terrified,*
  *the leaders of Moab will be seized with trembling,*
*the people of Canaan will melt away;*
*<sup>16</sup>   terror and dread will fall on them.*
*By the power of your arm*
  *they will be as still as a stone—*
*until your people pass by, Lord,*
  *until the people you bought pass by.*

They have just barely escaped the enemy's wrath, but Moses is thinking about the testimony to other nations. Of course, in this case it is largely so they will respect Israel's God and let the people through in peace, but God delights in manifesting his power so people who are lost and without knowledge of him will be awed by what a great God he is. What a shame that instead of being terrified and trembling when God is mentioned, he is often the subject of ridicule and jokes, and his people seen as buffoons.

Do you think God might want to change that? Could you be a vessel he would use to display his power and glory? Do you think he could work in your church in such a way that terror and dread would fall on the surrounding community? Do you remember how fear gripped all who heard what happened to Ananias and Sapphira? And how a deep sense of awe filled the early church?

*<sup>17</sup> You will bring them in and plant them*
  *on the mountain of your inheritance—*
*the place, Lord, you made for your dwelling,*
  *the sanctuary, Lord, your hands established.*

¹⁸ *"The Lord reigns*
 *for ever and ever."*

## "THY KINGDOM COME..."
It's all about God's kingdom reign – in your life, your family, your church, and, to the extent we can influence it, the world. It is the longing of our hearts for his kingdom to fully come on this earth when Christ returns. Then he will gather us, his people, and plant us in his dwelling place. Jesus said "In my Father's house are many mansions. I am going to prepare a place for you." Do you long for that sanctuary? Do you seek to enter into it as often as possible? One key way is through the worship we have been looking at in this chapter.

## MIRIAM LEADS THE WOMEN IN WORSHIP AND DANCING
¹⁹ *When Pharaoh's horses, chariots and horsemen went into the sea, the Lord brought the waters of the sea back over them, but the Israelites walked through the sea on dry ground.* ²⁰ *Then Miriam the prophet, Aaron's sister, took a timbrel in her hand, and all the women followed her, with timbrels and dancing.* ²¹ *Miriam sang to them:*

*"Sing to the Lord,*
 *for he is highly exalted.*
*Both horse and driver*
 *he has hurled into the sea."*

This is the first female prophet in the Bible. In Numbers 12:2 Miriam claimed that God spoke through her, but we don't know much about her prophetic ministry. She became jealous of her brother, wanting equal recognition as God's mouthpiece, and focused her complaint on Moses' Cushite wife. As a result her skin turned leprous (Numbers 12:10). But here she led the women of Israel in prophetic dance and worship.

Have you heard this story so often, or watched the movie so often, that you are not in awe of your God's power? When was the last time you were moved to lavishly praise God because of some great act he had done? Do you have a living relationship with God? Follow Moses' example and encourage those you influence, whether it be your church or your family, to become true worshippers.

# Part 3

## *Testing and Teaching in the Wilderness*

# 11

# RELIEF IS JUST AHEAD!
## *EXODUS 15:22-27*

I have often been asked how long someone should wait before leaving a difficult marriage, job, or church. My sense is that most leave way too soon. We tend to be like the Israelites on the exodus: At the first sign of difficulty we start crying. We fall apart. Life is tough. God doesn't seem to be coming through. We can't see that just ahead Elim awaits us; a place of refreshing springs and shady palm trees (seventy of them!). I have known couples who were separated. He finally decides to go for the divorce – just when his wife was thinking about reconciliation. He wasn't willing to give it enough time; he had suffered enough and was going to do things his way.

In this passage God wants to give you hope, and perseverance to hang in there.

### AFTER THE MIRACLE
*22 Then Moses led Israel from the Red Sea and they went into the Desert of Shur. For three days they traveled in the desert without finding water.*

If you didn't know the context, you could understand people panicking after three days without water. But only days before they had been liberated from 400 years of slavery in Egypt, with amazing displays of God's power. Then the Lord purposely placed them between Pharaoh's pursuing armies and the Red Sea. In a miracle you would think should give them an unshakable faith for years to come, God opened the sea, they crossed on dry ground, and Pharaoh's armies were destroyed. They just finished a glorious time of worship, and now they are on the road again. It says Moses led them — but really it is the pillar of cloud and fire, God's visible presence. And he leads them right into the desert. Everyone knows water is important in the desert. They had just walked through the middle of a sea — but now there is no water anywhere. One day might be bearable, but after three days the situation gets critical. Had God forgotten them? Does Moses really know what he is doing?

Miracles are great, but when it comes to truly strengthening faith, we have extremely short memories. We can experience a great miracle, and a couple days later be in despair and ready to give up. We can become so addicted to miracles that we can't handle the struggles of the desert.

Have you ever found yourself in a dry stretch after a great move of God in your life? Can you still trust him? Has he done enough that you can be confident he won't let you down? How would you be doing after three days without water? It is easy to feel betrayed by God — even angry at him. The great stories about victory and prosperity and God working out all your problems just don't seem true for you.

## PASTORING IN THE DESERT

And what about Moses? He was just as thirsty as everyone else, but was carrying a much heavier load. He was responsible for thousands of people. They all looked to him to make things work. He is the one they would stone if they got desperate. He had reluctantly accepted God's call to lead his people to a land flowing with milk and honey, and so far it has been a roller coaster ride. God displayed his power to Pharaoh - only for Moses' own people to rise up against him. They finally get out of Egypt - to find themselves trapped by the Red Sea. And now, after an incredible deliverance and worship service, they may all die of thirst.

If you are a pastor or leader you have probably ridden that same roller coaster. Sometimes it can be your fault. It is always appropriate to examine yourself and ask the Holy Spirit to search your heart. But chances are there is nothing wrong with you. Your faith isn't weak. You are not in sin. That's just the way it is. A big part of maturity is persevering through the lows and not getting carried away by the highs. You may have preached about all the great things God has for us in that Promised Land, but your people seem to be in a dry place. Some might be ready to leave for a more "successful" church with more pumped-up music. It's just not happening the way they say it should on TV. That is a tough spot for a pastor to be in. There is nothing wrong with preaching about God's blessings, but be sure to prepare your people for the dry stretches; that doesn't betray a lack of faith or negativity.

## HOPE DEFERRED

Perhaps the only thing worse than a gnawing thirst is getting your hopes up just to have them dashed. This could be the straw that breaks the camel's back. I can picture them seeing the oasis and hearing the water as they get closer. God finally came through! Suddenly they are praising him – until the first eager pilgrims drink some of the water. It's bitter!

*$^{23}$ When they came to Marah, they could not drink its water because it was bitter. (That is why the place is called Marah.)*

## BITTER WATER

Have you drunk some bitter water recently? Is there something you desperately need and want – that you have waited a long time for? Just when it seems it is finally yours, you find out you are at Marah instead of the Promised Land. Maybe it is a woman you thought was God's answer to years of praying for a wife – only to find out she is not as pleasant as you first thought. Or a job that promised you financial freedom that has become an unbearable burden. How do you respond when God disappoints you? When a pastor doesn't seem to deliver? When life seems more than you can handle?

*$^{24}$ So the people grumbled against Moses, saying, "What are we to drink?"*

It is the same familiar refrain repeated so frequently on this journey. As we have already seen several times, the people naturally turn to the one they think can help – their leader. Their pastor. Their husband, or father. They grumble. At this point there is no insurrection, but the heat is on. Remember when Jesus told the disciples to feed the multitude? They knew it was impossible. Moses can't just conjure up water for thousands of people! But both the disciples and the Israelites forgot who they are dealing with.

Are you in a dry place right now? Are you grumbling about it? Are you frustrated with someone over you because they are not offering relief and coming through for you? Does God seem to have turned a deaf ear? Are you in Moses' situation? People are looking to you for help, and you have absolutely no idea what to do!

## Fresh Water!
*²⁵ Then Moses cried out to the Lord, and the Lord showed him a piece of wood. He threw it into the water, and the water became fit to drink.*

Once again Moses did the right thing. He did the only thing he could do: He called out to God. The solution was simple. A piece of wood thrown into the water made it fit to drink. Not any piece of wood, but the one the Lord showed him. Was it a special kind of wood that somehow counteracted the bitterness in the water? Many possibilities have been offered. I don't think it had anything to do with the wood. I think it was a simple miracle God did in response to Moses' obedience to what could seem a silly command.

Some see in the wood a type of the cross. Certainly Jesus paid the price for the bitterness of this life. He doesn't instantly clear up every problem, but the power of the devil, and sin, and death, was broken at the cross. He experienced the most bitter death possible – for you. His presence will satisfy your soul's thirst.

Can you imagine what would have happened if Moses had gotten all logical and started arguing with God? Is God calling you to do something that seems crazy? Can you believe he knows what he is doing? Probably a mob of thirsty, frustrated people was watching as Moses tossed the wood in the water. What if nothing happened? What would he do then? Would the crowd be so angry they would kill him? Are you willing to step out in faith, with your whole church watching, to obey something that makes no sense to you?

## God's provision in the bitter times
Sometimes God sweetens the bitterness in your life and makes it bearable. He may provide fresh water from a rock. He is free to move as he wants in each situation. Moses would have made a

fool of himself if the next time they encountered bitter water he went looking for a stick and tossed it in. What God directed another pastor to do which brought tremendous blessing to his church may have nothing to do with your situation. Don't be too quick to line up and toss wood in the water! You need to hear from God for your situation. And the stick you threw in the water last year might not work this time.

Life is full of problems, but God has a way out of each one. Would it have been nice to have carts with ice cold water for the entire trip? Sure! Some people would "declare" that water was there, and was sweet, and would claim it in Jesus' name. They just can't stand the thought of having to go through hardship, but God may have you walking for a while without water. You will live! He won't let you die!

*There the Lord issued a ruling and instruction for them and put them to the test. [26] He said, "If you listen carefully to the Lord your God and do what is right in his eyes, if you pay attention to his commands and keep all his decrees, I will not bring on you any of the diseases I brought on the Egyptians, for I am the Lord, who heals you."*

## TESTING

Yep. It was a test. Remember school? Were you excited when the teacher announced a test? Not unless you were a brainiac, confident you would ace the test. Do you think you might be going through a test right now? The popular theology of endless blessings doesn't leave much room for testing, but God was finding out just how real their worship was. He is letting them see how much their faith had grown after walking through the Red Sea (not much!).

Could God be putting you to the test right now? They were fortunate that this test lasted only three days. That was about all they could take. I have seen people go through testing for years. God probably has great things in store and is doing a deep work in them.

## I AM THE LORD WHO HEALS YOU

This was actually an important step forward. God issued a new ruling and instruction, and gave an amazing promise; a promise that many today lay hold of as a blank check for healing. Let's look carefully at it:

- As with most of God's promises, it comes with a big condition. They have to listen carefully to the Lord. *And* do what is right in his eyes. *And* pay attention to his commands. *And* keep **all** his decrees. Wait a minute! That's impossible! Jesus is the only one who kept every command! If there is any chance of meeting this condition you will have to spend time with God so you can listen carefully to him. How are you doing on that? How is it going keeping all his decrees? It is easy to sail right over the condition and just grab hold of the promise, isn't it?

- This specifically covered diseases that God had brought on the Egyptians. There is no blanket promise of healing in every situation. We don't know exactly what those diseases were. What we do know is that every single one of these adults died in the wilderness over the next forty years. Of course, they didn't fulfill the condition of the promise.

- God may bring disease on you. This seems to imply it is in response to our unfaithfulness or sin. It may be some kind of correction. If you are ill, it is worth asking if God brought it on you for some reason. Apparently it's not always the devil.

- Having said all that, we can still joyfully affirm that God is a healer! He wants to heal. He has total power to heal. And it is always good to ask for the healing. Just be careful of "declaring" a healing when you really don't know what God might be doing in the person's life. It only makes you – and God – look foolish if it doesn't happen. If healing doesn't occur, take a look at how you're doing on the conditions.

*[27]{.sup} Then they came to Elim, where there were twelve springs and seventy palm trees, and they camped there near the water.*

## AN OASIS!

Ah, Elim. God is good. This is finally the campout they were hoping for by the Red Sea. It is so good to come across an oasis in the middle of the desert. They would love to stay there. But, alas, they still had a long journey and many battles ahead of them.

Thank God for the Elims in your life. Don't take them for granted, and don't get too attached to them. They are a taste of God's gracious provision, and encouragement that such places exist. There may be more of them along the way. In the meantime, hold onto the memory of how good it was. I see too many people today who feel Elim is their birthright as Christians. They settle down there to live the good life. No, this world is not our home. We are strangers and pilgrims here, and must be careful of getting too comfortable in Elim – perhaps to the point we no longer hear God or are unwilling to move on when he calls us back into the desert.

God led them both to Marah and to Elim; a place of bitterness and a place of blessing. Elim is even better when you have just been at Marah. God may keep you at Marah a little longer – but he will show you a log that makes it bearable. It's still no Elim –

but at least you will survive. Our lives tend to be a rhythm of Elims and Marahs. God doesn't owe you Elim. He never guarantees we will stay at Elim. In fact, Jesus told us there would be plenty of bitterness in this world.

## Relief Is Just Ahead

If only the people had hung in there a little longer, God had something so sweet waiting for them. Hang in there my brother. I can't tell you when you will reach Elim, but it will be right on time. Right in God's time. There are some beautiful moments, some gifts, which God has for us in the midst of this wilderness we call life. Enjoy them to the max while you are there. They are little boosts, steps along the way to heaven, which keep faith alive and refresh your soul. There may be an Elim just around the bend for you. Don't give up. God will give you the strength to keep going.

# 12

## THE DESERT OF SIN
### *EXODUS 16:1-12*

*¹The whole Israelite community set out from Elim and came to the Desert of Sin, which is between Elim and Sinai, on the fifteenth day of the second month after they had come out of Egypt.*

The Desert of Sin. What an appropriate name! Lots had happened in the month since they left Egypt! Certainly enough to give them a solid trust in God. They had just been refreshed at Elim, but now that seems a distant memory. They are back in the desert. Many Christians have the same experience after a powerful retreat or church service. You get home, or to work, and you are right back in the Desert of Sin.

Actually, the desert's name has nothing to do with sinfulness. It was probably named after the Semitic moon-deity Sin, who was worshipped in that region and may have looked like the moon. It's one of four places mentioned in this one verse:

1) Egypt – the place of slavery God delivered them from.

2) Elim – the place of God's gracious refreshing.

3) Sin – the desolate place they find themselves in at the moment; a place of scarcity and testing – and God's miraculous provision. As is often the case, Sin came

between the refreshing and an awesome encounter with God.

4) Sinai – the mountain that lies ahead, where God will display his glory as in few other places, and give them his law. Also a place of rebellion, because seeing God's power didn't keep them from sinning.

Interestingly enough, they only spent a few days at Elim, and a fairly short time at Sinai. They were in slavery 400 years, and in the desert for 40 years! But it's all preparation for an eternity in paradise!

Do any of these places describe where you're at right now? How do you handle the desert? Pay close attention to the lessons Israel learned at Sin!

## BEWARE OF GRUMBLING!

[2] *In the desert the whole community grumbled against Moses and Aaron.*

Grumbling, complaining, murmuring, moaning: different names for the same sin. If you are a leader, you might as well get used to them. Grumbling seems to come with the territory. Whether in your family or church, it can be a cancer that infects the whole body. It's common – and deadly.

How do you feel when your wife or kids complain about everything? It's the opposite of a grateful heart – and God hates it. Directly or indirectly, it reflects on him. He calls us to be content – and trust him in less-than-ideal situations. Resist the temptation to murmur. Train your children not to grumble. Don't tolerate it at home. Warn your church about it. Be careful not to fall into it yourself. And be pro-active; when people around you grumble, don't just silently sit there. Don't condemn them, but challenge them and offer a constructive alternative.

*³ The Israelites said to them, "If only we had died by the Lord's hand in Egypt! There we sat around pots of meat and ate all the food we wanted, but you have brought us out into this desert to starve this entire assembly to death."*

## MOSES AND GOD CONSPIRE TO KILL THEM!

With fear comes grumbling, and reality goes out the window. Egypt sounds great! After only a month, they actually romanticize slavery! Maybe they did eat plenty in Egypt – but they conveniently forgot the horrors of slavery. Desperate and hopeless, they prefer death. And they are deceived into believing God is determined to kill them, just days after his gracious provision of water. They probably left Egypt with provisions that lasted this first month. Now they're gone, and they lack the faith to trust that God won't let them starve!

They also question Moses' motives. Instead of a caring shepherd, he becomes a mass murderer, tricking them to leave Egypt so he can starve them. That has got to be one of the hardest things for a leader to take. Moses had left everything. He had nothing but headaches bringing them out of Egypt. Being accused of attempted homicide had to hurt! Whether it's your kids, wife, or church, it is dangerous to judge their motives. You don't know what is going on in their hearts! There is nothing wrong with feeling fear – but as almost every marriage seminar will teach you, express those feelings in "I" statements, instead of judging the other person. If you get accused, as Moses did, don't get defensive. Look at the fear behind it, let them talk about what they're feeling, and listen for what the Lord has to say.

## THE DANGER OF PROSPERITY PREACHING

The Israelites loved Elim. They were praising God after they crossed the Red Sea, ready to buy into the teaching that life with God is nothing but blessing and victory. Sadly, embracing that teaching can leave you vulnerable when God doesn't come through as you have been told he would. Can you imagine if Moses had promised abundant food, good weather, and victory over every enemy! This little bit of hunger would have been a real shock! But that is exactly what we do when we present a Christian life of pure blessing, joy, victory, and abundance. When it doesn't happen, we may blame God, the preacher – or ourselves. We may actually think death would be better. More likely, we will have fond memories of how good life was in the world, and may give up on God altogether.

If you are hungry and struggling right now, beware of romanticizing the past. Don't get angry at your pastor. Challenge thoughts of doom and desperation. Thank God for all he has done. Get into the Scriptures and be encouraged by his faithfulness. Don't get into a fake "positive confession." Be real about how painful it is – but look to God, and trust him for his provision.

*4 Then the Lord said to Moses, "I will rain down bread from heaven for you. The people are to go out each day and gather enough for that day. In this way I will test them and see whether they will follow my instructions. 5 On the sixth day they are to prepare what they bring in, and that is to be twice as much as they gather on the other days."*

## THE SECOND TEST

The first test was the bitter water of Marah. They didn't do too well on that one. Now they are going to be tested on how well they follow directions. How would you do on that? When you get that ready-to-assemble furniture, do you read the directions? Do you follow them? Or do you figure you know as well – or better – how to put it together? Do you study your car's owner's manual and strictly follow its guidelines for oil changes and maintenance? Failure to follow directions – whether for oil changes or traffic laws - often betrays a rebellious heart. You know better than the other person - or you just don't like being told how to do it. That is pride. Submitting to following directions from God and his Word is a critical foundation of the Christian life.

Following instructions for gathering manna may seem trivial. But if you don't follow instructions in the little stuff, chances are you won't in the important things either. That is the idea behind New York City's zero-tolerance approach to enforcing the law, responsible for making it one of the safest cities in the country. If people know they have to obey minor laws, they will develop a pattern of obedience, and be less apt to break the big laws. The same idea is behind training a dog to work for everything he gets. If he has to sit and wait to get fed, he will probably come when he's called. And that may save his life on a busy street.

## GOD WILL PROVIDE FOR YOU

God had not given the Sabbath law yet, but the principle was in place since creation. They could work as usual for six days, but on the seventh God would withhold the manna, and they would eat what they prepared the day before. If they failed to follow instructions they would go hungry. Human nature tends to chafe under the law – but along with the instructions came God's miraculous provision. Without Moses having to ask, God overlooked their grumbling, and graciously rained down bread from heaven. That is a pattern that continues until today: "Give us this day our daily bread." We trust God to provide day by day. That doesn't mean you can't store things up for a rainy day; we need to be wise n using what he gives us. But Jesus also clearly warns about getting caught up in material concerns:

> "Therefore I tell you, do not worry about your life, what you will eat or drink; or about your body, what you will wear. Is not life more than food, and the body more than clothes? Look at the birds of the air; they do not sow or reap or store away in barns, and yet your heavenly Father feeds them. Are you not much more valuable than they? Can any one of you by worrying add a single hour to your life?
>
> "And why do you worry about clothes? See how the flowers of the field grow. They do not labor or spin. Yet I tell you that not even Solomon in all his splendor was dressed like one of these. If that is how God clothes the grass of the field, which is here today and tomorrow is thrown into the fire, will he not much more clothe you—you of little faith? So do not worry, saying, 'What shall we eat?' or 'What shall we drink?' or 'What shall we wear?' For the pagans run after all these things, and your heavenly Father knows that you need them. But seek first his kingdom and his righteousness, and all these things will be given to you as well. Therefore do not worry about tomorrow, for tomorrow will worry about itself. Each day has enough trouble of its own. (Matthew 6:25-34)

Why is it so hard to follow what Jesus says, after all these years of seeing his faithfulness? Why are we so reluctant to seek his kingdom first? Why do we insist on seeking worldly wealth? Letting go of earthly concerns is incredibly freeing! Imagine how much grumbling would be eliminated! Live each day to the full! Trust God for what you need to make it through today!

## Your daily manna

We no longer go out to gather manna – but we should go every morning to meet with Jesus and feed our souls on the Word. Yesterday's great devotional time just doesn't carry over for today. Many people struggle with quiet time, and may resist it as legalism. Yet in over forty years of following Jesus, I have observed that making the effort to gather that manna every day is the single most important factor to spiritual health. You won't feel like it at times, but just as you shower, get dressed, and have breakfast every morning, make that devotional time an indispensable part of your daily routine. Trust that God will rain down bread from heaven for you.

*[6] So Moses and Aaron said to all the Israelites, "In the evening you will know that it was the Lord who brought you out of Egypt, [7] and in the morning you will see the glory of the Lord, because he has heard your grumbling against him. Who are we, that you should grumble against us?" [8] Moses also said, "You will know that it was the Lord when he gives you meat to eat in the evening and all the bread you want in the morning, because he has heard your grumbling against him. Who are we? You are not grumbling against us, but against the Lord."*

## Who are you really grumbling about?

When you complain about the one whom God has placed over you in authority, you are complaining about God. Moses couldn't give them daily meat and bread, but in response to their grumbling, God would move to prove himself and display his glory. He gave them all the bread they could eat. It may have been monotonous, eating the same manna every day, but it was utterly reliable. A Christian singer from the 80's, Keith Green, wrote a humorous song about it:

*So you wanna go back to Egypt, where it's warm and secure.*
*Are you sorry you bought the one-way ticket when you thought you were sure?*
*You wanted to live in the Land of Promise, but now it's getting so hard.*
*Are you sorry you're out here in the desert, instead of your own backyard?*

*Eating leeks and onions by the Nile.*
*Ooh what breath, but dining out in style.*
*Ooh, my life's on the skids.*
*Give me the pyramids.*

*Well there's nothing to do but travel, and we sure travel a lot.*
*'Cause it's hard to keep your feet from moving when the sand gets so hot.*
*And in the morning it's manna hotcakes. We snack on manna all day.*
*And they sure had a winner last night for dinner, flaming manna soufflé.*

*Well we once complained for something new to munch.*
*The ground opened up and had some of us for lunch.*
*Ooh, such fire and smoke.*
*Can't God even take a joke...Huh?...(NO!)*

*So you wanna go back to Egypt, where old friends wait for you.*
*You can throw a big party and tell the whole gang, that what they said was all*
*true.*
*And this Moses acts like a big-shot, who does he think he is.*
*It's true that God works lots of miracles, but Moses thinks they're all his.*

*Well I'm having so much trouble even now.*
*Why'd he get so mad about that cow, that golden cow.*
*Moses, he seems rather idle, he just sits around.*
*He just sits around and writes the Bible.*

*Oh, Moses, put down your pen.*
*What...Oh no, manna again?*
*Oh, manna waffles....*
*Manna burgers...*
*Manna bagels...*
*Fillet of manna...*
*Mannacoti...*
*Bamanna bread!*

Are you guilty of grumbling about God – because you are complaining about someone he has placed in authority? Are you content with what he has given you, or do you feel you deserve better? Has the greed and materialism of much of the church robbed you of simplicity and gratitude?

[9] Then Moses told Aaron, "Say to the entire Israelite community, 'Come before the Lord, for he has heard your grumbling.'" [10] While Aaron was speaking to the whole Israelite community, they looked toward the desert, and there was the glory of the Lord appearing in the cloud. [11] The Lord said to Moses, [12] "I have heard the grumbling of the Israelites. Tell them, 'At twilight you will eat meat, and in the morning you will be filled with bread. Then you will know that I am the Lord your God.'"

Right there, in the Desert of Sin, with all their murmuring, they get to see the glory cloud! God wants to display his glory! He will provide your daily needs! How much better to enjoy his glorious presence and receive his gracious daily provision with faith-filled, joyful, grateful hearts! Just like God was testing them, they were testing God. But Jesus said we shouldn't put God to the test!

- Have you been testing God?

- What are you grumbling about in your heart? The wife God gave you? Your job? Your pastor? Your congregation?

- How can you change your attitude so you can see God's glory?

- Are you taking advantage of the manna available to you every morning? What have you been missing out on because you haven't made the time and effort to go out and find what God has prepared for you?

We are no better than Israel. The Desert of Sin was not a pleasant place. But often it is in the desert that you see God's glory. When you are hungry, even manna can be a treat!

# 13

## HOW WELL DO YOU FOLLOW DIRECTIONS?
### EXODUS 16:13-35

God gave the Israelites manna for food – and as a test of how well they follow directions. The manna came with five important instructions. Let's see how well they did on the test – and how well we would do.

*¹³ That evening quail came and covered the camp, and in the morning there was a layer of dew around the camp. ¹⁴ When the dew was gone, thin flakes like frost on the ground appeared on the desert floor. ¹⁵ When the Israelites saw it, they said to each other, "What is it?" For they did not know what it was.*

*Moses said to them, "It is the bread the Lord has given you to eat. ¹⁶ This is what the Lord has commanded: 'Everyone is to gather as much as they need. Take an omer for each person you have in your tent.'"*

*¹⁷ The Israelites did as they were told; some gathered much, some little. ¹⁸ And when they measured it by the omer, the one who gathered much did not have too much, and the one who gathered little did not have too little. Everyone had gathered just as much as they needed.*

## First instruction: Gather just as much as you need

Oh, what a temptation for capitalists! The younger, stronger ones could gather far more than the elderly or infirmed. Survival of the fittest! Some would be greedy and gluttonous – and try to get as much as they *wanted*, instead of what they *needed*. Others might try to set up a business: packaging it, preparing it, buying it from those who chose to eat less, and selling it to those who could afford it.

There was an important principle here about living in community: God can be counted on to provide what we need. Self-discipline is needed not to grab more – and to leave enough for others. No one should go hungry! No one should hoard or over-consume to the detriment of others! If someone was lazy and didn't feel like going out to collect manna, they would go hungry! There was no welfare, although surely someone got manna for those who were physically unable to. It is a principle the Holy Spirit impressed on the early church:

> *God's grace was so powerfully at work in them all that there were no needy persons among them. For from time to time those who owned land or houses sold them, brought the money from the sales and put it at the apostles' feet, and it was distributed to anyone who had need* (Acts 4:33-35).

We should seek equality, especially within the church. It is sinful for some to be hoarding manna and getting fat while others barely have enough to eat! There are very efficient organizations to help wealthy Christians share with those who have less. When prosperity is taught we must guard against greed, and instead teach that God's abundant provision is meant to be shared with the less fortunate. There is also an important principle of being content with what God gives us:

> *Keep your lives free from the love of money and be content with what you have, because God has said, "Never will I leave you; never will I forsake you."* (Hebrews 13:5)

We can seek to establish these principles in society as well. The United States is experiencing a growing gulf between rich and poor. The church should be at the forefront of addressing that, and seeking greater equality. For centuries the church managed charities for that purpose. When the church failed, government stepped in, often with less than ideal results. Let's take back the leading role God intends for us in helping the needy and promoting greater equality!

This was potentially as much a test for Moses as for the community. Would he arrange for his family or friends to get more? Would he organize a corporation to collect the manna and sell it, instead of letting each person get what they needed? Would he accept bribes from those who had the means to pay him off? He could also be tempted to overlook others' abuses. In Acts five we have the story of Ananias and Sapphira, who tried to work the system for their own benefit. Peter was faithful in calling them out, and they both died.

Corruption is rampant in government – and even in the church! Guard yourself from favoritism or gaming the system. Moses got the same amount of manna as everyone else. It is wrong for a pastor to be in need while his congregation prospers. But, more frequently, the pastor lives the good life at his congregation's expense. There must be no hint of impropriety in your handling of material affairs!

[19] Then Moses said to them, "No one is to keep any of it until morning."

[20] However, some of them paid no attention to Moses; they kept part of it until morning, but it was full of maggots and began to smell. So Moses was angry with them.

**SECOND INSTRUCTION: DO NOT KEEP ANY OVERNIGHT**
It was mainly a matter of faith. Keeping some for the next day betrayed disbelief that God would provide enough manna in the morning. It also meant they either went hungry so they could save some for the next day, or gathered more than they should in the first place. God wants us to trust him for our daily needs. Be careful of focusing so much on preparing for the future that you never live for today!

Many bristle at the idea of being told what to do: "Who is Moses to tell me what I can do with my manna? Didn't I gather it? Don't I have the right to do what I want with it?" Whether it makes sense to us or not, if God has told us how to do something, we have to submit and do it. When the whole body walks in obedience, unity results. If one person started storing manna, others would follow, and the whole system of getting only what you need would fall apart.

There are always some, however, who refuse to pay attention to instruction. The fruit of their rebellion always stinks, as it did in this case. The maggots became a health issue for the entire community. Moses was rightfully angry, and so was God! The independent American spirit has fostered rebellion. At the end of the book of Judges we are told everyone did as they saw fit; the result was chaos. America is moving in that direction. It may not be popular, but don't stop teaching about submission to authority and following directions. Start at home with your own family.

*²¹ Each morning everyone gathered as much as they needed, and when the sun grew hot, it melted away. ²² On the sixth day, they gathered twice as much—two omers for each person—and the leaders of the community came and reported this to Moses. ²³ He said to them, "This is what the Lord commanded: 'Tomorrow is to be a day of sabbath rest, a holy sabbath to the Lord. So bake what you want to bake and boil what you want to boil. Save whatever is left and keep it until morning.'"*

*²⁴ So they saved it until morning, as Moses commanded, and it did not stink or get maggots in it. ²⁵ "Eat it today," Moses said, "because today is a sabbath to the Lord. You will not find any of it on the ground today. ²⁶ Six days you are to gather it, but on the seventh day, the Sabbath, there will not be any."*

Moses enforced God's rules. When they realized they couldn't get away with storing the manna, everyone started following directions. As a result, the community developed a rhythm. They got used to getting up every morning and finding that God had been faithful:

> *Because of the Lord's great love we are not consumed,*
> *for his compassions never fail.*
> *They are new every morning;*
> *great is your faithfulness.*
>
> (Lamentations 3:22-23)

## THIRD INSTRUCTION: GATHER DOUBLE ON THE SIXTH DAY

Once they had gotten the basic rhythm down, they were ready for something a little more complicated: Six days they went about their lives as usual, but the seventh was set aside for physical and spiritual refreshment. God likes to interrupt the rhythm of daily life to remind us who he is. Here it involved miraculous preservation of the manna until the following day. The lack of manna on the Sabbath reminded the Israelites that this was a supernatural provision, directly under God's control.

Although we rightly resist a legalistic observance of the Sabbath, we ignore it at our own peril. One day in seven we interrupt our routine, take the focus off self, and dedicate time to worship God, hear from him, and enjoy fellowship with his people. He knows we need it, and wants to refresh us.

Apparently most of them were learning that following instructions works, but there are always some who want to push the limits:

*[27] Nevertheless, some of the people went out on the seventh day to gather it, but they found none. [28] Then the Lord said to Moses, "How long will you refuse to keep my commands and my instructions? [29] Bear in mind that the Lord has given you the Sabbath; that is why on the sixth day he gives you bread for two days. Everyone is to stay where they are on the seventh day; no one is to go out." [30] So the people rested on the seventh day. [31] The people of Israel called the bread manna. It was white like coriander seed and tasted like wafers made with honey.*

We are not told whether these same people gathered double on the sixth day while still hoping to get more on the seventh. Again, it betrayed disbelief in God's word, and he was not pleased.

When you go out looking for something God hasn't intended for you, you are going to come up empty, or find yourself in a dark alley buying illegal manna. Either way you are drawn away from the Lord and miss out on his blessings.

## Fourth Instruction: Stay Where You Are on the Sabbath. Don't Go Out.

That's a hard one for a lot of us! We don't like being confined, or being told where we can or can't go. They already had to follow the cloud as one unified people. Now they are told there would be no travel on the Sabbath. They didn't even need to go out and get manna! He had taken care of that! No exceptions. *Everyone* had to do the same thing.

How would that go over in the church today? Do you think we have a hard time following instructions? I do! Don't go overboard, but try to re-establish a day of rest, a day dedicated to the Lord and to family. Start with your own family. Invite other families to join you. Slow down for one day, and then try to introduce it to your church.

*$^{32}$ Moses said, "This is what the Lord has commanded: 'Take an omer of manna and keep it for the generations to come, so they can see the bread I gave you to eat in the wilderness when I brought you out of Egypt.'" $^{33}$ So Moses said to Aaron, "Take a jar and put an omer of manna in it. Then place it before the Lord to be kept for the generations to come." $^{34}$ As the Lord commanded Moses, Aaron put the manna with the tablets of the covenant law, so that it might be preserved.*

## Fifth Instruction: Preserve Some Manna as a Memorial

This one was just for Moses – and it was the only command that was kept faithfully. Moses could have expressed concern about the manna spoiling – he had already seen only too many maggots. But he had also seen God's miraculous preservation of manna on the sixth day. He didn't ask any questions about what God told him to do.

Moses also had learned about delegation. God didn't mention Aaron, but Moses delegated the task to him, and Aaron faithfully completed it. Has God given you someone you can trust to carry out tasks? Do you feel you have to do everything? Or do you give others a chance to experience the blessings of obedience?

God is into memorials. Too few people today have any sense of where the church has come from or how God has worked through the centuries. The Jews have much to teach us here, with their observance of Passover and other significant events in their history!

What milestones have occurred in your life? In your family? In your church? Is there some physical evidence of God's faithfulness you can prominently display in your home or church? What traditions can you start to remind people of the good things God has done? The Lord's Supper is one such memorial. Make sure you give it the proper place in your church.

*35 The Israelites ate manna forty years, until they came to a land that was settled; they ate manna until they reached the border of Canaan.*

Once they reached the land flowing with milk and honey they were on their own. There is a time to grow up. God may spoon feed us or give us milk for a while, but the time comes when we need to eat solid food and learn how to care for ourselves as adults. Forty years is a long time to be eating the same food every morning, but it certainly established an unshakable confidence in God's provision.

Five simple instructions. None were really hard to keep. But we resist being told what to do. What instructions has God been giving you? What have you read recently in the Word which you know he wants you to follow? Are you consistent in enforcing the rules in your home or church? Do you only do it when you feel like it? Or just find it too much of a hassle? How are you doing on this test?

# 14

## DEALING WITH THE DRY PLACES
### *EXODUS 17:1-7*

Have you noticed that you tend to deal with the same issues in your life over and over again? I have been keeping a journal for over forty years. Looking back that far gives some real perspective! On the one hand I rejoice in growth and many great things the Lord has done. On the other hand I am deeply troubled by some recurring struggles. We can be very hard headed and slow to learn! As a father, you may get impatient with your kids for repeatedly making the same mistakes. If you are in leadership, you may get frustrated with how slow your people are to change. But don't be too quick to condemn them – or to condemn Israel out here in the desert. I am sure God has been very patient with you, as he has been with me!

Parts of this passage seem remarkably similar to Chapter 15. God knows we usually don't get it the first time; that's why Scripture is repetitious. Certain themes run throughout the Bible – sometimes in the same verse! Peter wrote: *So I will always remind you of these things, even though you know them and are firmly established in the truth you now have. I think it is right to refresh your memory as long as I live in the tent of this body* (2 Peter 1:12-13).

Israel was slow to learn. They barely started on their forty year journey, and already some disturbing patterns are emerging. You would think God's amazing provision of manna would be a daily reminder of his faithfulness, and would end their grumbling. Not so.

## WHEN GOD LEADS YOU TO A DRY PLACE
*[1]The whole Israelite community set out from the Desert of Sin, traveling from place to place as the Lord commanded. They camped at Rephidim, but there was no water for the people to drink.*

Israel's life was unpredictable - and not very pleasant. They never knew how long they would stay in one place, or where they would go next. The vague hope of a land flowing with milk and honey seemed very distant in the heat and drudgery of desert travel. We have what often is a hazy idea of heaven awaiting us, but if we're honest, too often it gets crowded out by the concerns of daily life.

This is not their first water problem. Just before bringing them to the oasis at Elim, the Lord miraculously sweetened bitter water. Now it looks like God isn't thinking too clearly. He has directed them to camp at a place with no water. Does that contradict your theology? Do you think you are assured of God's blessing if you are doing his will and walking with him? Most Christians probably do. Can you accept that he may take you to a dry place, with no apparent provision for your basic needs, where it feels like you are going to die? Maybe you are there right now and feel confused. Others may think you are in sin or lacking faith because you are in that dry place. That could be the case. It is good to examine yourself to see if you made a wrong turn. But if you are confident that God has you there, he wants to encourage you today. He has a purpose in it, and won't let you perish.

Nobody purposely chooses the dry place. But in our quest for the good life we may become hard of hearing. We get too comfortable, and are no longer sensitive to God's leading to pack up and move on, perhaps to a smaller house, a less hospitable climate, or a more challenging church. We are pilgrims on this earth, and may find ourselves moving around more than we would like. I certainly have.

## THE WRONG RESPONSES TO A DRY PLACE

*² So they quarreled with Moses and said, "Give us water to drink."*

*Moses replied, "Why do you quarrel with me? Why do you put the Lord to the test?"*

*³ But the people were thirsty for water there, and they grumbled against Moses. They said, "Why did you bring us up out of Egypt to make us and our children and livestock die of thirst?"*

When urgent needs aren't met, our perspective gets warped. Water is one of the most basic, along with food. But there are other needs – for love, for sex, for significance – that can also become life-controlling when they are unmet. You can hardly think about anything else! It is hard to have a strong faith at that point. Be careful to avoid one of Israel's wrong responses:

1. **Quarreling.** You may feel that your spouse, your pastor, or someone you hold responsible for the difficulty should be meeting your needs. It is easier to fight with them than with God. We don't see that the real battle is with the enemy of our souls. When you feel helpless, one thing you can do is quarrel. But chances are it won't solve anything, and will only make you feel worse.

2. **Demanding.** When you're desperate it is easy to get demanding: "Get me something to eat! Can't you see I'm starving?" "Make love to me!" "I need a raise!" Nobody likes having demands made of them, and it rarely results in your needs being met. Watch out for them!

3. **Putting God to the test.** Grumbling and unbelief are key ways we test God. Israel is getting good at it. God may test you, but don't test him! Verse 7 tells us they doubted that God was even among them – despite the manna and pillar of cloud and fire! God has promised he will never leave you or forsake you. Don't test him by questioning whether he is with you!

4. **Grumbling.** We have already seen how dangerous grumbling is.

5. **Distorting the facts, and assigning motives and blame.** In their eyes, Moses – not God, brought them out of Egypt. He is making them die of thirst; he actually wants them dead! And they regret this whole faith venture. Satan is the father of lies and will slip in his lies – or more frequently, half-truths – wherever he can. Be on the lookout for them and stand firm on the truth of God's Word. It really hurts if you are the one getting blamed – but don't let it get to you. Remember where it's coming from.

6. **Murder.** Yep. That's in the next verse. They are almost ready to stone Moses. Desperate people can do crazy things. Moses may have been exaggerating, but he apparently truly feared for his life.

*4 Then Moses cried out to the Lord, "What am I to do with these people? They are almost ready to stone me."*

## Wrong responses from a leader

1. **The why question.** In verse two Moses asked the very people who are struggling: "why?" But they are not thinking clearly and don't know why. To ask that of someone who is hurting gets you nowhere. As a leader,

try to understand where they're coming from and what is behind their request. Love them – don't interrogate them. Asking your wife why she is doing something that you find hurtful will rarely help the situation.

2. **The what question.** Of course Moses did right in such a desperate situation by crying out to the Lord. God was his only hope. But this was a cry of frustration. Moses was fed up. Not that we should judge his prayer. I am sure most of us would pray something similar. But it is far better to remind yourself of how you got to that place and express faith that God has a way out. When your wife is quarreling with you, instead of crying out to God "What am I to do with this woman?" try: "Thank you Lord for my wife. Thank you that you have made us one flesh. I know love is long-suffering, and you have called me to love her as Christ loves the church. Help me to lay down my life for her. I believe you have a way through this problem. Show me how I can truly love her." Do you sense the difference in those two cries?

3. **Fearing those God has entrusted to you.** When you fear your wife, your kids, or your congregation – when you fear people instead of God – you are headed for big trouble. You will lose your effectiveness as a leader. They have way too much control over you. Chances are they are partially motivated by fear themselves (the Israelites certainly were here), and your fear will just make things worse.

[5] *The Lord answered Moses, "Go out in front of the people. Take with you some of the elders of Israel and take in your hand the staff with which you struck the Nile, and go.* [6] *I will stand there before you by the rock at Horeb. Strike the rock, and water will*

come out of it for the people to drink." So Moses did this in the sight of the elders of Israel. ⁷ And he called the place Massah and Meribah because the Israelites quarreled and because they tested the Lord saying, "Is the Lord among us or not?"

## GOD'S RESPONSE

1. **The Lord answers.** They are God's people. He sent them on this mission. He called Moses. He has done amazing miracles. God has an answer to the problem. Wait for him. Listen to him. Do what he tells you to do.

2. **Lead.** Get rid of your fear. They're not going to stone you. God will protect you. They are just desperate. Don't hide. Get out in front of the people. Take your place of authority.

3. **Don't isolate yourself.** Out of fear or anger you may distance yourself from other leaders. They are the ones who will help you! Even if they have let you down, draw them in and share what God has called you to do. It will reassure the people that their elders are standing with you, and it shows your support for them. Even if you are upset with their seeming betrayal, you need them. You will be better off in the long run to include them.

4. **Grab hold of what God has given you.** In this case the staff had God's anointing. It represents authority to the people. God has used it in the past and they have seen its power. What staff has God given you? It may be a promise or a word from the Lord. Grab hold of it.

5. **Go.** Don't get paralyzed. There are times to wait, but often God moves when you get moving. Go to your wife. Go to the church. Go out into the community. It also communicates confidence and strength on your part.

6. **God will stand before you.** You are not alone! The people don't see the Lord, but Moses gets the assurance that as he steps out, God is right there with him. Does it encourage you to know God is standing before you as you make that difficult step of reconciling with your wife or confronting your church?

7. **God will provide – perhaps where you least expect it!** No Elim this time. Moses could have "declared" all day long that water would appear and nothing would have happened. He could have wracked his brain and tried to figure out how God would get him out of this jam – and never dream of striking a rock to produce water. It is easy for us to play God and try to come up with ways he could solve our problems. Let him be God, and be ready for something you would never dream of. 1 Corinthians 10:4 tells us this rock was Christ; Jesus was with them in the desert. The source of living water provided this life-giving water.

8. **Take a risk in front of your harshest critics.** It would be safer to strike the rock when nobody was around – just in case water didn't come out. These elders were not Moses' fans! They really might stone him or laugh him out of the camp if nothing happened! But faith calls us to take bold, risky, steps. Do you really believe God can heal or deliver someone from satanic bondage? Don't be afraid to pray for it in front of others!

9. **Obey.** It wasn't hard. All Moses had to do was get out there, take his staff, and strike the rock. Super easy! But it required significant faith, and it was risky. Carefully do whatever God tells you to do. Chances are it won't be beyond your abilities. But spiritually, mentally, and

emotionally it may seem almost impossible. Do exactly what God tells you do – and no more. Don't take for granted that what worked last time will work this time. We will see the tragic results of doing that in Exodus 20.

Wow! Another potential disaster averted because of one man's wise leadership. Without it, everyone might have died. Once again, one person who heard God and obeyed him saved a whole nation. Do you think he could still do that today? What is God calling you to do? What desperate situations do God's people find themselves in? Are you willing to be a Moses?

Massah means *testing* or *temptation,* and Meribah *strife*. They are not pleasant places. It is tough not having basic needs met. But God led them to this place. You may be there right now. It might seem there is no way out. You may be quarreling with someone, or testing God by your grumbling and lack of faith. You may be tempted beyond what you can resist on your own. God has a way through. He will provide! You're going to make it! It wasn't a mistake to leave Egypt, and it wasn't a mistake to follow Christ! He has all the life-giving water you need! He wants to refresh your soul right now – and get you through the dry place!

# 15

## THE FIRST BATTLE
### *EXODUS 17:8–16*

*⁸ The Amalekites came and attacked the Israelites at Rephidim.*

Isn't life great? Just what you need! No sooner does Moses resolve an internal problem than he faces an enemy attack. When will it ever stop? When do the blessings start? If it's not Pharaoh, it's squabbling and complaining among his own people. And now an attack from distant relatives, descendants of one of Esau's sons. They were most likely nomads, and water was a precious commodity. Their attack may have been provoked by God's abundant provision of water from the rock.

Unfortunately, that's life, whether you lead a church, a business, or a family. Sin has affected us at every level. The devil is always that lurking lion, looking for someone to devour. Thank God for moments of peace. Enjoy them. They're generally not the norm, especially if you are moving forward in God's purposes. You may be tempted to sacrifice spiritual progress to get away from the battles, but you won't find peace that way. Especially not God's *shalom* - total well-being.

Was Israel ready to fight? They did leave Egypt armed for battle (Exodus 13:18), but at the same time God sent them on a roundabout route because he knew they weren't ready; they might be tempted to turn back to Egypt (13:17). They were probably too deep into the wilderness to turn back now, to say nothing of having to get across the Red Sea. So God allows this first battle – and first victory.

Do you believe God allows the battles that come into your life, family, ministry, and work? Are you able to get beyond the fear and discouragement to see his hand and purpose in allowing them?

> ⁹ Moses said to Joshua, "Choose some of our men and go out to fight the Amalekites. Tomorrow I will stand on top of the hill with the staff of God in my hands."

## INTRODUCING JOSHUA

Moses is learning he doesn't have to do everything, and delegates the fighting to Joshua. This is the debut of the man who will lead Israel into the Promised Land, although we don't know a whole lot about him. Moses changed his name from *Hoshea* (salvation) to *Joshua* (God saves) – and his name was given to our Lord (*Jesus* is the Greek translation). He must have been quite young at this point. Joshua became Moses' indispensable aide – probably even closer than his brother Aaron. He was a great warrior, and had probably already distinguished himself in some way for Moses to entrust this task to him. With an inexperienced commander, Moses might have felt pressured to oversee the selection of the soldiers for such an important battle, but he wisely refuses to micromanage. He trusts Joshua to choose the men he wants to fight with, and doesn't question his choice. Moses won't have any part in the battle; Joshua will be on his own, while Moses watches from the hill.

Obviously, there are times when we need to be in the thick of battle, but often our motives are wrong: "If I don't fight, they might not do it right and we might lose the church!" It's hard to trust others to do the job right, especially when they are young and inexperienced. That's why great wisdom and divine guidance is so important in choosing those who work with you. It is much easier to put someone into a position than take them out later! Trust that God has provided them, is with them, and will help them carry out their task. Be careful of micromanaging! Give them room to make their own choices, fight some battles - and get the glory for the victory! Recognize your own calling - and limitations.

Moses was already up in years, and God hadn't called him to be a warrior. He was more of a pastor, but that doesn't mean he totally removed himself from the situation. Some leaders give a man a task and then disappear. He needs to know you're backing him up, standing with him, and watching to see how things go. You're on his side. At any point in the battle Joshua could look up to the hill and see Moses standing there with upraised hands. New strength and confidence would flow into him! Perversely, there are men who secretly hope their young, virile Joshua fails, so they can look good. If you tell your Joshua you are going to be on the hill, be there! There's nothing worse than being in battle and looking to the man who sent you and promised to be with you— and he's nowhere to be seen!

Moses set the timeframe: tomorrow. If Joshua got overly zealous and decided to get his men together for a sneak attack that night, he probably would have been slaughtered. He needed the covering and support Moses provided. A young man entrusted with an important task can get puffed up and feel he no longer needs to submit to the old man. Many battles are lost and much damage done by men who feel they know how to fight better than their Moses. They may even mock him: "Great, Moses. You're going to be safely up on the hill while you send me into the battle!" "What's up with the staff? You still think you're at the Red Sea? We need swords, not some ridiculous staff you're holding up." Be careful of those rebellious attitudes. They can get you in big trouble.

## THE STAFF

What was the deal with the staff? It wasn't magic – but it was an instrument God had chosen. Much like the ark was a symbol of God's presence and power, and would be used in battle, the staff symbolized God's presence. It demonstrated God's power to Pharaoh as it turned into a snake and back into a staff. God directed Moses to stretch it out over the sea – and it opened. Later, the same outstretched staff closed the sea. We have just seen the rock pour out life-saving water when struck by that staff. But the staff could also be misused. When Moses angrily struck a rock with the staff after God had instructed him to speak to it, God judged him, denying him entrance to the Promised Land.

It's not stated here, but it was probably God who instructed Moses to stand on the hill and keep the staff outstretched. Moses' faith and obedience unleashed God's power to win the battle. It's not unlike Jesus directing the leper to wash in a pool. There was nothing miraculous about the water, but that faith-inspired obedience was necessary to receive the healing.

*[10] So Joshua fought the Amalekites as Moses had ordered, and Moses, Aaron and Hur went to the top of the hill. [11] As long as Moses held up his hands, the Israelites were winning, but whenever he lowered his hands, the Amalekites were winning.*

## TEAMWORK BRINGS VICTORY

That's rough for Joshua – and humbling! His victory didn't depend on his great fighting skill, but on whether Moses' hands were up or down (presumably with the staff in them)! Joshua was doing his part, but it was in partnership with Moses. Moses had to do his part or his young assistant would be defeated. You may have zealous young men under you, or you might be that zealous

Joshua. God wants to teach us that we need each other. The young warrior needs the support and spiritual oversight of his Moses. He needs to be submitted to that leader and follow his orders. Moses needs to realize how critical his prayers and spiritual warfare are to the survival of his Joshua. How tragic when competition, envy, or rebellion enter the picture! How many battles are lost because we don't follow this basic model?

According to tradition, Hur was Moses' brother-in-law (his sister Miriam's husband), and possibly the grandfather of the famous artisan of the tabernacle, Bezalel.

*[12] When Moses' hands grew tired, they took a stone and put it under him and he sat on it. Aaron and Hur held his hands up—one on one side, one on the other—so that his hands remained steady till sunset.*

### SOMEONE TO HOLD YOUR HANDS UP
Thank God for Aaron and Hur! Had it not been for them, Israel would have lost that battle! Too bad many leaders have no one to hold their hands up! Do you? Are you willing to admit you're tired? That you can't do it all alone? Will your pride allow other men to help keep your hands steady?

Did Moses look at Joshua fighting down in the valley and feel a little envy? Or awe? Or rejoicing? It's funny the range of feelings that vigorous young men can provoke in an older man. Was it hard for Moses to acknowledge he had to sit down on a rock while Joshua was cutting down scores of Amalekites with his sword? Was there a part of him that would have loved to be in the thick of battle? Maybe the only man Moses ever killed was that Egyptian so many years before. Did he think about that?

Are you an Aaron or a Hur? How can you help hold your pastor's hands up? Are you willing to humble yourself for that lowly task?

Or are you thinking "If it was me, I wouldn't have to sit down. I wouldn't need anyone to help me."? We don't hear much more about Hur. What if that was the most important thing he ever did? What if the most valuable service you could perform was holding up another man's hands? Are you willing to do it?

*¹³ So Joshua overcame the Amalekite army with the sword.*

Well, yes, with quite a bit of help from the Lord. And Moses' faithfulness. We don't know the exact mechanics of the victory. We do know God had a big part to play in it. And so often that's the way he chooses to work. Sure, there are plenty of battles where God miraculously destroys the enemy. But he loves to get us involved. He wants us to learn how to fight. He wants to teach us the importance of team work, just like the Father, Son, and Holy Spirit function as a team. Without an army, Moses could have stood there all day with his arms up, and the Amalekites would probably have killed him. Without the godly covering, intercession, and faith of their leader, the best fighting men would have been defeated. It took Joshua a while to learn that lesson. Years later, after his glorious victory at Jericho, he was soundly defeated at Ai because he thought he didn't need God (Joshua 7).

*¹⁴ Then the Lord said to Moses, "Write this on a scroll as something to be remembered and make sure that Joshua hears it, because I will completely blot out the name of Amalek from under heaven."*

## WRITE DOWN WHAT GOD DID

This is our first indication that Moses could write. God commanded him to write down Israel's experiences so we can remember them today. The many prophecies which we see fulfilled in the Scriptures validate their authority. God's vow here was finally carried out in a dramatic but tragic chapter of King Saul's life (1 Samuel 15).

Why was God particularly intent that Joshua hear this story? Perhaps to remind him that it wasn't just his skill which won that victory, or to encourage him in future battles. If you don't have a journal, start one, and record the victories God gives you. Reflect on his work in your life, and your own battles. We have short memories, and a journal is very useful in giving us perspective and reminding us of what God has done.

*[15] Moses built an altar and called it The Lord is my Banner (Jehovah-Nissi). [16] He said, "Because hands were lifted up against the throne of the Lord, the Lord will be at war against the Amalekites from generation to generation."*

Moses recognizes that an attack on God's people is an attack on God himself. It is a beautiful way of portraying the battle: the Amalekites lifted up their hands against God's throne, so Moses lifted up his hands with the symbol of God's power to show that no one will push God from his throne. In addition to the scroll, Moses built an altar, a place of worship and thanksgiving to God for his victory. We don't build altars today, but there may be photos – even a Facebook posting – that are visible reminders of what God has done.

It gets lost in translation, but the Hebrew word for banner is related to the word for staff, and is used for the pole the bronze serpent was placed on in Numbers 21:8. This banner may not be cloth at all, but rather refers to God as their standard, the rallying point they must look to.

It's bad enough to endure God's anger for a moment, but imagine having him at war with your family from generation to generation. Are there nations today that have so scorned God that he is continually at war with them? Are there nations still experiencing his blessing because of the faithfulness of past generations? Is there a point at which that favor will run out as we continue to turn away from him?

It would have been easy to despair when a powerful enemy appears on the horizon. It might have been one more thing pushing Moses to give up this whole venture. Instead it turns into a great learning experience for everyone involved. Faith is built. A young man is raised up and taught how to fight and win battles God's way – an indispensable skill as they enter the Promised Land. Battles aren't fun. You may be in one right now – or see one coming your way. Are you ready for it? What can you learn from Israel's experience here that will help you prevail?

# 16

## MOSES THE FAMILY MAN
### *EXODUS 18:1-12*

*¹Now Jethro, the priest of Midian and father-in-law of Moses, heard of everything God had done for Moses and for his people Israel, and how the Lord had brought Israel out of Egypt.*

Do you ever feel like you have no one to talk to about your struggles? No one to speak into your life -while you are constantly giving to others? One of the hazards of leadership is loneliness. In the midst of all the problems on the Exodus, this intimate chapter reminds us that Moses is a man. A family man. Sometimes the leader's personal life gets lost in the pressures of ministry, but here Moses receives some much-needed advice and gets a short break from his very challenging job.

We know very little about Moses' family, so we have to be careful of speculation. We do know he spent forty years in Midian. The Midianites were descendants of Abraham's son Midian, born in his [very] old age, after Sarah's death, to his wife Keturah (Genesis 25:1-2). They worshiped a multitude of gods, so we don't know what a "priest" in Midian did. God had not yet established a priesthood, although this chapter shows that Jethro had some knowledge of God. He may have been unhappy at losing Moses' service, or having his daughter's life disrupted, but he didn't just write Moses off. It took considerable effort to get news of what was happening in Egypt (this was long before the internet, cell phones, or TV!). He probably inquired of passing caravans.

² After Moses had sent away his wife Zipporah, his father-in-law Jethro received her ³ and her two sons. One son was named Gershom, for Moses said, "I have become a foreigner in a foreign land"; ⁴ and the other was named Eliezer, for he said, "My father's God was my helper; he saved me from the sword of Pharaoh."

⁵ Jethro, Moses' father-in-law, together with Moses' sons and wife, came to him in the wilderness, where he was camped near the mountain of God. ⁶ Jethro had sent word to him, "I, your father-in-law Jethro, am coming to you with your wife and her two sons."

## WHAT ABOUT MOSES "SENDING AWAY" HIS WIFE?

Much speculation has swirled around Zipporah, and Moses "sending her away." We don't know when or why it happened. God called *Moses* to Egypt, but when he left Midian he took his wife and sons with him. That could point to a healthy family life, but perhaps they should have stayed behind. Did he send her away after the "bridegroom of blood" incident (Exodus 4:25)? Or after things got ugly in Egypt? They were still together as a family at this point, since they came to visit him.

Some have used this verse to justify divorce, pointing to the objection Moses' brother and sister had to his "Cushite" wife in Numbers 12:1: *Miriam and Aaron began to talk against Moses because of his Cushite wife, for he had married a Cushite.* Was it the same woman? Some think he divorced and remarried. Others suggest Zipporah died. But the Midianites were a dark-skinned people often called *Kushim*, the Hebrew word for dark skinned Africans. Further confusion has been created by some translations using "Ethiopian" instead of "Cushite." But the Hebrew word in the text is Cushite, and traditional Jewish scholarship affirms that it was Zipporah. Why did Miriam and Aaron wait so long to object to her? It may have been simmering under the surface for years, as they waited for the right moment to use it against Moses. It certainly is not unusual for families to nurse grudges or offenses and then unleash the criticism at the opportune moment. Chances are they lumped all dark-skinned people together under one (probably negative) name.

As with many scriptural debates, we can't definitively say what the answer is. We are wise not to become too dogmatic, and to acknowledge that God apparently prefers to keep us guessing at times. Don't build doctrines on a couple obscure verses! There is no way this should be used to justify divorce. It is easy to get caught up in insignificant details and controversies and miss the main message of a passage. The focus of this chapter clearly is not his marriage.

## WHAT WE CAN SAY ABOUT MOSES' MARRIAGE

Moses did have a cross-cultural marriage. He never felt the need to defend it, and God never judged it, although it did complicate his life, as a cross-cultural marriage usually does. Moses was multi-cultural: Jewish birth, Egyptian upbringing, and forty years in Midian with a Midianite wife. The perspective which that heritage gave probably contributed to his humility and helped in his leadership. But it can elicit negative reactions from family members, and perhaps from the Israelites.

As the stage is set for this chapter's message, we can make several observations about his marriage:

1. Whatever was involved in "sending them away" must have been painful for all involved. Even if it was a difficult marriage, as it appears it might have been from their only recorded interaction (in Exodus 4), separation is difficult.

2. Moses obviously had his hands full, and conceivably there could be times when sending the family to the in-laws would be the best option.

3. You almost get the feeling that Jethro pushed Zipporah to come with him on this trip, perhaps in hopes of healing the marriage. There is no indication that she wanted to come, or that Moses sent for her.

4. She is never mentioned again in the Bible, so possibly any effort to restore the family failed, and she returned home with Jethro.

5. Perhaps even more surprising for someone of Moses' stature, his sons disappear from Scripture as well. It is interesting that Jethro calls the boys "*her* sons."

*⁷ So Moses went out to meet his father-in-law and bowed down and kissed him. They greeted each other and then went into the tent. ⁸ Moses told his father-in-law about everything the Lord had done to Pharaoh and the Egyptians for Israel's sake and about all the hardships they had met along the way and how the Lord had saved them.*

A family visit can be bitter sweet: You're happy to see someone you know so far from home – but they bring their own problems. You might expect Moses to grab his wife and take *her* into his tent, but the warm greeting and tent meeting is with Jethro. Zipporah is notably absent from the picture. It must have been exciting for Moses to share the many amazing things God had done with his father-in-law, but Zipporah doesn't seem to be present there either.

*⁹ Jethro was delighted to hear about all the good things the Lord had done for Israel in rescuing them from the hand of the Egyptians. ¹⁰ He said, "Praise be to the Lord, who rescued you from the hand of the Egyptians and of Pharaoh, and who rescued the people from the hand of the Egyptians.* **¹¹** *Now I know that the Lord is greater than all other gods, for he did this to those who had treated Israel arrogantly."* **¹²** *Then Jethro, Moses' father-in-law, brought a burnt offering and other sacrifices to God, and Aaron came with all the elders of Israel to eat a meal with Moses' father-in-law in the presence of God.*

If Jethro had been involved with multiple gods, Moses' testimony convinced him that Yahweh was supreme. His heart seems open, and this may have been the start of a new faith pilgrimage for him.

God knows that Moses is at a breaking point. He has sent Jethro with the wisdom and love to confront Moses, and show him how to survive the pressures of his job. This may have been the last time Moses ever saw his family. Is there anything in Moses' family story that reminds you of your own? Perhaps alienated children? A difficult marriage? Are you in need of some sort of break from the pressures of ministry or work? What can you learn from Moses that would help your own family life?

This encounter left a lasting impact on both Jethro and Moses, as we will see in the counsel Moses was given.

# 17

## SOMEONE TO LOOK OUT FOR YOU
### *EXODUS 18:13-27*

¹³ The next day Moses took his seat to serve as judge for the people, and they stood around him from morning till evening. ¹⁴ When his father-in-law saw all that Moses was doing for the people, he said, "What is this you are doing for the people? Why do you alone sit as judge, while all these people stand around you from morning till evening?"

### THE INDISPENSABLE LEADER

Moses may have thought this would impress Jethro and his family. He's important! He's busy from morning until evening! People are seeking him out! He sits in the seat of judgment! But Jethro isn't impressed! He is a pragmatist, and though the crush of the crowd may have stoked Moses' ego, it wasn't efficient, and he could see how it wore on Moses.

Too many pastors and church leaders have yet to learn the simple lesson of this passage. Too often we are exhausted, doing way too much in the church, and feeling satisfied because we are so needed. No one else can do what I do! Yet it's often pride –no one can do it as *well* as I can – that prevents us from entrusting the work to others. If you are in leadership, God has delegated his authority to you. He has given you a job to do, and he expects you to delegate authority and tasks to others. Sometimes a job is given without the corresponding authority, setting the person up for failure, or we can give someone authority without making their responsibilities clear. Proper delegation is essential if an organization or church is to grow.

<sup>15</sup> Moses answered him, "Because the people come to me to seek God's will. <sup>16</sup> Whenever they have a dispute, it is brought to me, and I decide between the parties and inform them of God's decrees and instructions."

There's nothing wrong with what Moses is doing. It's good that people are coming to seek God's will! It's good they are going to a godly leader to settle their disputes, instead of going out into the desert. And it's good that Moses' decisions are based on God's decrees and instructions. What's wrong is the unstated belief that he is the only one capable of doing it.

Where does your family go to seek God's will? If you are a pastor, where does your church go? Do you base your counsel on God's instructions – or the world's wisdom? Are you willing to step into disputes and trust God to use you as a peacemaker? Make sure you don't fall into the error of intervening in every problem, as though you alone have the necessary insight.

<sup>17</sup> Moses' father-in-law replied, "What you are doing is not good. <sup>18</sup> You and these people who come to you will only wear yourselves out. The work is too heavy for you; you cannot handle it alone.

## Do you have someone looking out for you?

Would you get defensive if someone like Jethro said "what you are doing is not good?" Many of us would. Moses was doing the best he could. He had never been taught anything else. He spent most of his life herding sheep in the desert! At home and on the job you may be doing your best. You are sincere; knocking yourself out trying to do it right. But there may be a better way.

Humble yourself. A teachable spirit is very important. Have you ever asked for suggestions on how to do it better?

Unsaved parents or relatives often have great perception and good advice. Don't be too quick to write them off just because they're not in church! They know you and may have more genuine concern for your wellbeing than others. They may actually have a better way of doing things! Don't resent someone who comes to you with honest insight! Receive it!

Too often no one looks out for the pastor. If you see a pastor doing too much and wearing himself out, go and lovingly confront him. Express genuine concern for his well-being, and offer an alternative. Be ready to do what you can to relieve his burden!

*[19]Listen now to me and I will give you some advice, and may God be with you. You must be the people's representative before God and bring their disputes to him. [20]Teach them his decrees and instructions, and show them the way they are to live and how they are to behave. [21]But select capable men from all the people—men who fear God, trustworthy men who hate dishonest gain—and appoint them as officials over thousands, hundreds, fifties and tens. [22]Have them serve as judges for the people at all times, but have them bring every difficult case to you; the simple cases they can decide themselves. That will make your load lighter, because they will share it with you. [23]If you do this and God so commands, you will be able to stand the strain, and all these people will go home satisfied."*

## WISE COUNSEL FOR GODLY LEADERSHIP

1. Do you have anyone giving you good advice? You need someone, like Jethro, who can speak into your life. Many people are full of advice – but be careful whose advice you listen to!

2. Make sure God is with you! His presence and anointing are essential!

3. Even with the amazing benefits of the New Covenant – certainly way beyond Israel's primitive faith – people still need someone to represent them to the Lord. You are their intercessor. Even though the Holy Spirit indwells them and they can go directly to Christ, you can still represent them before God.

4. When people bring you disputes and problems, don't feel intimidated! You don't need to have all the answers! Bring them to God.

5. Your main job is two-fold:

    a. First, teach them God's word, so they can be equipped to make their own decisions.

    b. Second, show them how to live and behave. People learn much more from example than from preaching. If your life doesn't match up with what you're teaching, you are failing in your leadership. Many years ago a pastor told me he required someone seeking counseling to participate in church activities. Is that unfair or manipulative? No! A large portion of the disputes Moses was mediating – and church members' problems – would be solved simply by getting sound biblical teaching and observing godly models. For example, there is great ignorance among young people today of what the Bible teaches about marriage. Sound teaching, along with modeling and mentoring by mature couples, would eliminate much of the need for marital counseling.

6. God's kingdom is not a democracy! The people didn't elect these leaders! Moses chose and appointed them! That is one of your most important tasks! Jesus spent a whole night in prayer before choosing his disciples. Your wise choices can make or break the church.

7. Make sure they are capable. Nice people aren't necessarily capable. And make sure they are God-fearing. Plenty of capable people lack an intimate relationship with Jesus as their Lord. Finally, they must not be motivated by dishonest gain.

8. Use great discernment in *where* you appoint them. Someone who should be over thousands will be frustrated if assigned a group of ten. On the other hand, the person over fifty must be ready to handle the added responsibility.

9. Make sure they are representative. These were selected from *all* the people. The early church learned the danger of ignoring one ethnic or age group, and appointed deacons. Take care that so-called "minority" groups are included in the upper levels of authority.

10. They were to *serve* as judges. Jesus taught that leaders are servants, not lording it over others.

11. They were to serve at *all times*. Servant leadership impacts all of life. It's not a 9-5 job or something done a few hours a week. It can be costly.

12. Share the load with others! There really is an easier way! Don't worry about working yourself out of a job! As you

evaluate what you're doing, first entrust it to the Lord. Then start praying and looking for helpers. Do you have too much work around the house? Who can help you? Your wife? Your kids? Is there too much to do in the church? Start developing and training people who can help you. Here there were capable men just waiting to be asked! That is probably true for your church as well!

13. Leadership is a strain! If you try to do too much, or fail to follow the guidelines given in God's word, you will burn out!

The result of doing things God's way is satisfied people. If your people are dissatisfied, don't get down on them – look for what is causing it! When people are heard, cared for, properly represented before God, and given good teaching and example, they should be satisfied!

*[24] Moses listened to his father-in-law and did everything he said.*

## LISTEN AND ACT

Moses was known as the most humble man on earth. Maybe this is one reason why. He listened to advice! And he did what he was counseled to do! So few people really listen! Position and power ruin too many pastors! Even those who listen often fail to follow through and do the work of making things better.

How is your hearing? Do you welcome input from others? Do you truly listen to them? Do you act on wise counsel? Do you do everything you should – or only go half way, and then say it wouldn't have worked anyway?

*[25] He chose capable men from all Israel and made them leaders of the people, officials over thousands, hundreds, fifties and tens. [26] They served as judges for the people at all times. The*

difficult cases they brought to Moses, but the simple ones they decided themselves.

## AN ORGANIZATIONAL STRUCTURE THAT WORKS

This simple structure is a great model for any organization. It is hard to pastor, disciple, or have a real relationship with more than ten people. Jesus had twelve. The next level is over five small group leaders. The leader of hundreds only had two leaders of fifties under him, while the leader of thousands was over ten leaders of hundreds. Moses invested in the leaders of thousands, who kept him abreast of what he needed to know. Only when something couldn't be settled by one of the other leaders was it brought to him. He had no need to know everything going on in the community.

If you have been entrusted with authority, use it with confidence. Don't bother the person over you with every little thing; ask for wisdom to discern when you need to pass something on. If you are over a leader of a smaller group, let them learn, and respect the decisions they make. Offer gentle counsel when needed, but everyone benefits when they learn to deal with things on their own. You really don't want them overly dependent on you.

*27 Then Moses sent his father-in-law on his way, and Jethro returned to his own country.*

Did Moses "send away" Jethro, like he had Zipporah? Was Jethro hoping the family would travel with Moses? Moses may have been nice but firm: "I really can't deal with having my family here. You need to go on home." Of course, he was 80 at this point, and perhaps wasn't feeling the need for a woman as he had when he was younger. Probably Zipporah and the boys left with her father.

It's tough to balance family and ministry. Too often family gets neglected, especially with responsibilities like Moses had. Whatever was going on in his family, he didn't let it keep him from what God called him to do. Foster your family relationships, and include people around you who really care about you and can speak into your life. Sometimes we cut ourselves off from the very people who truly care for us. Hopefully your wife has that insight, but that's not always the case. She may be too close. Keep your eyes open for whom God brings your way. Listen to them, and put their advice into practice as God leads you.

# PART 4

## *MOUNT SINAI: MEETING GOD*

# 18

# THE PROPOSAL: GOD'S INVITATION TO COVENANT RELATIONSHIP
## *Exodus 19:1-9*

Do you long for a deeper spiritual experience? A real encounter with God? Do you ever have doubts if Christianity is even real? If Moses was feeling any of that, God was about to overwhelm him. Sure, he had been in regular communication with God since the burning bush. He had seen God's power displayed in the plagues and the opening of the Red Sea. He ate manna every day just like every Israelite – a constant reminder of God's faithfulness and provision. But that is nothing compared with what he is about to experience – essentially a face to face encounter with God.

I have seen all too many attempts to produce great spiritual experiences and make God show up in church. It is interesting that none of what we see in Exodus took place in the tabernacle (not yet built) or the temple (many years away). Could we be missing something by trying too hard to make God appear in our buildings?

*¹On the first day of the third month after the Israelites left Egypt— on that very day—they came to the Desert of Sinai. ²After they set out from Rephidim, they entered the Desert of Sinai, and Israel camped there in the desert in front of the mountain.*

## Mount Sinai Desert Campground

Another campout! (Well, they had one just about every night!) It's not in an ideal location. They have just come into a huge desert – not exactly the land flowing with milk and honey they had been promised. They had been traveling three months – more than enough time to reach Canaan if they had taken the direct route. But God wasn't interested in saving time. He still had much to do before they were ready for the Promised Land. It is often in the desert that we have the most meaningful encounters with God, and humanity has never witnessed anything quite as intense as what happened here at Mount Sinai.

Do you feel like you are coming into a desert? Does it strike fear in your heart? Are you frustrated and tired of tramping around? Are you ready to settle into the good life you have been promised in the Lord? Or have you already been in the desert way longer than you feel necessary? Trust God. You may need that desert for a life-changing encounter with him, free of the many distractions that crowd our lives when things are going well.

Mount Sinai (also known as Mount Horeb) is 7, 497 feet (2,285 meters) high, and located near the southern tip of the Sinai Peninsula in modern Egypt. It's uncertain exactly which mountain Israel camped at. The Mount Sinai we know is devoid of vegetation, with jagged, rocky peaks. The easier route to the top takes about 2 ½ hours. Pilgrims also climb the 3,750 "steps of penitence" to the top. Whichever peak it was, and whichever route he took (no steps back then!), Moses was about to go up. And down. And up. Over the coming days he would be going up and down eight times. He must have been in good shape for an 80-year-old! Of course the idea of meeting with God would be a strong motivator!

# The Proposal: God's Invitation to Covenant Relationship

*³ Then Moses went up to God, and the Lord called to him from the mountain and said, "This is what you are to say to the descendants of Jacob and what you are to tell the people of Israel: ⁴ 'You yourselves have seen what I did to Egypt, and how I carried you on eagles' wings and brought you to myself. ⁵ Now if you obey me fully and keep my covenant, then out of all nations you will be my treasured possession. Although the whole earth is mine, ⁶ you will be for me a kingdom of priests and a holy nation.' These are the words you are to speak to the Israelites."*

## Invitation to Covenant

No commands. Nothing to fear. God is making a loving proposal to Israel, not unlike an offer of marriage. He finally has the people where he wants them, and has their undivided attention. Now he can get down to business and propose the covenant he has been longing to make for all eternity. Hopefully they have been impressed with his rather unusual "courtship" up to this point and will accept his offer.

Three things he has already done should make their decision easy:

- He judged Egypt and freed them from slavery.
- He carried them on eagles' wings. What a beautiful picture of how God cares for us!
- He brought them to himself, wooing them as a lover.

As with any covenant, including the marriage covenant, there is a condition. For Israel, it's simple, but their experience will prove that it is hard:

- Fully obey God.
- Keep his covenant.

If they do, here is his offer:

- **They will be his treasured possession.** The whole earth is God's. It's not like he really needs anything. But he has chosen this particular nation (largely based on Abraham's faithfulness and promises made to him) from all the nations of the earth. Do you feel special? What's not to like about being God's possession?

- **They will be a holy nation.** Unique in all the earth, they will be set apart and dedicated to worshipping and serving God, while keeping themselves free from the world's corruption. That implies some loss of freedom, and submission to the boundaries God lays down.

- **They will be a kingdom of priests.** The New Covenant concept of the priesthood of all believers isn't all that new. Levi may have had the official duties, just like pastors carry out official duties today, but God's intent was for all his people to minister before him and serve as intercessors and mediators with the world.

It sounds like a great offer for this ragged bunch of ex-slaves. But it would be a rocky courtship and even rougher marriage; essentially ending in divorce. Did God make a mistake choosing them? I'm confident he didn't. Did you make a mistake choosing your wife because your relationship has been difficult? Study God's interaction with his "bride" and you may gain insights into his purposes for your marriage and how to deal with a less-than-perfect relationship.

Moses probably had been with these people less than six months, and it hasn't been easy. God graciously enabled him to perform great miracles to gain their trust. So far Moses has been true to his word, but they still are not too sure about him. Now he has something really great to offer them, although if they are anything like us, they might have preferred an offer of wealth and happy, long lives.

When was the last time you went "up the mountain" to meet with God? If you preach or teach his word, do you seek him and wait on him until you are confident you have something fresh that is really from God's heart? God was very clear about exactly what Moses was to say. He couldn't add anything or take anything away from God's word.

*⁷ So Moses went back and summoned the elders of the people and set before them all the words the Lord had commanded him to speak. ⁸ The people all responded together, "We will do everything the Lord has said." So Moses brought their answer back to the Lord.*

Do you think you have it rough delivering God's Word? Moses brought God's Word down the mountain - and then went back up with the peoples' answer. Initially he spoke to the elders, who probably took the offer back to the people. The response was a unanimous and prompt "yes." Perhaps too quick, without really thinking through all its implications, but then few couples understand the implications of the marriage covenant either.

*⁹ The Lord said to Moses, "I am going to come to you in a dense cloud, so that the people will hear me speaking with you and will always put their trust in you." Then Moses told the Lord what the people had said.*

## GOD AFFIRMS MOSES AS LEADER
God really does stand behind his servants. Though meeting God in the dense cloud would be great for Moses, the real purpose was to impress the people so they would always trust him. Some are hesitant to trust too much in a pastor or leader, and a certain amount of caution is good, especially when they do things that

are not of God, or bring a word that's not from the Lord. But God knows this trust relationship is critical for the proper functioning of the nation. If you are a pastor, make sure you do nothing to betray your peoples' trust. God will affirm your call if you are faithfully serving him. If you are part of a church, it's important that you can trust your pastor. If that trust has been betrayed, pray for reconciliation and forgiveness, but you may need to look for a new shepherd, someone you believe God can really work through.

Didn't God know what the people said? Surely he did, but for some reason he chooses to use us to deliver has word, intercede for the people, and communicate to him what is in their hearts. That position as spokesman for God (prophet) and representative of the people (priest) carries great responsibility. Together with ruling (king), they make up the three primary roles God has given us. If you function in any of them, be aware that God Almighty has entrusted you with an extremely important task.

The nation has accepted God's proposal. Now they must get ready for the "wedding day," which will be the most dramatic wedding ever witnessed! Have you accepted God's offer of eternal life in Jesus Christ? Are you aware of the great privileges inherent in it?

# 19

# THE WEDDING: SEALING THE COVENANT
## EXODUS 19:10-25; 20:18-21

It seems like few couples today actually get married, and those who do often want a dramatic wedding:

- On a remote mountain peak.
- On the beach.
- Exchanging vows as they parachute down to their waiting families.

But even the most dramatic wedding today can't compare with the "wedding" God put on for his chosen people.

*[10]{} And the Lord said to Moses, "Go to the people and consecrate them today and tomorrow. Have them wash their clothes [11]{} and be ready by the third day, because on that day the Lord will come down on Mount Sinai in the sight of all the people. [12]{} Put limits for the people around the mountain and tell them, 'Be careful that you do not approach the mountain or touch the foot of it. Whoever touches the mountain is to be put to death. [13]{} They are to be stoned or shot with arrows; not a hand is to be laid on them. No person or animal shall be permitted to live.' Only when the ram's horn sounds a long blast may they approach the mountain."*

Another trip down the mountain, another task. This is a matter of life and death. If Moses neglects to communicate everything God told him, or downplays the seriousness of disobedience, somebody is almost certain to die.

## CONSECRATION IS REQUIRED

It would take two days to get ready, washing their clothes and making sure appropriate boundaries were in place. The third day carries special importance to God. Jesus rose on the third day. Make sure you are ready for the third day.

For centuries, preparing to meet with God was taken very seriously. Saturday night was bath night. In the days before hot showers, it was usually the only bath of the week. You were symbolically cleansed for the Lord's Day. Clean clothes – Sunday best – were laid out. No one would dream of coming to church in the same jeans or overalls they had been wearing all week. In the best of the tradition, these externals were accompanied by self-examination and confession of any sin. Even after arrival in church, there was usually a prayer of confession near the beginning of the service to make sure everyone was ready to meet with God and hear his Word. Did some of that become mere ritual? Absolutely! But they sensed a need for consecration before entering God's presence that has been largely lost today. When was the last time you heard a sermon about consecration, or how to prepare yourself to meet with God? Where is an appropriate fear of God In the casual informality that characterizes most of our churches?

## BOUNDARIES

Nobody likes limits, and there surely would be an uproar today if we started enforcing the limits Scripture places on who can be part of the fellowship of believers. But we put limits on our children for their well-being:

- "No, you can't spin in the washing machine."
- "No, eight-year-olds can't drive the car."

In the same way, God puts limits on what we can do. This passage is a very graphic description of the consequences of breaking God's boundaries, but the result is just as serious when we violate other limits he imposes.

There are always people who want a "taste" of sin, to see what it's like. Just like the prohibition to eat the fruit in Eden made it that much more tantalizing, it would be so tempting to quickly reach out and touch the mountain to see what would happen. Maybe you would receive divine power that God was trying to deny you! When God says "don't touch" he is serious. You do no one a favor by watering down his prohibitions. Similar to someone being electrocuted, at Sinai they couldn't even lay a hand on the offender, or they would die as well. The offender had to be stoned or shot with arrows. And if you didn't keep your dog on a leash (and he was one of those dogs that don't always listen to you), he would die too if he happened to touch the mountain.

It's not that God is unapproachable. We just have to come in his timing and on his terms. In this case the sounding of the ram's horn would give the okay. For us it is through faith in Jesus Christ, symbolized in the waters of baptism. Through Christ we can "touch the mountain."

*14 After Moses had gone down the mountain to the people, he consecrated them, and they washed their clothes. 15 Then he said to the people, "Prepare yourselves for the third day. Abstain from sexual relations."*

## NO SEX

In addition to the individual preparation, Moses consecrated the congregation, possibly by prayers and sprinkling of water (blood would come later). Details aren't given, but everyone had to be there. If someone felt he could skip that service, he might be in for a rude awakening.

Moses adds another prohibition that wasn't mentioned earlier. Maybe he snuck it in on the end because he knew it would be controversial: "Who is Moses to tell me I can't have sex? What does my relationship with God have to do with my bedroom anyway?" Our culture finds Scriptural prohibitions on certain sexual practices, or even delaying sex until marriage, hopelessly antiquated and out of place. But as one of the closest expressions on this earth of the union found in the trinity, sex is intricately connected with spirituality, and perhaps provides the greatest risk of corruption.

How would anyone know if this prohibition was ignored? Would a couple in bed who found the moment irresistible really think "We can't do this because we're supposed to be consecrated to God?" It certainly is a great test of obedience, not unlike what a young unmarried couple experiences today. No one else may know, but God knows what goes on behind closed doors – and in your mind.

*[16] On the morning of the third day there was thunder and lightning, with a thick cloud over the mountain, and a very loud trumpet blast. Everyone in the camp trembled. [17] Then Moses led the people out of the camp to meet with God, and they stood at the foot of the mountain. [18] Mount Sinai was covered with smoke, because the Lord descended on it in fire. The smoke billowed up from it like smoke from a furnace, and the whole mountain trembled violently. [19] As the sound of the trumpet grew louder and louder, Moses spoke and the voice of God answered him.*

## SHOCK AND AWE

That is about as dramatic as it gets! Can you imagine a church service like this? Some may try to copy it, but they couldn't approach this third day. Take some time to try and picture and feel what was going on. It was a day unlike any other. You wake up to thunder and lighting, and the thickest cloud you have ever seen. A shrieking trumpet blast. Even the toughest men tremble. But somehow, amidst the fear, Moses gathers the people and they march out to the foot of the mountain. They are going to meet with God. Tremendous fire breaks through the cloud, sending up even more smoke. You can feel its heat. The mountain and the ground you're standing on shake. You cover your ears from the un-ending and unbearably loud trumpet blast. Suddenly you hear Moses speak. His speech impediment is gone, along with any hesitancy he might have had before Pharaoh. We don't know what he spoke – but in response, perhaps for the very first time, you hear the very voice of God. God answers to a man! What an incredible confirmation of Moses as his chosen leader! Can you picture yourself as Moses in this scene? What would you say to get the whole "service" going?

What has happened to awe and fear in our churches? Obviously it is a different time, but do you think we should take meeting with God and hearing from him a little more seriously?

[20] *The Lord descended to the top of Mount Sinai and called Moses to the top of the mountain. So Moses went up* [21] *and the Lord said to him, "Go down and warn the people so they do not force their way through to see the Lord and many of them perish.* [22] *Even the priests, who approach the Lord, must consecrate themselves, or the Lord will break out against them."*

All the fire and smoke were just setting the stage. Like Elijah witnessing the drama before hearing the still small voice, Moses ascends through the cloud and meets with God. Can you imagine the people watching him go up? They probably thought they would never see him again. If Moses had any reservations about another climb up the mountain, they're not mentioned. He goes up only to be told to go down once more - to warn them again not to come up. All the fire and smoke wouldn't be enough to keep some from violating the clear command, nor would it keep them from building a golden calf in a few days. Just because Moses could approach God didn't mean everyone could. Priests would be allowed, but special consecration was needed for them.

Earlier (verse 11) it said God would descend in the sight of all the people – but apparently that didn't mean actually seeing the Lord. These narratives raise issues for some people – especially Muslims – about the verse "No one can see God and live" (Genesis 32:30, Exodus 33:20), but there is no real contradiction.

*[23]{.sup} Moses said to the Lord, "The people cannot come up Mount Sinai, because you yourself warned us, 'Put limits around the mountain and set it apart as holy.'"*

## BEST TO ERR ON THE SIDE OF CAUTION

It seems like Moses wasn't quite clear on what God was saying. Could the priests come up? He had understood no one else could. Before doing something foolish, he needs to know exactly what God wants.

*[24] The Lord replied, "Go down and bring Aaron up with you. But the priests and the people must not force their way through to come up to the Lord, or he will break out against them."*

*[25] So Moses went down to the people and told them.*

Moses was right in his instinct for caution. Only one man, Moses' brother Aaron, would be able to accompany him. If you're not sure about something, it is better to err on the conservative side.

If Moses had taken God's words as meaning all the priests could come up, there would have been a great slaughter that day. You may seem too legalistic to some, but don't risk God's wrath because you relax his commands too much!

Exodus continues, in chapter 20, with the Ten Commandments. But after the commandments are given, the narrative returns to conclude the experience of Moses and the people that day on Sinai:

*20:18 When the people saw the thunder and lightning and heard the trumpet and saw the mountain in smoke, they trembled with fear. They stayed at a distance 19 and said to Moses, "Speak to us yourself and we will listen. But do not have God speak to us or we will die."*

*20 Moses said to the people, "Do not be afraid. God has come to test you, so that the fear of God will be with you to keep you from sinning."*

*21 The people remained at a distance, while Moses approached the thick darkness where God was.*

What a way to end a wedding! The bride remains at a distance, cowering in fear! It reminds me of a very young girl in an arranged marriage, scared of the hulking man she's marrying. In this case there is nothing wrong with their fear. In fact, God purposely wanted to instill fear in them. The thunder, lightning, trumpet sound, and smoking mountain all had their desired effect. They might have been able to tolerate those things, but God's voice was too overwhelming, and that was what God wanted. He never expected to speak directly to the crowd. He would speak to Moses, who was his mouthpiece. Moses would communicate his word to the people, much as a preacher hears from God and brings that word to his congregation. Yet today every believer has the opportunity to hear God for himself. There is no need to remain at a distance! You can enter directly into God's presence through the blood of Jesus!

God pushed the limit a bit on revealing himself to test them, letting them hear his voice. How would they respond? It appears they responded appropriately, with reverence, respect, and fear. It is that fear that should keep them from sinning – although it didn't. As we end this astonishing section, our challenge is to instill a healthy awe and fear of God in believers today, so they too will be kept from sinning.

Moses had been through some rough times with Pharaoh and the people, but meeting with God like this would make it all worthwhile. This was clearly the experience of a lifetime!

Pastor, you have the great privilege of ushering your people into God's presence. There may be times when you want to get them away from the city to a retreat where they can really meet with God. Don't neglect taking your own time to go up the mountain and meet with God! And don't be surprised if your experience, like that of Moses, may involve some ups and downs (mountain tops and valleys).

Father, you have the same privilege with your family. Have you ever considered a different kind of vacation where you get away as a family to meet with God? And make sure you take some time to go up and meet with God yourself.

It's an amazing chapter, isn't it? Almost overwhelming. Read it through a few times in your Bible. Let it impact your view of God and ministry.

# 20

## HOW TO DEFEAT YOUR ENEMIES
### EXODUS 23:20-33

*[20] "See, I am sending an angel ahead of you to guard you along the way and to bring you to the place I have prepared. [21] Pay attention to him and listen to what he says. Do not rebel against him; he will not forgive your rebellion, since my Name is in him. [22] If you listen carefully to what he says and do all that I say, I will be an enemy to your enemies and will oppose those who oppose you. [23] My angel will go ahead of you and bring you into the land of the Amorites, Hittites, Perizzites, Canaanites, Hivites and Jebusites, and I will wipe them out.*

Have you heard someone called "so heavenly minded they're no earthly good?" Moses was on Mount Sinai, enjoying intimate fellowship with the Lord of the universe! It would have been easy to forget about the people waiting for him below, but God chooses this time to remind him of the journey they're on. Mountain-top experiences should impact your daily life. At the same time, all the distractions of daily life can make you lose sight of your destination. God has a calling on your life, a job for you to do, a purpose and a destiny. Thank God for the times of refreshing fellowship on the mountain top! They reaffirm that God will take care of everything along the way. But Moses had a critical part to play. And so do you.

## MOSES' RESPONSIBILITIES

- **Listen to God.** To make sure Moses gets the message, God says the same thing three different ways. Pay attention. Listen to what he says. Listen *carefully* to what he says. God will speak and tell you what to do! That is great news when you are traveling in a desert and conquering new territory. It is good news for you if you are unsure about what you're supposed to do at home, on the job, or in your church. There is just one problem: God knows we are hard of hearing. We are too involved in other things to pay attention to the inner nudges of the Spirit. We fail to listen carefully, and misinterpret God's word. It's one thing to mess up if you have no family or church responsibilities. It's another if your wife and children are depending on you to hear from God, or if other believers – be it a small group or a mega church – are relying on you. How is your hearing? Do you practice listening to God? Do you get the message clearly? Or are you in such a rush, with so many thoughts running through your head, that the message gets garbled? Moses would never have made it through the desert without that angel leading the way (better than Waze or a GPS!). And you won't make it through your desert if you are not listening to God and led by his Spirit.

- **Obey.** Listening is essential – but it is worthless if you don't do what God says. Selective obedience doesn't work. God says Moses must do *all* he says to do. We think we are doing great if we can manage 75% obedience. After all, God knows our intentions are good, and we are under grace, right? Maybe, but the Bible never allows for less than 100%. I'm afraid I don't quite make that, and you won't either. That is where sincere repentance and

God's gracious forgiveness come in, but our hearts must be dedicated to doing everything God tells us to do. And why not? Don't you believe he really does know the best way to the Promised Land? Why take shortcuts that he knows will get you in serious trouble? How are you doing on that obedience? It affects not only you – but everyone God has placed under your authority. It is an awesome responsibility.

- **Don't provoke God.** Rebellion is lethal. Like witchcraft. Moses has been very submissive – but God knows rebellion is a possibility even for Moses, and must warn him about it. The Orthodox Jewish Bible says not to *provoke* God. In this case it is provoking God's messenger. It makes sense to be on good terms with the one providing such essential help. When you start doing things your way and resist instructions you prefer not to follow, you rebel and provoke the Lord. And this sin will not be forgiven! It is almost like blasphemy of the Holy Spirit! We are rebels by nature. Watch for rebellion rising up in your heart against those in authority - in government, work, and the church. Choose to submit to them. Is there any place you can detect a rebellious spirit in your heart? Are you provoking the very one who can help you the most?

Leadership isn't easy! There is a price to pay and a burden to carry, but it is balanced by the blessing of hearing God's voice and seeing him move as you obey him. You have the power to bring great blessing into your family and church! But don't forget about the *"if,"* which is present in almost all of God's promises. Yes, he is sovereign. He is determined to get his people to Canaan. But he still chooses to work through us, and a lot depends on whether we hear him and obey what he tells us to do. Moses' part really isn't that hard, as we have already seen in a number of examples: Stretching out his staff over the sea, striking the rock, throwing a log into the water. In comparison, God goes overboard on what he offers us.

## God's Promises to Moses and Israel

- **He is sending his angel ahead of them.** He is preparing the way. All Moses has to do is follow him.

- **That angel will *guard* them along the way.** *Keep* and *protect* are other possible translations. Will there be danger? Absolutely! But Moses can put fear aside in faith that the angel will protect them, just like God protected them from Pharaoh's armies.

- **God has a place prepared for them.** Jesus told us he went to prepare a place for us. The future is in God's hands. He has good things prepared for you.

- **He will *bring us* to that place.** There would be many times when that looked doubtful. Most of them would die in the wilderness. It took forty long years to get there. But there is absolute assurance that God would bring them to the Promised Land.

- **God will be an enemy to their enemies.** Someone messes with his boy, and he's going to take care of them. Just make sure you are clear on who is truly an enemy. God is not necessarily going to be someone's enemy just because you don't like them.

- **He will oppose those who oppose you.** When you are walking in obedience to the Lord, the devil and his agents will oppose you, but you can be assured God himself will oppose them. Just don't count on him to oppose those you resent because they are standing in the way of your own selfish plans.

- **God will wipe out their enemies.** He is bringing them right into the middle of a vast enemy. Just because God guides you and is with you doesn't necessarily mean it will be easy, but God will *wipe them out*. That sounds great – but it would include some fierce fighting by Israel. Do you like the idea of your enemies being wiped out? Are you ready to fight, if it is required?

That is some impressive encouragement! The same general principles apply to your walk today. Let them strengthen you!

## Who was this angel?

What does it mean that God will not forgive rebellion against the angel because his *Name is in him*? I have never heard of God's Name – meaning his very power and nature – residing in an angel. It may have been Jesus himself guiding and guarding his people. If you are intrigued, check out these Scriptures where the distinction between God and his messenger are blurred: Genesis 16:10, 19:1,21; 31:11,13, Exodus 3:2,4; Judges 2:1-5; 6:11-12,14; 13:3-23; Zechariah 3:1-6; 12:8.

*24 Do not bow down before their gods or worship them or follow their practices. You must demolish them and break their sacred stones to pieces. 25 Worship the Lord your God, and his blessing will be on your food and water. I will take away sickness from among you, 26 and none will miscarry or be barren in your land. I will give you a full life span.*

## Demolish every idol

The Promised Land would present a whole new danger: other gods and pagan practices competing for their attention (to say nothing of beautiful women!). But absolutely no compromise or concession could be made to them. No ungodly practices could exist among God's holy people. The only response is total destruction, removing every trace of anything ungodly. It is the same response we are to have to sin in our lives and the church. We must demolish it completely.

Some Christians would love to demolish other religions and ungodly practices in their nation today. But we are not establishing a physical kingdom as Israel was. We are a city set on a hill, a light shining in the darkness; an alternative, spiritual, kingdom to what the world is offering. We are salt. In some ways our job is harder, because we live in the midst of the world. There have always been those who wanted to establish utopian communities or retreat to monasteries, but Jesus sends us into the darkness of the world with the message of the Kingdom of God.

There are tremendous promises made here – and only one condition: They must worship the Lord. Not just sing worship songs and have nice services, but lift God up, bring him glory and honor, and make him Lord in all of life. Be careful of thinking you are truly worshipping him just because you have a great worship band! The word can also mean *serve* him, dedicated to doing the work of the Kingdom.

## GOD'S PROMISES IN RESPONSE TO OUR WORSHIP

- **Blessing on our food and water.** That had already been an issue on this Exodus journey. Drinkable water remains a problem in much of the world – and could get far worse. God wants to provide the necessary food and water for us – not to be gluttons, but to meet our daily needs. This is a tough promise to trumpet to a bunch of starving refugees – who may love Jesus more than any of us. Though the principle remains true, we can't just grab on to every physical promise made to the nation of Israel. And we certainly can't judge someone starving to death as lacking real faith.

- **Sickness removed from our midst.** God had already promised to keep them free from illnesses brought on the Egyptians. Here is a more blanket promise of healing, but also one specifically made to Israel at that time.

- **No miscarriages or infertility.** In general, bearing children is God's gift to women, and barrenness is seen in the Old Testament as a curse. God can open a barren womb, but be careful of putting an even heavier burden on a couple struggling with infertility, as though they weren't properly worshipping God.

- **A full life span.** God's intention for us from the beginning includes children and a healthy, good, long, life. We should pray for that and seek it. God clearly is sovereign over all those areas. But Jesus had neither children nor a long life. Paul had a stubborn thorn in the flesh and died relatively young – and childless. Again, these physical promises don't always carry over into the spiritual kingdom of the New Covenant.

*27 "I will send my terror ahead of you and throw into confusion every nation you encounter. I will make all your enemies turn their backs and run. 28 I will send the hornet ahead of you to drive the Hivites, Canaanites and Hittites out of your way. 29 But I will not drive them out in a single year, because the land would become desolate and the wild animals too numerous for you. 30 Little by little I will drive them out before you, until you have increased enough to take possession of the land.*

## VICTORY

Here is another tremendous promise of victory – and an important principle as we face our own enemies: God is determined to wipe them out. He went to the extreme of sending his own Son to die on a cross to do so.

## GOD'S WEAPONS

- **Sending his terror on them.** An intense and paralyzing fear.

- **Throwing them into confusion.** Disrupting their plans and turning them against each other.

- **Making them turn their backs and run.**

- **Sending an advance army of hornets.** The meaning of the Hebrew word is unclear, but it is some agent that would drive out the enemy armies.

Our God is a mighty warrior! These are awesome manifestations of his power! Surely he can still do this today – and you have every right to pray he would!

## THE REASON FOR DELAY

We may struggle with the timing of their defeat. We would love to see every trace of the enemy miraculously removed right now. But in his wisdom, God does it little by little. He knows how much you are able to handle. It is similar to the house swept clean of demons that Jesus referred to in Matthew 12:43-45: When an enemy is removed, it must be replaced by something of the Spirit. We must occupy and take possession of the land. As we increase in strength and faith, we will be ready to take possession of more that God has prepared for us. When God directed Israel to fight against an enemy and gain additional territory, he assured them of victory. They couldn't fight every enemy at the same time, however. And they didn't have the numbers or skill to care for the land and keep it free of human or animal invaders. Don't be discouraged because there are still enemies troubling you. Deliverance usually is not instantaneous. It is a step by step walk of obedience and victory.

*31 "I will establish your borders from the Red Sea to the Mediterranean Sea, and from the desert to the Euphrates River. I will give into your hands the people who live in the land, and you will drive them out before you. 32 Do not make a covenant with them or with their gods. 33 Do not let them live in your land or they will cause you to sin against me, because the worship of their gods will certainly be a snare to you."*

## ADDITIONAL REQUIREMENTS MADE OF THE PEOPLE

God now defines the boundaries of their land and repeats his commitment to give all the inhabitants into their hands. But there are some things they would have to do:

- **They had to drive them out.** God will grant you victory over your enemies – but you must have the will and determination to cast them out. Too many get weary and discouraged at this point and never do. Israel didn't, and Judges 1 & 2 detail the devastating consequences – something seen all too often in Christians.

- **They could not make a covenant – any kind of agreement – with them or their gods.** Paul warns us about the dangers of an unequal yoke (2 Corinthians 6:14-18). The most common covenant believers make with unbelievers is marriage. Be careful of any agreements you make in your mind or daily life with the devil or any of his servants.

- **They could not allow them to live in their land.** Again, Judges describes their failure here. It seemed extreme - and too much trouble - to destroy them all. Instead of totally destroying the sin in our lives we often leave traces – and it becomes a snare. You may be called a fanatic if you get serious about removing ungodly music, entertainment, and other influences from your life. But why play around with something that could cause you to sin against God, especially with all that he has just said he is going to do? Why knowingly allow something that will be a snare?

What about your life? Have you gotten tired of the battle? Have wild animals come in to desolate places that you haven't really taken possession of? Are there snares caused by ungodly alliances or traces of sin you have neglected to fully address? Are there things you need to drive out of your life? What about those people God has entrusted to your care, especially as a husband, father, or pastor? Are you providing godly leadership to bring them into the fullness of all God has for them?

# 21

# ARE YOU READY TO MEET GOD?
## *EXODUS 24*

*¹Then the Lord said to Moses, "Come up to the Lord, you and Aaron, Nadab and Abihu, and seventy of the elders of Israel. You are to worship at a distance, ² but Moses alone is to approach the Lord; the others must not come near. And the people may not come up with him." ³ When Moses went and told the people all the Lord's words and laws, they responded with one voice, "Everything the Lord has said we will do." ⁴ Moses then wrote down everything the Lord had said.*

## WE WILL OBEY EVERYTHING!

Moses descended Mt. Sinai to bring God's law to his people. Can you picture this massive crowd listening as he proclaims it? It's not clear whether Moses called for a response, or if it was spontaneous, but they gladly received it: This is a good word, and we want to obey it. As on other occasions, they are unanimous – and maybe a little hasty – in agreeing to do *everything* God commanded.

It's good to give the church an opportunity to sincerely consider if they are ready to obey what God has spoken. How great to have unanimous affirmation, like Israel! But talk is cheap. It is easy to go forward or raise your hand in church; it can be a different story the next day when that decision is put to the test at home or work. At least Israel's response is a step in the right direction.

## WRITE DOWN WHAT GOD SPEAKS

We don't know if God told him to, but Moses wrote down everything God said while it was still fresh in his mind. Thank God for diligent leaders who keep good records of what God has spoken! With that completed, God calls Moses back up for another session. This time the seventy elders, along with Aaron and his sons, will accompany him.

If you are a pastor and have had a powerful encounter with God, you have the opportunity and privilege of bringing others with you to meet with God. It could be on a retreat or at your home. Even here, though, it is Moses alone who can actually approach God, while the others are worshipping.

*He got up early the next morning and built an altar at the foot of the mountain and set up twelve stone pillars representing the twelve tribes of Israel. ⁵ Then he sent young Israelite men, and they offered burnt offerings and sacrificed young bulls as fellowship offerings to the Lord.⁶ Moses took half of the blood and put it in bowls, and the other half he splashed against the altar. ⁷ Then he took the Book of the Covenant and read it to the people. They responded, "We will do everything the Lord has said; we will obey." ⁸ Moses then took the blood, sprinkled it on the people and said, "This is the blood of the covenant that the Lord has made with you in accordance with all these words."*

It's hard to know the exact chronology here. It seems that Moses verbally shared the law, got their agreement to obey it, prepared the elders to go up with him, and then wrote down what he had shared. The next morning there was a more formal ceremony as he read what he had written.

## PREPARING FOR WORSHIP
Though precise instructions regarding corporate worship had not been given, Moses takes it very seriously. It reminds me of what a pastor might do today:

- Gets up early in the morning to prepare himself, meet with the Lord, and have plenty of time to get ready for the service.

- Goes to the church (the foot of the mountain) and spiritually prepares the place for a meeting with God. If the Lord's Supper is to be shared, he may get the communion table ready.

- Has some sort of representation (like the stone pillars) of the various groups that make up the congregation. It might be a banner for each small group.

- Has a group of young men who arrive before others, and prepare the atmosphere with prayer and worship. They might be a prayer or worship team. Notice the conscious effort to involve both elders and young men.

- At this point the people arrive. The blood from the sacrifices reminds me of bringing a congregation into God's presence with confession and assurance of sin forgiven through the shed blood of Jesus Christ.

- Shares the Word of God.

- Calls for a response from the people. It is great to remind them that they are part of a New Covenant, and encourage them to renew their commitment to Christ.

- The focus on covenant leads naturally into celebrating the Lord's Supper. Instead of sprinkling blood on people (externally), everyone has the opportunity to partake (internally) of the cup that symbolizes the blood of the New Covenant.

*⁹ Moses and Aaron, Nadab and Abihu, and the seventy elders of Israel went up ¹⁰ and saw the God of Israel. Under his feet was something like a pavement made of lapis lazuli, as bright blue as the sky. ¹¹ But God did not raise his hand against these leaders of the Israelites; they saw God, and they ate and drank.*

## EATING AND DRINKING IN GOD'S PRESENCE

With the congregation dismissed after agreeing to the covenant, Moses and the elders go up the mountain. Think about the indescribable beauty of this shining blue pavement! The expectation is that men could not survive in such a glorious divine presence, but God had called them up, and doesn't raise his hand against them.

What did they eat and drink? It is striking that food and drink are part of such a solemn and glorious occasion! And yet that is very much in keeping with other glimpses we get of God's heart. It reminds me of the Lord's Supper. God likes meals! Did they bring it with them? Or did God himself provide it? We don't know.

## CAN YOU SEE GOD AND LIVE?

Again, the issue of how they could see God and live comes up. We skirted it earlier, but let's give it the attention it deserves.

First, notice that Moses only describes what was under God's feet. That may have been all they saw, similar to Isaiah's vision of God in Isaiah 6, where he only describes the throne, the train of his robe, and the surrounding seraphs. The blinding light would make it impossible to actually see God. Ezekiel has a similar vision of a form on a throne (Ezekiel 1:26-28). The Hebrew word translated "saw" in verse 11 (to see in a vision) is different than the word in verse 10 (seeing with your eyes). Another account of this experience (Deuteronomy 4:15) says: *You saw no form of any kind the day the Lord spoke to you at Horeb out of the fire.*

## BIBLICAL TEXTS THAT ALLUDE TO SEEING GOD

*So Jacob called the place Peniel, saying, "It is because I saw God face to face, and yet my life was spared."* (Genesis 32:30)

*"When there is a prophet among you,*
  *I, the Lord, reveal myself to them in visions,*
  *I speak to them in dreams.*
*But this is not true of my servant Moses;*
  *he is faithful in all my house.*
*With him I speak face to face,*
  *clearly and not in riddles;*
  *he sees the form of the Lord.* (Numbers 12:6-8)

*"We are doomed to die!" he said to his wife. "We have seen God!"* (Judges 13:22)

*"As I looked, thrones were set in place,*
  *and the Ancient of Days took his seat.*
*His clothing was as white as snow;*
  *the hair of his head was white like wool.*
*His throne was flaming with fire,*
  *and its wheels were all ablaze.* (Daniel 7:9)

Some of these were probably visions. Even Moses, speaking to God face to face, only saw his form. And no one actually describes him.

## BIBLICAL TEXTS THAT DENY THE POSSIBILITY OF SEEING GOD
This verse seems to specifically prohibit seeing God's face: *"You cannot see my face, for no one may see me and live."* (Exodus 33:20)

*No one has ever seen God, but the one and only Son, who is himself God and is in closest relationship with the Father, has made him known.* (John 1:18)

*Who alone is immortal and who lives in unapproachable light, whom no one has seen or can see. To him be honor and might forever. Amen.* (1 Timothy 6:16)

So what are we to conclude? It is possible to be in the overwhelming presence of God and even get hints of his appearance, but it seems likely that no one has ever actually seen him in all his glory.

## MOSES DOESN'T GO ALONE
*12 The Lord said to Moses, "Come up to me on the mountain and stay here, and I will give you the tablets of stone with the law and commandments I have written for their instruction." 13 Then Moses set out with Joshua his aide, and Moses went up on the mountain of God. 14 He said to the elders, "Wait here for us until we come back to you. Aaron and Hur are with you, and anyone involved in a dispute can go to them."*

Glorious as it was to see the pavement before the Lord, Moses gets to actually go up to God and stay there with him, primarily to get the stone tablets with the law. But Moses doesn't go alone; Joshua goes with him. Joshua wasn't included among those God called to go up, but apparently wherever Moses went, Joshua went. And God didn't strike him down! Do you have a Joshua you take with you into God's presence?

Hur had not been mentioned either (unless he was among the 70 elders). He and Aaron are left in charge while Moses and Joshua go up. I don't know if they were aware of it when they went up, but that crew was to stay there the whole 40 days Moses was on the mountain top. It's hard to know exactly how that worked out, since Aaron had his unfortunate incident with the golden calf while Moses was on the mountain.

## ARE YOU READY TO PAY THE PRICE TO MEET WITH GOD?

*15 When Moses went up on the mountain, the cloud covered it, 16 and the glory of the Lord settled on Mount Sinai. For six days the cloud covered the mountain, and on the seventh day the Lord called to Moses from within the cloud. 17 To the Israelites the glory of the Lord looked like a consuming fire on top of the mountain. 18 Then Moses entered the cloud as he went on up the mountain. And he stayed on the mountain forty days and forty nights.*

Meanwhile Moses' "congregation" is left at the bottom to witness these amazing displays of God's glory. They probably had no idea if they would ever see Moses again, especially as the days drag on.

Moses (and Joshua) had to wait six days just to get the go ahead to enter the cloud! Surely there is some significance to those six days, and God calling him on the seventh day to enter into communion with him. Perhaps the six days God worked creating the earth? Six days in preparation for the Lord's day?

Many people long to be in leadership. You might picture Moses entering that cloud and wish you could be there, but don't be too quick in asking for what Moses had. It doesn't say it here, but that was a forty day fast. No food or drink. No internet or TV. No sex. Maybe Moses had an idea of what was coming and knew it would be better to send Zipporah and the boys back home with Jethro.

You say you want to meet with God? Are you really ready for a forty day fast? Are you willing to just wait six days for the word to proceed? Or would you figure it's just not happening after a couple days, and go back down? Do you get impatient if God doesn't show up in the first half hour of a worship service? Do you feel like a few hours waiting on God for personal fellowship is about all you can take? How serious are you about being a leader and getting to know God? He shows up in his time, not ours. He calls us into the glory cloud when he wants to. Are you ready for that consuming fire to purge your flesh?

# 22

# A Golden Calf Emerges from the Fire
## *Exodus 32*

This is one amazing chapter. Of course we have all seen *The Ten Commandments* and know about the golden calf. But in the midst of the drama there are some profound messages.

Moses has been on the mountain forty days, receiving the Law directly from God himself. He went up in a blaze of glory. God awed the nation with his majesty and validated Moses' leadership. The recently freed Hebrew slaves had seen plenty to bolster their faith:

- Plagues that destroyed the land of Egypt
- Passing through the Red Sea on dry ground
- God's physical presence in the pillar of fire and cloud
- Water from a rock
- The daily provision of manna

That would seem like enough to establish their faith and cement their commitment to the God who delivered them from slavery. Think again. After just forty days they are ready to turn to other gods.

We are quick to condemn them. But remember, they are fresh out of hundreds of years of slavery and have only known Moses for a few months. Someone in a supportive church community who is receiving regular encouragement could probably survive a dry spell for several months or even years, but they are like children at this point. Mommy or Daddy being gone forty days is a lifetime for a kid. They can't take it anymore.

*[1]When the people saw that Moses was so long in coming down from the mountain, they gathered around Aaron and said, "Come, make us gods who will go before us. As for this fellow Moses who brought us up out of Egypt, we don't know what has happened to him."*

## ABANDONMENT BY A SPIRITUAL LEADER
They had been warned that anyone touching the mountain would die. Moses not only touched it, he climbed it, amidst all the quaking and fire and smoke. After forty days they probably thought he was never coming down. Like so many of us, they put a time limit on when God was supposed to come through for them. Their patience was limited. They had just left Egypt and are in the middle of a wilderness. They feel Moses has abandoned them.

Like a foster child who has never had the chance to bond with a parent, they quickly latch on to another "spiritual father." They were never too sure about Moses anyway, and hadn't formed a real attachment to him. To them, Moses represented God. They still felt it was "this fellow" Moses who brought them out of Egypt; they haven't grasped that it was God's work. Everything they knew about God was wrapped up in this one man – and with him gone, their faith fails. It's not that different from some churches which revolve around a charismatic pastor. It's not uncommon for the church to fall apart when that pastor leaves or dies.

So what do they do?

1. They seek out the person closest to the missing leader. If you feel abandoned by a pastor, you will probably go to an assistant pastor or elder. Your natural tendency is to seek out someone else in spiritual leadership.

2. They ask for gods to lead them. They don't yet have the concept of monotheism. Probably influenced by the religion in Egypt, they feel there are a multitude of gods to choose from. If one doesn't work, you can try another. It may sound silly, but people do it all the time today.

3. They express dismay at the loss of their leader.

Have you ever been let down by someone in spiritual leadership? Perhaps they failed to follow through on promises made to you? Or weren't there when you needed them? It serves as a wake-up call to how man-centered our faith can become, when that pastor takes on a larger-than-life role for you, and your whole relationship to God is undermined if they don't come through. They were right in going to Aaron – but as we will see in a moment, Aaron had serious problems of his own. Be careful of putting too much weight on a man.

## ABANDONMENT BY GOD

On a deeper level, with Moses gone the people have no sense of God's presence, despite all that he has done. They don't know him yet. Their faith hasn't developed. There is fear of what will happen to them without Moses. You would think the tremendous miracles they had witnessed would be a life-long confirmation that God was with them. Not so. As we have already seen in Exodus, people have amazingly short memories when it comes to miracles, and our experience confirms that. If you base your faith on miracles it seems you need a steady supply. We are prone to doubt and unbelief.

People typically feel abandoned by God when he doesn't answer prayer as they hoped he would:

- When a loved one dies.
- When healing doesn't come.
- When things go terribly wrong and it feels like God doesn't care.

God had made it very clear he was going to take them to the Promised Land. We know he is not an evil or capricious God who would deliver his people from Egypt only to let them die in the wilderness, but they didn't have that confidence yet, and they didn't have a community of committed believers surrounding them to encourage them. There was no Bible. The Tabernacle hadn't been built, and there were no regular worship services. Their religion was very primitive.

Somehow they feel they can make their own gods to replace the one who abandoned them. That seems ludicrous to us – but we constantly make gods to suit our needs. Are you tempted to follow a god of your own making? Sometimes it's a woman; sometimes a businessman who promises you wealth and power. Jesus promised he would never leave you or forsake you. If you feel far from God, guess who has moved?

*² Aaron answered them, "Take off the gold earrings that your wives, your sons and your daughters are wearing, and bring them to me." ³ So all the people took off their earrings and brought them to Aaron. ⁴ He took what they handed him and made it into an idol cast in the shape of a calf, fashioning it with a tool. Then they said, "These are your gods, Israel, who brought you up out of Egypt."*

*⁵ When Aaron saw this, he built an altar in front of the calf and announced, "Tomorrow there will be a festival to the Lord." ⁶ So the next day the people rose early and sacrificed burnt offerings and presented fellowship offerings. Afterward they sat down to eat and drink and got up to indulge in revelry.*

## WEAK LEADERS

When Moses went up the mountain he entrusted the people to Aaron. He had no choice; he had important business to do with God. A pastor can't possibly be there all the time, but when the shepherd is gone the wolf sees the opportunity to ravage the sheep. Aaron should have provided leadership in Moses' absence, but instead he allowed the people to lead him. Whether he was a people-pleaser, or lacking in any real relationship with God, or just weak and cowardly, he failed miserably, and was responsible for the deaths of thousands of people.

Aaron should have stood up boldly and said "Are you crazy? After all God has done for you? I cannot and will not make gods for you! There is only one God and you should have seen enough of his glory to know you can't mess around with him! Stop this silliness right now. Moses will be back. God will continue to go before you in the pillar of fire and cloud!"

## THEIR NEW GOD

God had moved the Egyptians to give their jewelry to the Israelites when they left. Now Aaron asked for this gold. Be careful of those who go after your gold! They may be wanting it to make their own idol! How the people could really believe that a silly gold calf which Aaron made from their earrings was the god who brought them out of Egypt just confirms how vulnerable people are to spiritual deception. And Aaron made it worse by building an altar before it and proclaiming a festival to the "LORD"! He was mixing aspects of true faith with their idolatry, and further adding to their confusion. It's not unlike what has happened when the Gospel is brought to a new country and elements of an indigenous religion are mingled with Christianity.

## PASSING THE BLAME

We see further evidence of Aaron's weakness when Moses confronts him:

*21 He said to Aaron, "What did these people do to you, that you led them into such great sin?"*

*22 "Do not be angry, my lord," Aaron answered. "You know how prone these people are to evil. 23 They said to me, 'Make us gods who will go before us. As for this fellow Moses who brought us up out of Egypt, we don't know what has happened to him.' 24 So I told them, 'Whoever has any gold jewelry, take it off.' Then they gave me the gold, and I threw it into the fire, and out came this calf!"*

Aaron knows Moses is furious, and does what most people do when confronted with wrong-doing: deny it and pass the blame. Moses can see right through it, and places full responsibility on Aaron. He can't believe his brother was so easily influenced and led astray. It's tragic when someone in authority actually *leads* people into sin.

Moses had his share of problems with the people, and Aaron hopes he can get his sympathy by reminding him – correctly – that they are prone to evil. As Satan did in the garden, Aaron mixes truth and lies. He comes up with this fantastic story of a calf somehow emerging from the fire!

We all make mistakes. It takes maturity to be honest and accept responsibility for what you have done, and bear the consequences. Passing the blame and lying is cowardly. It is always better to be honest, ask for mercy, and do what's necessary to set things right.

Don't be a wimpy leader like Aaron. Be careful of being a people-pleaser and giving in to things you know aren't right. If you are still trying to run from something you have done wrong, it is better to take responsibility and pay whatever price has to be paid.

## THE TENDENCY TO IDOLATRY

It's not in our nature to stay faithful to God. We need constant encouragement, feeding from the Scripture, help from God's Spirit, and shepherding by godly leaders to keep us from going astray. Our natural tendency is to idolatry. Of course we are not so ignorant as to think a calf we fashion out of gold could be a god. But we have plenty of idols today. Most confessing Christians spend far more time in front of the computer and the television than they do in God's presence; they are more influenced by the culture than the Word of God.

This probably was their first real party since leaving Egypt, and they let it all out! They were eating and drinking (most likely strong drink) and engaging in revelry (the Hebrew word probably refers to orgies). They were shouting (what Joshua thought were war cries), and singing and dancing. They were running wild and out of control and had become a laughingstock to their enemies, who apparently were close enough to be aware of what was happening. Once godly restraint has been removed, our natural tendency is to go wild. God has established authority in society and in the church for a reason.

This is the discouraging part of the story. Next we will see the amazing contrast Moses offers, in an almost Christ-like rescue of his people, but there is plenty here to reflect on. If God has placed you in leadership, learn from Aaron's poor example. Don't be a people-pleaser! Take responsibility for your mistakes! Stand up for what you know is right. If you feel let down by God or a pastor, you have every right to feel hurt, angry, and dismayed. But don't let your fear and anger blind you to the great record God has with you – and with millions of other people through the millennia. Don't give up! Don't turn to other gods! Fight the natural human tendency to idolatry!

# 23

# THE HEART OF A MAN OF GOD
## *EXODUS 32*

Moses was enjoying amazing fellowship with God and receiving laws to govern the nation, which God was gracious enough to write on stone tablets. Moses was blissfully unaware that his people were engaged in mass revelry, drunkenness, and idol worship, but he's about to get a rude awakening. The mountain top experience is being interrupted by an emergency down in the camp.

*⁷ Then the Lord said to Moses, "Go down, because your people, whom you brought up out of Egypt, have become corrupt.*

Read that verse carefully. Do you notice anything unusual about the way God refers to Israel? They are *your* people, Moses, whom *you* brought out of Egypt. God is distancing himself from them, not unlike a father who talks to his wife about *your* son when the kid messes up – but *my* son when he does well!

### AN OFFER THAT COULD SEEM HARD TO REFUSE
*⁸ They have been quick to turn away from what I commanded them and have made themselves an idol cast in the shape of a calf. They have bowed down to it and sacrificed to it and have said, 'These are your gods, Israel, who brought you up out of Egypt.'*

⁹ *"I have seen these people," the Lord said to Moses, "and they are a stiff-necked people. ¹⁰ Now leave me alone so that my anger may burn against them and that I may destroy them. Then I will make you into a great nation."*

God seems ready to give up on them very easily. Is he just speaking in anger? Could God speak rashly – like we do – in the heat of the moment? Or is it a test of Moses' commitment to them? God isn't backing away from his promise to form a nation or get them to the land flowing with milk and honey. It would just be much smaller; the descendants of the one man who remained faithful to him. But God had tried that before, with Noah, and it wasn't that successful.

Would you have been tempted by God's offer? Moses hadn't known these people that long, and he already had plenty of bad experiences with them. How liberating to be free of their constant complaining! Here was a chance to shape a people without all their baggage! But Moses knows he was charged with bringing them to Canaan – and it looks like he has actually grown to love them.

Israel is frequently called stiff-necked, but all of us continually test God's patience and give him headaches. It would certainly seem easier to destroy them (and us), but fortunately there is someone to intercede for them (and us).

¹¹ *But Moses sought the favor of the Lord his God. "Lord," he said, "why should your anger burn against your people, whom you brought out of Egypt with great power and a mighty hand? ¹² Why should the Egyptians say, 'It was with evil intent that he brought them out, to kill them in the mountains and to wipe them off the face of the earth'? Turn from your fierce anger; relent and do not bring disaster on your people. ¹³ Remember your servants Abraham, Isaac and Israel, to whom you swore by your own self:*

*'I will make your descendants as numerous as the stars in the sky and I will give your descendants all this land I promised them, and it will be their inheritance forever.'"* [14] *Then the Lord relented and did not bring on his people the disaster he had threatened.*

## THE NATION SAVED BY MOSES' INTERCESSION

This is the first of two amazing prayers in this chapter. Several things are noteworthy:

- Unlike the rest of the nation, which lacked a real commitment to the Lord, Moses clearly has made the Lord *his* God.

- In what almost seems like a game, Moses turns God's words around on him: "They're *your* people who *you* brought out of Egypt. Don't try to hand them off to me!" It is an important perspective for a pastor to keep in mind: God may have given you authority over a church, but they are still *his* people.

- In a pattern often seen in Scriptural prayers, Moses builds a case with God (as if God had forgotten this in the heat of his anger!):

    o "You have already worked mightily on their behalf. You brought them out of Egypt. After doing all that, it doesn't make sense to destroy them."

    o With remarkable perception, Moses recognizes that God has a broader concern than just Israel: "What about your reputation? Remember, you want to glorify yourself in all the earth. Do you really want word to get out that you are an impulsive God who delivers his people only to destroy them?"

- o "You will break your word; your promise; your covenant. Remember Abraham? You swore by yourself in making that promise! You certainly can't back down!"
- With that strong case, Moses makes a simple but obvious request: "Don't do it. Turn from your anger." And amazingly, God listens, and relents.

It may be hard to understand the idea of God "relenting," but throughout Scripture his promises and warnings are usually conditional on our response. He may threaten judgment – but if we repent and turn back to him, he will withdraw the punishment. This dramatically demonstrates the importance of an intercessor or priest: Someone with a clear head who knows the Lord, and is willing to come between God and a sinful people, going boldly before him in prayer. We may not understand all the dynamics, but somehow God has chosen to work together with us, and has ordained prayer as a means of influencing the Lord of the universe.

Having saved his people from destruction, Moses needs to get down there and take care of business. There may be intercessors who stay in their prayer closets, but the pastor needs to wade right into the mess and set things right.

*$^{15}$ Moses turned and went down the mountain with the two tablets of the covenant law in his hands. They were inscribed on both sides, front and back. $^{16}$ The tablets were the work of God; the writing was the writing of God, engraved on the tablets.*

*$^{17}$ When Joshua heard the noise of the people shouting, he said to Moses, "There is the sound of war in the camp."*

[18] Moses replied: "It is not the sound of victory,
it is not the sound of defeat;
it is the sound of singing that I hear."

## Down from the Mountaintop

Can you imagine this trek down the mountain? Moses has been fasting forty days; he must be starving. But more importantly, he's not sure what he is going to find when he gets down there. For God to be so angry, he knows it's going to be bad. He knows he has a tough job in front of him. Deuteronomy 9:15 tells us the mountain was ablaze with fire. Moses is going to make a dramatic entry.

We are reminded that he isn't alone: Joshua has been with him the entire time. Perhaps they were discussing together how to respond to the crisis. This was on-the-job training for the one who would assume leadership of the nation when Moses died. It is a great example of the need for spiritual leaders to pour themselves into a younger person who can carry on the work. Take them with you wherever you go! Let them see you in prayer and in some of the agonizing struggles a pastor experiences.

It is a little odd that Moses didn't give his precious cargo to the younger man to carry, but it had been entrusted to him, and it was among the most valuable treasures man had ever been given: tablets inscribed by God himself with his laws! Aside from the replacement tablets, can you think of anything else on this earth that bears God's handwriting?

As they approach the camp, the shouting grows louder. It was so intense that Joshua thinks it is the sound of war. But Moses recognizes it as singing – and not in sweet worship to God, but the bawdy singing of drunken revelry. What songs were they singing? Maybe work songs from back in their slave days? Or some kind of pagan worship song they had learned in Egypt?

[19] *When Moses approached the camp and saw the calf and the dancing, his anger burned and he threw the tablets out of his hands, breaking them to pieces at the foot of the mountain.* [20] *And he took the calf the people had made and burned it in the fire; then he ground it to powder, scattered it on the water and made the Israelites drink it.*

## MOSES' ANGER

Now it's Moses' turn to get angry. On the mountain he couldn't see what God had seen. That was a good thing, or he might have agreed with God's plan to destroy them. His burning anger leads to two dramatic responses:

- Moses casts down the tablets God had written, breaking them into pieces, like a guy punching a hole in a wall or throwing something. Imagine finding some of those pieces today! Perhaps Moses felt God's holy laws were useless with such a rebellious bunch. It was a rash act, but no more rash than God's intent to destroy all the people. It might be better to smash some tablets than kill someone. God never rebukes Moses, and, later, graciously replaces the tablets.

- It's hard to picture exactly how it was done, but Moses gets rid of their new god, destroying the calf, mixing it with water, and making them drink it. So much for all their gold! Rebellion can be very costly! And humiliating!

Was Moses wrong to get so angry? There is no suggestion that he was. God was angry too. It does sound abusive to make them drink the golden water. We can do rash, destructive things in our anger. Be careful! In your anger do not sin!

[25] *Moses saw that the people were running wild and that Aaron had let them get out of control and so become a laughingstock to*

*their enemies. ²⁶ So he stood at the entrance to the camp and said, "Whoever is for the Lord, come to me." And all the Levites rallied to him.*

## MOSES DRAWS THE LINE

Moses seems to have found his voice! Do you remember his argument with God at the burning bush? Apparently he had some kind of speech problem. That's how Aaron got involved in the first place – he was to be his spokesman. Well, Aaron is in discipline and has nothing to say! Moses seems quite capable of speaking!

A dramatic situation calls for a dramatic response. He issues a bold challenge: If you are ready to repent, leave this idolatry, commit to God, and come to me. When people are running wild, totally out of control, they need someone in authority who will stand up, proclaim God's Word, and call them back to the Lord. Aaron was a weak leader who just looked on and let them go wild. Sometimes leaders will sit back and let people self-destruct. Not Moses. He told God he was ready to go the distance with this stiff-necked people, but he can only move ahead with those who are truly for the Lord.

There is a place for patience and giving people time to deal with their sin and idolatry, but there are too few bold men like Moses, ready to get up and take a stand for truth and righteousness. You can't build a church with people who are not really committed to Christ! Yes, you want to be inclusive and loving, but the Bible makes very clear statements about who can and cannot enter the kingdom. You may fear you will lose most of your church if you make this kind of call. Moses apparently lost most of Israel. Only the Levites, his own tribe, rallied to him. And that may have been more out of tribal loyalty than true devotion to God. Their commitment is about to be tested.

*²⁷ Then he said to them, "This is what the Lord, the God of Israel, says: 'Each man strap a sword to his side. Go back and forth through the camp from one end to the other, each killing his brother and friend and neighbor.'" ²⁸ The Levites did as Moses commanded, and that day about three thousand of the people died. ²⁹ Then Moses said, "You have been set apart to the Lord today, for you were against your own sons and brothers, and he has blessed you this day."*

## PURIFYING THE NATION
Up to this point the tribe of Levi had not been separated out as the priestly tribe, but their zeal and faithfulness were rewarded by being appointed to serve God.

God may have relented from destroying the nation, but they would still have to pay for their sin, and God apparently had told Moses what to do. Judgment on sin is ruthless: brothers, friends, and neighbors would die. It's not unlike what Jesus portrays happening in the last day, when family members will turn on each other (Matthew 10:25, 35, 36). Are you willing to purify your home, your family, and your church? No, I'm not talking about killing them off, but scriptures like 1 Corinthians 5 lay out procedures for church discipline – procedures which are rarely followed today. Too many fathers and pastors are cowards in dealing with sin in their homes and churches! The laws God gave Moses imposed the death penalty for many things we routinely overlook – like rebellion in our children or sexual sin. No wonder our churches are weak! Could it be time to take the "sword of the Lord" and boldly deal with the sin in our midst? It will be painful, and will evoke a great outcry!

*³⁰ The next day Moses said to the people, "You have committed a great sin. But now I will go up to the Lord; perhaps I can make atonement for your sin."*

*³¹ So Moses went back to the Lord and said, "Oh, what a great sin these people have committed! They have made themselves gods of gold. ³² But now, please forgive their sin—but if not, then blot me out of the book you have written."*

*³³ The Lord replied to Moses, "Whoever has sinned against me I will blot out of my book. ³⁴ Now go, lead the people to the place I spoke of, and my angel will go before you. However, when the time comes for me to punish, I will punish them for their sin."*

*³⁵ And the Lord struck the people with a plague because of what they did with the calf Aaron had made.*

## BACK TO THE MOUNTAIN

Moses still isn't finished – and neither is God. We're not told exactly why the Levites stopped the killing, but God makes it clear: one way or another, whoever sins against God will pay for it. Moses can intercede and stay God's hand for a while; he can buy time and call the nation to repentance. But many more people die from plague, and ultimately God will "blot out of his book" everyone who refuses to follow him. He wouldn't be just if he didn't.

Deuteronomy 9 tells us that this trip involved another forty days of fasting. Hopefully Moses got a chance to eat while he was back in camp – maybe left-overs from the interrupted festivities! It also tells us that Moses feared God's anger and wrath – but went up the mountain anyway!

Moses makes no great argument this time. His prayer is desperate, and extreme: "Forgive them, or send me to hell. Blot my name out of your book." It reminds me of Paul in Romans 9, willing to be accursed if that would mean Israel's salvation. Moses is offering to bear God's anger for the peoples' sin. He is taking a Christ-like position of self-sacrifice. It is an amazing expression of the great love he has for his people. Deuteronomy 9 tells us he also requested forgiveness for Aaron.

It is remarkable that Moses understands that somehow atonement must be provided. Someone must pay for the sin, and he is willing to. We know that only a perfect sacrifice could satisfy God's wrath; only the sacrifice of his own Son could provide atonement. Moses shows additional insight with the idea of a "book" containing the names of those who would enter God's kingdom. God ignores Moses' request to bear the peoples' punishment, which would not be just either. Those who sin must die. All Moses can do is plead for mercy. He has nothing else to stand on. He has done what he can to purify the camp. Now it is in God's hands.

This has been an ugly wound for the nation, from which they can only very slowly recover. They are sobered, and in mourning for the many dead. Fear of God has replaced their revelry. But somehow, after God's judgment we must still pick up the pieces and move on. Moses' mission remains intact: He will still lead the people. God's promise hasn't changed: They will still make it to their destination – although God can't bring himself to speak of a "Promised Land" at this point. It is just "the place I spoke of." He also offers his angel to go before them. That sounds like a good deal, but the next chapter will reveal that Moses isn't satisfied with that. He knows God has distanced himself. His presence will no longer go with them – he will send his angel instead. Moses can't bear that distance from his God. Without the Lord's presence, he feels there is no way he can do it.

## COULD YOU DO WHAT MOSES DID?

I am overwhelmed at what I see in Moses here. It is hard to lead God's people! It is very costly: Weeks of fasting, being wildly unpopular, making agonizing decisions, and spending hours in prayer interceding for a people who only cause you headaches. But we are seeing the heart of a true man of God; a heart fully revealed in Jesus Christ. I am tremendously grateful for Jesus and the price he paid for my sin! For the forgiveness and atonement he provides. For my great high priest who is interceding for me! But I am also mindful that he calls me to lay down my life just as he did, and love with his agape love. That is a tremendous challenge. Are you willing to do it, with his help?

# 24

# I WON'T GO WITHOUT GOD'S PRESENCE
## EXODUS 33

*¹Then the Lord said to Moses, "Leave this place, you and the people you brought up out of Egypt, and go up to the land I promised on oath to Abraham, Isaac and Jacob, saying, 'I will give it to your descendants.'*

They have spent several months at Horeb, and what a time it has been!

- Glorious manifestations of God's power.
- Unanimous agreement to follow his laws (only to break that promise a few days later).
- The golden calf.
- Moses fasting 80 days on the mountaintop in God's presence.

Despite all our ups and downs, God's plan for "salvation history" is unchanged; ultimately, nothing will stand in the way of him establishing his kingdom. The nation was only saved from destruction by Moses' intercession, and now it is time to move on. But God won't claim ownership of the people; they are still the ones *you* (Moses) brought out of Egypt. And he has a surprise for Moses.

## God will not go with them

*² I will send an angel before you and drive out the Canaanites, Amorites, Hittites, Perizzites, Hivites and Jebusites. ³ Go up to the land flowing with milk and honey. But I will not go with you, because you are a stiff-necked people and I might destroy you on the way."*

Apparently God is still angry with them. He has found out what they are really like (and it's not good), so he decides to keep his distance to avoid destroying them. It's almost like he doesn't trust himself. Moses saved them once, but if they act out again God is afraid he might just annihilate them, so he will let his angel go with them. God is giving them the land, but withdrawing his presence. Do they have any choice? If you had to choose between an earthly paradise and God being with you, what would you choose?

Could this be why there are times when it seems God is nowhere around? Could it be we are stiff-necked like Israel, and God just chooses to keep his distance? Maybe he is nauseated by the shows we put on in his name, or by the hypocrisy of people deep in sin singing about how much they love him. Perhaps we will still make it to the Promised Land – but without the glory of his presence. Maybe we should follow God's example at times and send an assistant to deal with a problem, so we don't hurt somebody!

*⁴ When the people heard these distressing words, they began to mourn and no one put on any ornaments. ⁵ For the Lord had said to Moses, "Tell the Israelites, 'You are a stiff-necked people. If I were to go with you even for a moment, I might destroy you. Now take off your ornaments and I will decide what to do with you.'" ⁶ So the Israelites stripped off their ornaments at Mount Horeb.*

I wonder what ornaments they had left after Aaron used their gold to make the calf. Maybe other types of jewelry? Apparently taking off ornaments is a way of humbling ourselves and getting in a place to hear from God. If we are serious about hearing from him, maybe there are times when we should leave all our adornments and come together in the equivalent of sackcloth and ashes.

It seems odd that God appears indecisive about what to do with them. He still feels so much anger and disgust he is afraid he will destroy them if he is with them even for a moment! He certainly has the power to do that! He seems to lack self-control! In effect he is buying time, cooling down, so he can figure out what to do next.

I am surprised that the people would be so impacted by God's decision. They were ready to go back to Egypt and follow a different god of their own making, but just like many fickle Christians today, when they start to experience God's distance and judgment, they get serious and mourn the loss of his presence.

## BACKGROUND: MOSES' PRACTICE OF MEETING WITH GOD

At this point we are given insight on how Moses met with God. The mountain-top conferences were nothing new. Sometimes we want the mountain top experiences without cultivating a daily relationship with God. With all the responsibility he was carrying, Moses probably needed to meet with God daily just to get strength to go on, and direction for the day ahead. Jesus also had a habit of meeting with his Father early in the morning (Mark 1:35). And you? Do you have a "tent of meeting" – a private place where you can meet God daily for worship, fellowship, prayer, and hearing from him?

*⁷ Now Moses used to take a tent and pitch it outside the camp some distance away, calling it the "tent of meeting." Anyone inquiring of the Lord would go to the tent of meeting outside the camp. ⁸ And whenever Moses went out to the tent, all the people rose and stood at the entrances to their tents, watching Moses until he entered the tent. ⁹ As Moses went into the tent, the pillar of cloud would come down and stay at the entrance, while the Lord spoke with Moses.¹⁰ Whenever the people saw the pillar of cloud standing at the entrance to the tent, they all stood and worshiped, each at the entrance to their tent. ¹¹ The Lord would speak to Moses face to face, as one speaks to a friend. Then Moses would return to the camp, but his young aide Joshua son of Nun did not leave the tent.*

That is an amazing relationship with God!

- Moses got the tent, found a place for it wherever they happened to be at the time, and pitched it. He prepared to meet with God, making sure nothing got in the way. Maybe it was one of the first things he did in a new place. So much for the excuse of missing your devotions because you are traveling!

- Moses pitched it away from the crowd and its distracting noise. It was a holy, sacred place, used for nothing else. Most of us don't have the space or money to have an exclusive room or building set aside – but there may be a closet or corner somewhere in your home you can use.

- Moses held regular "office hours" there. People who needed to hear from God would go to the tent, presumably share their concern with Moses, and wait for the response he received from God. Do you wish there was a "tent of meeting" you could visit to get a word from the Lord? If you are in ministry, do you make that available to your people, and seriously seek the Lord to get a word for them?

- Moses enjoyed intimate, face to face (not literally), fellowship with God. Prayer is not difficult – it should be like talking with a friend. They had a deep relationship. God spoke to him. If you want to hear from God, you may need to get away from the crowd and make your own "tent of meeting." Far better to have that place of communion with God than a "man cave"!

The community's support was impressive. They knew their survival depended on Moses being in tune with God. Wouldn't it be great if our families and others around us would realize that! Everyone knew where Moses was going as he passed through the camp. There was something mysterious and awesome about him meeting God in the tent: Everything stopped, they arose, stood at the entrance to their tents, and watched him. As the pillar of cloud moved to the tent's entrance, worship rose up throughout the camp. What a glorious spiritual support for their leader as he met with God! Do you give that kind of support to your leaders? If you are in leadership, is there a way you could foster that in your people?

We don't know how much time Moses spent there. Certainly it wasn't hurried. Eventually he returned to camp, and daily life continued. Except for Joshua. He had been there as Moses talked with God, and stayed in the tent. Why?

- Maybe he was so overwhelmed with God's presence that he wanted to.

- Maybe he stayed there worshipping and ensuring the atmosphere was spiritually prepared for Moses' next meeting.

- Maybe God talked with him.
- Did he stay to make sure no word that might come from God would be lost?
- Or was he just guarding it from any curious intruder?

It is one more critical step in the preparation of the leader who would take them into the Promised Land. If you are an aspiring leader, are you willing to spend that kind of time? If you are already a leader, do you take a Joshua with you into your intimate fellowship with the Lord?

## BEHIND THE SCENES IN THE TENT OF MEETING

Devastating as the experience was with the golden calf, it led to deeper intimacy between God and Moses. That is one of the blessings that often comes from our trials. Somehow, one of those face-to-face meetings was recorded. Let's listen in:

*12 Moses said to the Lord, "You have been telling me, 'Lead these people,' but you have not let me know whom you will send with me. You have said, 'I know you by name and you have found favor with me.' 13 If you are pleased with me, teach me your ways so I may know you and continue to find favor with you. Remember that this nation is your people."*

Have you ever read something in the Bible or received a word from the Lord that doesn't seem to connect to your daily experience? That appears to be how Moses was feeling.

- The assignment is clear: Moses is to lead the people. But he knows he can't do it by himself. He had counted on God's presence with him, but this was probably after God said he would no longer go with them. If not God, then who? Moses needs to know. Maybe he hadn't yet heard it would be an angel, or wasn't happy about that. If I am confident God is with me I can do just about anything. The feeling that I might not be in his will or that he's not with me is frightening.

- God told Moses he knows him and approves of him. He has found favor with God. That's good to know, but Moses wants more: "Teach me! I want to know you! I want to do whatever it takes to continue in your favor!" It reminds me of hearing "God loves you and has a wonderful plan for your life" so many times. Great. But how can I have a relationship with him so I can experience that love? What am I supposed to do? How am I supposed to live? What is his plan for me? Pastor, get beyond the motivational hype, and give your people solid teaching and help in actually knowing God. There is an appalling lack of real relationship with God and knowledge of his ways. By the way, God does know you by name. He knows you intimately. And he loves you, warts and all. If you are in Christ, you are his adopted son, and you are favored!

- Moses has extra leverage, which he uses freely: "Remember, this is *your* people, God. They're not mine. You are doing yourself a favor by helping me be the most I can be." If you are a leader, feel free to use that same argument with the Lord.

*14 The Lord replied, "My Presence will go with you, and I will give you rest."*

God is not very verbal, is he? In what appears to be a reversal of his earlier refusal to go with them, God promises his Presence *would* go with them. Or is he just promising to be with Moses? At any rate, Moses' first request is answered, and God offers him something he hasn't requested: rest. If you think back on the last few months of Moses' life (confronting Pharaoh, leading the people out of Egypt, crossing the Red Sea, dealing with their complaints, extensive fasting, the golden calf) we can see why Moses could use rest. Sometimes Christian leaders feel that exhaustion is part of their call. They neglect God's command to separate a day for rest to recharge the batteries and spend time with the Lord. God wants to give you rest! Your circumstances may not be restful, but he can *give* you that rest!

*[15]{.sup} Then Moses said to him, "If your Presence does not go with us, do not send us up from here. [16]{.sup} How will anyone know that you are pleased with me and with your people unless you go with us? What else will distinguish me and your people from all the other people on the face of the earth?"*

Did Moses miss what the Lord just said? Does he need extra assurance? Or is he "addicted" to God's presence?

1. Without God's Presence, life is not worth living. I can't go on; I have to have his Presence. That is where life is found. Some have suggested that hell is simply the absence of God's presence. Too many people leave whatever taste they have of God's Presence at church. We need to live in his Presence every day. It is too easy to move ahead on our own and leave him behind, or let TV and the internet take the place of God's Presence. Do you need to get back to the "tent of meeting"?

2. It is important for others to know that God is pleased with me, with you, and with your church. If there is no evidence of God's Presence, there is no way they can know that. If God is with you and moving with you in whatever you are doing, it will be evident to others, and will draw them to you, and to Christ. A church without

God's Presence is just a social club or show, and is not attractive on a deep level.

3. One of the key distinguishing marks of the believer is God's Presence with him. Without that, there really is not much difference between you and the people of the world.

*[17] And the Lord said to Moses, "I will do the very thing you have asked, because I am pleased with you and I know you by name."*

It seems like God frequently repeats himself, maybe to make sure we get the message. He had just told Moses he is pleased with him and knows him by name, and since that is the case, Moses' request is granted. Moses is making headway, so he gets bold.

*[18] Then Moses said, "Now show me your glory."*

Moses probably had seen more of God's glory than any of us, but there is something about his glory that makes you want more. Moses isn't thinking of what he can get out of the relationship or the mansion he can get in the Promised Land. He's not thinking about his success leading the people. He just wants to see God's glory. Do you have that longing for God?

*[19] And the Lord said, "I will cause all my goodness to pass in front of you, and I will proclaim my name, the Lord, in your presence. I will have mercy on whom I will have mercy, and I will have compassion on whom I will have compassion. [20] But," he said, "you cannot see my face, for no one may see me and live."*

God is very gracious with Moses, but you get the feeling that Moses doesn't really understand what he is asking for. What will God do?

1. He will cause his goodness to pass in front of Moses. Do you believe God truly is good? Though he wouldn't

actually see God, Moses would have an overwhelming sense of God's goodness.

2. He will proclaim his name (the Lord) in his presence.

3. God is providing amazing self-revelation, but he is concerned he might be giving up too much to Moses. He retains his sovereignty. Moses can influence him, but God will have mercy and compassion on whom he chooses.

As privileged as Moses is, he cannot see God's full glory. He cannot see his face, because it would kill him. Moses' request may have been answered on the Mount of Transfiguration, when he was able to see Jesus' face shining with God's glory (Matthew 17:3).

*21 Then the Lord said, "There is a place near me where you may stand on a rock. 22 When my glory passes by, I will put you in a cleft in the rock and cover you with my hand until I have passed by. 23 Then I will remove my hand and you will see my back; but my face must not be seen."*

In what theologians call "anthropomorphisms" God expresses very human characteristics: his hand, his back, his face. Somehow he takes Moses and puts him in a cleft in the rock.

- What would it feel like to be covered there by God's hand?
- What happened as God was passing by?
- Was Moses trying to sneak a peek?
- What exactly did Moses see when he saw God's back?

The chapter ends with this tantalizing picture – but without any description of happened. Perhaps it was beyond Moses' ability to record.

Do you hunger for God's Presence? Is it more important to you than anything else? Do you have a "tent of meeting" where you can truly meet with God? Or has it been a long time since you have enjoyed "face to face" communion with God, talking with him as you would with a friend? Are you confident God is going with you on the path you are taking in life? Or have you left him somewhere along the way – possibly without even knowing it?

# 25

## THE END OF THE CRISIS
### EXODUS 34

It is certain to come, whether it's a new marriage, a new baby – or a new nation: The first crisis. Israel is only a few months old, and they have just had theirs. It almost ended up destroying them, but they squeaked through. In this chapter the last traces of the mess are cleaned up, and they are ready to move on.

They came close to losing God's presence with them. Moses agonized over that possibility – and finally ended up getting a glimpse of God's back and the assurance that God would go with them. With things pretty much back to normal, it's time for Moses to spend another 40 days fasting in God's presence, and receive replacements for the stone tablets he broke.

*¹The Lord said to Moses, "Chisel out two stone tablets like the first ones, and I will write on them the words that were on the first tablets, which you broke. ²Be ready in the morning, and then come up on Mount Sinai. Present yourself to me there on top of the mountain. ³No one is to come with you or be seen anywhere on the mountain; not even the flocks and herds may graze in front of the mountain."*

When I was a kid I got in big trouble if I broke something. Breaking tablets written by God himself would seem worse, but all God does is remind Moses that he broke them. That's it. Moses does have to chisel out new tablets and climb the mountain again, but he knew that amazing fellowship with the Lord of the universe awaited him at the top. Far better than hanging out with those problematic Israelites! Moses was clearly told not to bring anyone else, so this time Joshua may have stayed below.

*⁴ So Moses chiseled out two stone tablets like the first ones and went up Mount Sinai early in the morning, as the Lord had commanded him; and he carried the two stone tablets in his hands. ⁵ Then the Lord came down in the cloud and stood there with him and proclaimed his name, the Lord. ⁶ And he passed in front of Moses, proclaiming, "The Lord, the Lord, the compassionate and gracious God, slow to anger, abounding in love and faithfulness, ⁷ maintaining love to thousands, and forgiving wickedness, rebellion and sin. Yet he does not leave the guilty unpunished; he punishes the children and their children for the sin of the parents to the third and fourth generation."*

Once again the exact chronology of events in Exodus is unclear. Could this have been God's response to Moses' request to see his glory at the end of chapter 33? Many think it is. We see more of his love than his majesty and power. It is these characteristics that demonstrate his glory, and we reflect his glory as we display them.

## CHILDREN PUNISHED FOR THEIR PARENTS' SIN?
Many believers have struggled with what God says here. First the good news:

- He is Lord, sovereign, reigning in unparalleled power.

- He is compassionate and gracious. He understands us and bestows his favor on us because he wants to. It is not based on what we deserve.

- He is slow to anger. Yes, he got angry about the golden calf, but they had been provoking him for a while! If you read about what happened throughout Israel's history, you would have to agree he was extraordinarily patient with them. And what about us today? We are way beyond ripe for judgment, but he still holds back his anger.

- He is loving, maintaining love to thousands. Before anger or judgment, he is love.

- He forgives wickedness, rebellion, and sin. And that is before Christ paid for our forgiveness on the cross!

That sounds great, and it is. It's the "but" (*yet*, verse 7) that causes concern.

- He doesn't leave the guilty unpunished. He wouldn't be just if he did. These are the unrepentant who insist on continuing in their sin, not those who have received his forgiveness.

- That punishment continues on to the third and fourth generation. That is sobering, and sounds unfair. But this verse must be taken in the context of the revelation Moses already received in the second of the Ten Commandments (Exodus 20:4-6): *"You shall not make for yourself an image in the form of anything in heaven above or on the earth beneath or in the waters below. You shall not bow down to them or worship them; for I, the Lord your God, am a jealous God, punishing the children for the sin of the parents to the third and fourth generation of those who hate me, but showing love to a thousand generations of those who love me and keep my commandments."*

Far from being unfair in punishing innocent children, the punishment is for those who *continue to hate him*. In fact, God is incredibly gracious: the punishment is to the *fourth* generation; his love is shown to a *thousand* generations! There will be a tendency for a generational curse to follow those who hate God. It will be harder for their children to follow the Lord. But God's love will automatically be shown to the children of those who love and obey him.

*⁸ Moses bowed to the ground at once and worshiped.⁹ "Lord," he said, "if I have found favor in your eyes, then let the Lord go with us. Although this is a stiff-necked people, forgive our wickedness and our sin, and take us as your inheritance."*

Again, this seems repetitious, since God already promised he would go with them in chapter 33. Perhaps Moses is emboldened by God's declaration of compassion and forgiveness to intercede for the people and get further confirmation that God will go with them. That is his primary concern.

## A NEW COVENANT
*¹⁰ Then the Lord said: "I am making a covenant with you. Before all your people I will do wonders never before done in any nation in all the world. The people you live among will see how awesome is the work that I, the Lord, will do for you. ¹¹ Obey what I command you today. I will drive out before you the Amorites, Canaanites, Hittites, Perizzites, Hivites and Jebusites. ¹² Be careful not to make a treaty with those who live in the land where you are going, or they will be a snare among you. ¹³ Break down their altars, smash their sacred stones and cut down their Asherah poles.¹⁴ Do not worship any other god, for the Lord, whose name is Jealous, is a jealous God.*

Again, God goes far beyond what we might expect. Despite their grievous sin, he is making a covenant with them; not because he feels so great about them, but in response to Moses' intercession. Any covenant involves two parties. For his part, God promises:

- To do wonders before them unequalled anywhere else on earth
- To do awesome work on their behalf which others will witness.
- To drive out the pagan nations currently in the Promised Land.

To experience these blessings, the nation of Israel must:

- Obey his commands.
- Never make a treaty with the pagans in the land, since they would be a snare that would pull them from the Lord.
- Break down all evidence of their idolatry.
- Worship God alone. Part of his very character is jealousy! He will not tolerate any other god in our lives.

*15 "Be careful not to make a treaty with those who live in the land; for when they prostitute themselves to their gods and sacrifice to them, they will invite you and you will eat their sacrifices. 16 And when you choose some of their daughters as wives for your sons and those daughters prostitute themselves to their gods, they will lead your sons to do the same.*

This command reminds me of Paul's command to not be yoked with unbelievers (2 Corinthians 6:14). We are to be a sanctified people, separated from those who do not worship God. We are *in* the world but not *of* the world. Marriage to an unbeliever is particularly problematic, as noted here. Israel's history confirms the danger of inter-marriage. When we get too cozy with the world, they invite us to take part in their lifestyle, and the believer generally ends up being influenced by the unbeliever.

We may not feel much danger of prostituting ourselves to idols or eating food sacrificed to them, but Jesus gave us a broader view when he said *"No one can serve two masters. You cannot serve both God and money."* (Luke 16:13) Far too many believers are trying to do just that – and the Lord almost always ends up losing out. We risk inciting his jealous wrath.

Verses 17-26 contain various commands, mostly regarding feasts and offerings.

*²⁷ Then the Lord said to Moses, "Write down these words, for in accordance with these words I have made a covenant with you and with Israel." ²⁸ Moses was there with the Lord forty days and forty nights without eating bread or drinking water. And he wrote on the tablets the words of the covenant—the Ten Commandments.*

I wonder how Moses felt about another forty day total fast!

Once again we see the support for Mosaic authorship of these books. We know he could write (his Egyptian education came in handy), and God commanded him to write down his words. The first time God himself had written the commands on the tablets; this time Moses wrote them.

## MOSES' RADIANT FACE

*²⁹ When Moses came down from Mount Sinai with the two tablets of the covenant law in his hands, he was not aware that his face was radiant because he had spoken with the Lord. ³⁰ When Aaron and all the Israelites saw Moses, his face was radiant, and they were afraid to come near him. ³¹ But Moses called to them; so Aaron and all the leaders of the community came back to him, and he spoke to them. ³² Afterward all the Israelites came near* him, and he gave them all the commands the Lord had given him on Mount Sinai.

Have you ever seen a glow on the face of someone who has spent extended time with the Lord? How about you? Do you run the risk of people being afraid to come near you because of the radiance of God's presence? Moses (called the most humble man on earth) didn't take advantage of it by setting himself above others, but sought to maintain fellowship with all the people.

*³³ When Moses finished speaking to them, he put a veil over his face. ³⁴ But whenever he entered the Lord's presence to speak with him, he removed the veil until he came out. And when he came out and told the Israelites what he had been commanded, ³⁵ they saw that his face was radiant. Then Moses would put the veil back over his face until he went in to speak with the Lord.*

It appears Moses took the veil off to speak with God, and to convey God's Word to the people. The rest of the time the veil covered his face. Paul refers to Moses' veil in 2 Corinthians 3 when he talks about the glory of the New Covenant being greater than what Moses experienced. Paul explains that the veil was kept in place so the Israelites wouldn't see the glory fading. How sad that many believers never come close to the depth of fellowship Moses had!

## THE END OF THE CRISIS
And that's it. It's the end of their first crisis as a nation. They will head back into the desert, get a tabernacle so they can learn how to approach God themselves, and have a chance to put into practice the law they have just received. There will be more crises. In fact, none of that generation will make it to the Promised Land. Not even Moses! They will spend the next forty years wandering around in that desert.

It has been a brutal time for all involved. For Moses: extensive fasting, sleepless nights, and intense intercession. For his brother Aaron, the second in command, a devastating fall. And, for multitudes, death by the sword and plague. What are some of the key lessons learned?

- One tribe, the Levites, chose to stand up for the Lord. They were rewarded with the priesthood. God always honors those who honor him. Are you in a situation where you are tempted to compromise? Is it time for you to take a stand for the Lord?

- Don't play with God. Israel was learning that God is dead serious about obedience. He means what he says. He is a jealous god and will not put up with idols. He wants a people who truly follow him and worship him. Sin is serious. Are there any idols in your life? Is there any sin you need to deal with before you experience God's judgment?

- One man saved the nation. Were it not for Moses' intercession, God would likely have destroyed them all. Moses' steadfastness, obedience, and intimacy with God are remarkable. Moses stands as a tremendous example of what one man can do, especially when he is serious about being in God's presence. What can you draw from his experience for your own leadership? Are you in a situation where it seems you are the only one really seeking God?

- God ends up making a covenant with them, promising to do great and mighty things on their behalf. Talk about making up! God wants to do great and mighty things for you too!

Maybe you are in the midst of a crisis, or have just come through one. Can you handle it like Moses did, and end up seeing God's glory as you get close to him? Could you be the one who comes through as a leader and intercessor to help others make it?

There can be serious consequences of sin – whether yours or someone else's. But Israel's experience gives us hope to press on, hang in there, pray, and allow it to deepen our relationship with God. Wouldn't it be great if your family saw your face radiant because you had been in God's presence?

Whether you are in crisis or things are great, God wants to speak with you. Will you give him that time? Are there some things you have been needing to talk to him about?

# 26

## GIFTS OF CRAFTSMANSHIP
### *EXODUS 35:30–36:7*

*³⁰ Then Moses said to the Israelites, "See, the Lord has chosen Bezalel son of Uri, the son of Hur, of the tribe of Judah, ³¹ and he has filled him with the Spirit of God, with wisdom, with understanding, with knowledge and with all kinds of skills— ³² to make artistic designs for work in gold, silver and bronze, ³³ to cut and set stones, to work in wood and to engage in all kinds of artistic crafts. ³⁴ And he has given both him and Oholiab son of Ahisamak, of the tribe of Dan, the ability to teach others. ³⁵ He has filled them with skill to do all kinds of work as engravers, designers, embroiderers in blue, purple and scarlet yarn and fine linen, and weavers—all of them skilled workers and designers."*

When God has a job to do in his house, he will provide what is needed to get it done. Moses certainly didn't have the time or skill to do all this artistic work, but he does have an important role to play: He introduces these artisans to the whole nation, and recognizes God's call on them. How many Bezalels are languishing in the church because their Moses is too threatened, too busy, or too disinterested to notice their gifts and validate them before the whole congregation? The leaders in God's house need to be aware of what the Lord wants to do – even if it involves some creative work that may seem unimportant compared with the pastor's preaching. They need to be aware of the diversity of the Spirit's giftings, affirm them, and give people the opportunity to exercise their gift and teach others.

## THE LORD CHOSE THEM, GIFTED THEM, AND FILLED THEM WITH HIS SPIRIT

Even at this early stage in Israel's faith walk, giftings of the Holy Spirit were recognized! Specifically, God filled them with:

- His Spirit
- Wisdom
- Understanding
- Knowledge
- All kinds of skills (engravers, designers, embroiderers, weavers)

Does it surprise you that craftsmen would also have wisdom, understanding, and knowledge? It seems that the manual skill was accompanied – and enhanced – by the spiritual abilities.

What is even more impressive to me is that they were also given teaching skills. Could it be that God generally gifts someone who has a certain ability with the teaching gift, to pass it along to others who may not be supernaturally gifted? Do we encourage our gifted people to teach? Do we give them that opportunity? Do we try to find students for them?

Have you been filled with the Spirit? Do you need wisdom, understanding, and knowledge? Some of that is gained through experience and study, but some is supernaturally imparted by the Spirit of God. Seek him for it! Have you been filled with a gift for the benefit of the whole church? It may not be limited to the lists of gifts we commonly study in the New Testament! Is your church open to a variety of giftings? Is there a gift you have which has never been recognized by the church because it doesn't fit the expected mold?

We may have a hard time understanding the great architecture, paintings, sculpture, and other artwork that fills ancient cathedrals, but in the past those gifts were recognized and encouraged. Are our warehouse-type church buildings really more spiritual? Are we missing out on beautiful expressions of the Spirit of God in artwork?

## DO IT GOD'S WAY

*"¹ So Bezalel, Oholiab and every skilled person to whom the Lord has given skill and ability to know how to carry out all the work of constructing the sanctuary are to do the work just as the Lord has commanded."*

These craftsmen were gifted, but the gifts operated in submission to the Lord. It's easy for creative types to do their own thing, apart from the covering of the church, and not necessarily as directed by the Lord. Obviously there is room for individual creativity, but this was a special task involving God's tabernacle. Do you think it's possible for God to guide you as you do wood working? Landscaping? Painting?

When it comes to God's house, we need to do it God's way. He no longer dwells in tabernacles, but as we work together to build God's house today, we need to make sure we're following his Word, and are under the supervision of his appointed authority.

*² Then Moses summoned Bezalel and Oholiab and every skilled person to whom the Lord had given ability and who was willing to come and do the work. ³ They received from Moses all the offerings the Israelites had brought to carry out the work of constructing the sanctuary. And the people continued to bring freewill offerings morning after morning.*

## INVOLVE THE ENTIRE COMMUNITY

There is a beautiful participation by the whole community, similar to what we should see in the church today.

- Moses called all the workers together. Someone needs to take the initiative in gathering the workers and motivating them to get going.

- That leader, or someone working with him, needs to distribute the resources necessary to do the work. There was order in the receiving and distribution of offerings, with Moses coordinating it. This ensured integrity and good stewardship of the gifts.

- There may be some who are gifted, but are unwilling to work. They will have to answer to the Lord for refusing to use their gifts, but it is not our place to pressure them to work. They will end up being more of a hindrance than help in doing a work of excellence.

- The entire community was supportive of the work, and willing to provide for those who were gifted. Without their participation, nothing would happen. Those who have the resources to give are just as important as the workers. These appear to be special, freewill, offerings, as opposed to the tithe required to support God's work. In fact, they seem so excited about the project that they keep bringing offerings every morning.

*[4] So all the skilled workers who were doing all the work on the sanctuary left what they were doing [5] and said to Moses, "The people are bringing more than enough for doing the work the Lord commanded to be done." [6] Then Moses gave an order and they sent this word throughout the camp: "No man or woman is to make anything else as an offering for the sanctuary." And so*

*the people were restrained from bringing more, ⁷ because what they already had was more than enough to do all the work.*

What a great problem! When was the last time you heard any church or ministry say "Stop giving, we have too much!"? The problem was so severe that work stopped on the sanctuary while the workers spoke to Moses!

These were just-released slaves who barely knew about God, didn't have his Word or the Holy Spirit, and didn't have the privilege of salvation through Jesus! Why is it that we have to drum up support for the work of the church today, when we have been given so much more? Why isn't there more excitement for building God's house today? Could it be we're not doing it God's way? Are we more concerned about building a house for *our* glory, than for His? May we have such tremendous excitement and support for the work of God's house today!

# Part 5

## *Authority and Rebellion*

# 27

## Will you enter the Kingdom?
### Numbers 9:15-23

In this passage Moses literally has the last word. Actually, he doesn't say a word, and it is only his name that finally appears as the very last word in the passage. At first glance this passage doesn't seem to belong in a study on Moses' leadership. It was the *Lord's* command, and the pillar of fire and cloud, that was leading them. And that's the way it should be. In the church *He* is Lord, and it is *his* voice we seek to hear. But he chooses to use us as his delegated leaders and mouthpieces, as seen in the final words of the chapter: *in accordance with his command through Moses*.

### Submission to God

Without authority there is chaos. The book of Judges is a great example of that, where *everyone did as he saw fit* (Judges 21:25). That could describe our culture. Talking about authority and submission sparks a huge outcry of control, abuse, and rigidity. But a relationship with God starts by acknowledging his authority as Lord and submitting to him. Remember when Eve decided to listen to the serpent instead of God? That's what got us into trouble in the first place, isn't it? The opposite of submission is rebellion. And it has plagued our race ever since.

## Submission means obedience

Most Christians acknowledge Jesus as their Lord and confess a desire to do his will, but Jesus seems to have an issue with many of us:

> "Not everyone who says to me, 'Lord, Lord,' will enter the kingdom of heaven, but only the one who does the will of my Father who is in heaven. Many will say to me on that day, 'Lord, Lord, did we not prophesy in your name and in your name drive out demons and in your name perform many miracles?' Then I will tell them plainly, 'I never knew you. Away from me, you evildoers!' (Matthew 7:21-23)

This is one of the most sobering passages in Scripture. These are church-going believers. I'm sure they knew the latest worship songs and could quote many Bible verses. And they weren't just warming a pew. They were prophesying and casting out demons and performing miracles. Jesus never denies that they did great things. The problem was they were doing their *own* thing. Just because something is good doesn't mean it is God's will. The call is to submit *all* of life to his leadership. This is a salvation issue. We're not talking about God chastening us for a time or losing some eternal rewards; they cannot enter the kingdom of heaven. And Jesus says *many* are affected.

That message isn't popular. It doesn't preach well on TV. But authority and submission are at the heart of our faith. We believe God has absolute authority, which Jesus clearly demonstrated, over sickness, demons, death, and nature. Authority demands obedience. Demons have to submit, and we have to submit. Some say submission is a sign of weakness: if you can't manage your life, you defer to God or someone else to make your decisions. Actually, it takes more strength to voluntarily submit!

## DELEGATED AUTHORITY

In Numbers 9, God's authority was visibly present in the pillar of cloud and fire, but he spoke through Moses, his designated authority. Disobeying Moses was like disobeying God. In the church, God delegates his authority to apostles, pastors, and elders. He gives them authority to heal, speak his word, and lead his people. He also expects us to obey authority in government, at school, and in the workplace, so society can run smoothly: *Let everyone be subject to the governing authorities, for there is no authority except that which God has established. The authorities that exist have been established by God* (Romans 13:1). He established man as head of the family. Both parents have authority over their children. Where authority breaks down, there is anarchy. If it is a nation we call it a "failed state." In many ways our society is a "failed society," where authority is scorned, children run wild, schools are ineffective, and rebellion is rampant.

## AUTHORITY BEGINS AT HOME

Respect for authority – ultimately the authority of God, his Word, and his church – begins in the home. Children need to learn it from infancy. If Biblical authority is not established, with dad honored as head of the home and mom respecting him and upholding his word, children will be rebellious at school and, eventually, in the workplace and in church. We are seeing the devastating fruit of that breakdown in authority. At the same time, possibly the majority of men have no idea how to exercise loving biblical authority. Authority and submission have been painted as hopelessly out of touch, chauvinistic, and suffocating. The church desperately needs to teach families what godly authority and submission look like.

## Abusive authority

Israel suffered for hundreds of years under the abusive authority of Pharaoh. That would be enough to make anyone rebellious and fearful of submission. Sinful man is capable of horrendous abuses of authority. Perhaps you have suffered under a tyrannical father, a pastor on a power trip, or a demanding boss. That doesn't excuse us from obeying God's delegated authority; it does call for great wisdom and guidance from the Holy Spirit in choosing whom we submit to.

God's authority is righteous and good. Israel was just learning about it, and God gave them a very simple, daily lesson in obedience:

*15 On the day the tabernacle, the tent of the covenant law, was set up, the cloud covered it. From evening till morning the cloud above the tabernacle looked like fire. 16 That is how it continued to be; the cloud covered it, and at night it looked like fire.*

## The glory cloud

Making the tent of meeting was also a lesson in obedience: God gave detailed plans, and Moses oversaw the work, making sure everything was done exactly as God specified. There was no room for individual initiative or changing the design. Now the tabernacle was ready, and the glory cloud of God's presence covered it. At night the cloud looked like fire.

Additional details are given in the parallel passage in Exodus 40:34-35:

*Then the cloud covered the tent of meeting, and the glory of the Lord filled the tabernacle. Moses could not enter the tent of meeting because the cloud had settled on it, and the glory of the Lord filled the tabernacle.*

God's glory also *filled* the tabernacle, and was so overwhelming that not even Moses could enter! When we follow God's plans we can expect to see his glory. Maybe it is absent in our services at times because we're not doing things God's way! But we are about to see that there was more involved here than basking in God's glory. It's like us leaving the glow of a great worship service to go out and walk in obedience through the desert all week.

[17] *Whenever the cloud lifted from above the tent, the Israelites set out; wherever the cloud settled, the Israelites encamped.*

## FOLLOW THE CLOUD

The lesson was very simple: Your life is controlled by God. You don't have the freedom to take off just because you feel like it. And no matter how much you like a place, you have to pack up and move on when God says to.

It is tragic when a glory cloud moves on from a church and the people aren't aware of it. Instead of spiritually packing up the tent and moving along with God, they stay where they're at. The tabernacle is still beautiful. It was built according to God's plan, but he isn't there anymore. He will only inhabit it when the people are walking in obedience to him, where he has directed them to be.

[18] *At the Lord's command the Israelites set out, and at his command they encamped. As long as the cloud stayed over the tabernacle, they remained in camp.*

## A 100% CORPORATE EXPERIENCE

The entire nation moved. There was no room for individualism or doing your own thing. If someone got impatient with the long stay in one place and decided to set off on his own - without the manna, quail, and water God provided - chances are he would die in the desert. Israel encountered enemies along the way, and their unity was critical to their survival in battle.

They had to move as one people or everything could fall apart. Doesn't it make sense that the same concept applies to the church today? God has a plan and destination for us, and places us in a body of believers that will lead us to maturity and prepare us for eternity. He places authority in that body in the form of pastors and elders. When we choose to become part of a local church we are acknowledging our belief that God has placed those leaders there, and we are willing to submit to them.

The rugged American individualist has a real problem here: "Nobody is going to tell me what to do or how to live my life." Pastors who seek to exercise godly authority are called controlling or abusive. And, indeed, abuses can occur. Back in the 70's the shepherding movement sought to establish proper authority and submission in the church. Unfortunately, members' basic life decisions were controlled and the movement got a bad name. In the process, valid teaching on submission was also discredited.

## LIFE REVOLVED AROUND GOD'S MOVE

*[19] When the cloud remained over the tabernacle a long time, the Israelites obeyed the Lord's order and did not set out. [20] Sometimes the cloud was over the tabernacle only a few days; at the Lord's command they would encamp, and then at his command they would set out. [21] Sometimes the cloud stayed only from evening till morning, and when it lifted in the morning, they set out. Whether by day or by night, whenever the cloud lifted, they set out. [22] Whether the cloud stayed over the tabernacle for two days or a month or a year, the Israelites would remain in camp and not set out; but when it lifted, they would set out.*

This may seem very arbitrary. You might have real issues obeying Moses' orders. There was no way you could live your life! Your wife might be ready to serve a delicious meal or get intimate when the cloud lifts and you have to pack up. It could be in the middle of the night. It would be one thing if there was some logic to it; if God posted a schedule so you would know what to expect. He really didn't seem to care about the inconvenience this constant movement caused. But the people learned that obedience was not optional. From infancy, children learned to watch the cloud and listen for Moses' order. Everyone did it.

## FOLLOWING THE CLOUD TODAY

Today we don't have the cloud. A cloud might seem easier, but we have something better: The Holy Spirit indwelling us. Ideally, we have more freedom, and constant guidance. In reality, it seems much easier to disobey the Spirit's leading, or be too busy to even hear what he says. God expects more of us than Israel's child-like faith and obedience. He has given us the resources, and expects us to act more like adults. But many of us find it hard to figure out where God is telling us to go and what to do along the way. Certainly he gives us freedom in many areas, as long as it is pleasing to him, within the guidelines of Scripture, and led by the Spirit. But we need to invest the energy in learning how to discern his will. Jesus said it is only those who *do* the Father's will who enter the kingdom. But without the cloud, how can you know what he wants?

Perhaps you are young in the Lord and afraid you might miss out because you're not doing God's will. Figuring out what he wants can seem intimidating! I have a simple question for you: Would you be willing to follow the cloud? Start there. Watch what God is doing and follow him. He will meet you where you are at. I have five suggestions that may help you discern God's will. But to start, just come before God each morning and ask him to show you one thing in the Bible you should do that day. Read until something calls your attention – and do it. You will find that things start falling into place! That can also work if you are a veteran Christian who has gotten so caught up in the routine that you have lost sight of the cloud!

## Discerning God's Will

- Immerse yourself in Scripture and seek to put all of it into practice. When you are habitually submitting to God's Word and walking in obedience, it will be easier to figure out his will in specific situations.

- Cultivate your prayer life. Learn to listen to God and hear the still small voice of the Spirit. Clear your life of some of the noise. Give him a chance to speak! Get in the habit of asking for his direction in daily decisions, and you will be ready to hear him when something big comes along.

- Share your life with other believers. Develop relationships with godly peers who really know you. Seek their counsel and confirmation when decisions need to be made. Submit yourself to the leadership of your church and seek guidance from them on major issues. Walking together as a body (like Israel did here) makes it much easier to stay in God's will.

- If you feel dread or lack peace, don't move. Unless you are sure the cloud is moving, stay where you are. If it is God telling you to move and you are open to him, he will let you know.

- Be aware of how easily the sinful nature can cloud our judgment. Some examples: being guided by lust or appearances in your selection of a mate, choosing a job simply because it pays better or offers more status, or selecting a mission field or new church because of its desirable climate.

God wants you to know his will! It is not some huge mystery, but it does require some work on our part.

## THE NECESSITY OF OBEYING MOSES

*²³ At the Lord's command they encamped, and at the Lord's command they set out. They obeyed the Lord's order, in accordance with his command through Moses.*

Moving a group of slaves from Egypt to the Promised Land was a massive undertaking. If they were to make it, they had to honor and obey Moses. The relationship wasn't always the best. They had not elected him or had any choice in who would lead them; he arrived on the scene and announced what God had sent him to do. As we have seen, they were quick to blame Moses for any problems. They were still thinking about going back to Egypt. They had even given up on him at one point and made a new god, the golden calf. But in the end they had to trust that Moses was hearing from God and had their best interests in mind, even when it was annoying and it seemed they would never get out of the desert. Forty years of packing up and following a cloud and Moses' commands can get old! We will see how seriously God supported Moses' authority and dealt with those who questioned it.

Unfortunately, despite the fact that we have infinitely more resources (the full Word of God, salvation in Christ and a personal relationship with him, the fullness of the Holy Spirit, more media to teach and equip than ever before in history), we exemplify what would have been a disastrous turn of events for Israel.

## A HOUSE DIVIDED...

It's not hard to imagine:

- Aaron, humiliated by his brother after the golden calf incident, gathers a disgruntled group around him. They make another calf and head off on their own toward Canaan.

- Joshua gets tired of chafing under the old man (Moses). He has seen God's glory and doesn't feel that the restrictions on who can enter the holy place are fair. He gathers zealous young people who love worship, and promises that they can all have glowing faces like Moses.

- Bezalel gathers craftsmen frustrated with having to follow set plans for the tabernacle. He teaches that God gave them creativity. In his group each person will have the opportunity to express himself.

- A great chef taps into the discontent with the quail and manna, and promises a more appetizing diet. He makes Moses look like he is holding back on the best food and probably keeping it for himself.

- Another claims knowledge of a direct route to the holy land and tells the people God has shown him in a dream how to get there in a month.

On and on it goes. It sounds distressingly like the church today.

## Authority and freedom

I am seriously concerned about the lack of authority and submission in the church. Does that mean I am in favor of a Catholic system of a pope and total control from above? Certainly not! In the early church there were various men who functioned as apostles and exercised authority over their churches, and there were false apostles competing with them. Just read about Paul's effort to maintain his place of authority in 2 Corinthians.

There is no lack of apostles today, but few who demonstrate biblical signs of apostleship, and too many who seem to be in it for the glory and money.

Nor am I advocating that the church exercise total control over people's lives. We are definitely not talking about a Jim Jones or cult-like situation. Within the context of following the cloud the Israelites were free to:

- Marry who they wanted (as long as it was a believer)
- Have as many children as they wanted and teach them at home
- Eat what they wanted (within the guidelines of the law)
- Wear what they wanted (also governed to a certain extent by the law)

You get the picture. God never intends us to be in bondage to a man. What God did order was where they could set up their tents (in tribal groupings to maintain order and provide authority over them; see Numbers 2), and where they could go and when (following the cloud). They had to move as a group. God places us in a body today, and I believe we need to walk together with the other members of that body as we move toward maturity in his purposes for us (see Ephesians 4). Within that there is great freedom.

## UNITY IN DOCTRINE

So how can we make sure we are all following the same doctrine and headed in the same direction? I believe we should follow the example of the early church. Beginning in Acts 15, when there was disagreement on a doctrinal or ethical issue, apostles and church leaders from around the world came together in prayer, to seek God and find a solution. Their decision was shared with the churches, and out of respect for the apostolic leader and a healthy fear of God, the believers submitted to it. The same procedure was followed in defining the nature of Christ and what books should be in the Bible. They were called ecumenical councils. The Catholic church has continued to rely on them. Various attempts have been made to reproduce that communication and unity, such as the World Council of Churches or the World Evangelical Fellowship. Within various denominations the leaders of all the churches may get together to determine what their stance will be. But too often it seems to be man's organization, and we fail to see true apostolic authority at work.

Many have noted the alarming growth of internet-based ministries which correct others' doctrine and pose as great authorities on biblical and theological matters. Everyone becomes an authority, and no one knows who to believe. This highlights the urgent need to re-establish true biblical authority in the church – and perhaps (horrors!) even have some means of verifying that someone on the internet is providing solid teaching.

## WILL YOU ENTER THE KINGDOM?

Do you want to experience God's authority and power in your life? You can - to the extent that you submit your entire life and plans to him. What do you think would happen if a church decided to practice what Israel did here? Do you think we might see the fire of God and his glory cloud in that church? Are you in a beautiful church that has been "left behind" because they failed to move in the Spirit as God told them to?

Don't be one of those whom Jesus tells he never knew! Take a good look at what you are doing – even good things like healing the sick!

- Are you willing to submit your life to God's authority? Can you confidently say you are doing God's will? Or have you taken it upon yourself to do what you want?

- Are you properly submitted to spiritual authority?

- How do you respond to authority at work or school? To the police and the laws of the land? As long as it doesn't violate God's commands, do you seek to be submissive in every situation? Or would you call yourself a rebel?

# 28

# Rebellion: Complaints and Discontent
## Numbers 11:1-34

In the last chapter we saw the importance God places on authority and submission. Unfortunately Israel did not get the message. We will spend the next ten chapters looking at the disastrous results of rebellion. Perhaps it is no coincidence that it was right after receiving the law, building the tabernacle, and moving on toward the Promised Land. Here they are rebelling against God himself, but as God's delegated authority, Moses has to deal with it.

Unsubmissive rebels are often exposed by their complaining and discontent:

*¹Now the people complained about their hardships in the hearing of the Lord, and when he heard them his anger was aroused. Then fire from the Lord burned among them and consumed some of the outskirts of the camp.*

How would you feel at this point in the exodus? Being in that wilderness, with no control whatsoever over your life, and having to move at God's whim couldn't be easy. You may be in the midst of some tough circumstances as well, but that doesn't justify complaining. Hard as it may be, God calls us to praise him and thank him - even when the road gets rough. Complaining spreads like cancer through a church, family, or workplace. It accomplishes nothing, and God hates it. Why? We are essentially saying he doesn't know what he is doing. We're not submitting to what he has sovereignly placed in our path. We lack the faith that he could change things and make them easier if he wanted to, and we may be angry that he doesn't.

We sin not only when we complain about God, but about anyone he has placed over us in authority. That doesn't mean you can't pray about it, cry out to God about it, and speak to the person in charge to try and improve the situation. But the complaining spirit arouses God's anger, and when he gets angry, things can turn ugly: Fire consumed the outskirts of the camp. Whether that included people or not is unclear, but it definitely got their attention. Once again, they naturally run to Moses.

*2 When the people cried out to Moses, he prayed to the Lord and the fire died down. 3 So that place was called Taberah, because fire from the Lord had burned among them.*

Moses intercedes, faithful as usual, and the fire stops. But, like many of us, the people were slow to learn:

*4 The rabble with them began to crave other food, and again the Israelites started wailing and said, "If only we had meat to eat! 5 We remember the fish we ate in Egypt at no cost—also the cucumbers, melons, leeks, onions and garlic. 6 But now we have lost our appetite; we never see anything but this manna!"*

Now they are complaining about what God has specifically, miraculously, supplied in response to their earlier groaning. There are several red flags in these verses:

- **The "rabble."** The problem started with the mix of foreigners who joined the Israelites on their trek to the Promised Land. That is not intended to point the finger at foreigners, but these were outsiders who lacked a full understanding of God's purposes. There tends to be "rabble" in any group, and not necessarily foreigners. Watch out for them. Don't cater to them, but be aware of the trouble they can cause. Their complaining quickly spread to the rest of the Israelites.

- **Craving.** We have all had cravings, and often do whatever is necessary to satisfy them. It is especially easy to crave what we can't have, whether it be food or some pleasure. It is normal to have a healthy appetite, and craving can seem innocent. But it is a short step from craving to lust; in fact the Hebrew word used here means lust. Be careful your cravings don't control you and lead you into sin. Watch for lust and craving in yourself, your family, and others you may be responsible for. Don't be afraid to confront it before it causes them serious problems.

- **Wailing.** Weeping. Really? Is it all that bad? When we fall into rebellion and a complaining spirit, the importance of what we're missing gets exaggerated. You begin to feel you can't live without it.

- **"If only."** That can be applied to so many things. Media seems to encourage it:

    o   If only I had a house like the one on HGTV.

    o   If only I was as good looking.

    o   If only I could afford that.

    o   On and on it goes. The unfortunate truth is that you won't be satisfied when you get it. If you have that complaining spirit there will always be another "if only."

- **Nostalgia.** The good old days; perhaps before you came to Christ. The hard labor as slaves is forgotten; all they can remember is the good food they enjoyed in Egypt. The tendency is to blame whoever took you away from that situation, and regret the decisions you have made. In the extreme, you may go back to Egypt in search of the good life. Sadly, usually it is not the same, and it rarely was as good as you remember it anyway. Sure, the food there was free, just like prison food is free. Do they really want to go back to being slaves, though?

- **Losing your appetite.** Nothing satisfies. You don't love her anymore. You can't stand the thought of going to work. Church is doing nothing for you. Even sex is unappealing (that's when you know things are really bad!). God wants to give you zest for life – in whatever circumstances he has allowed. When you lose your appetite, take a look at yourself and see if a rebellious, discontented, spirit has crept in.

## IN CASE YOU FORGOT: A DESCRIPTION OF THE MANNA

*7 The manna was like coriander seed and looked like resin. 8 The people went around gathering it, and then ground it in a hand mill or crushed it in a mortar. They cooked it in a pot or made it into loaves. And it tasted like something made with olive oil. 9 When the dew settled on the camp at night, the manna also came down.*

It doesn't sound very appealing, especially when you have to eat the same thing month after month, but it was reliable and free.

# Rebellion: Complaints and Discontent

## Moses Loses It

*<sup>10</sup> Moses heard the people of every family wailing at the entrance to their tents. The Lord became exceedingly angry, and Moses was troubled. <sup>11</sup> He asked the Lord, "Why have you brought this trouble on your servant? What have I done to displease you that you put the burden of all these people on me? <sup>12</sup> Did I conceive all these people? Did I give them birth? Why do you tell me to carry them in my arms, as a nurse carries an infant, to the land you promised on oath to their ancestors? <sup>13</sup> Where can I get meat for all these people? They keep wailing to me, 'Give us meat to eat!' <sup>14</sup> I cannot carry all these people by myself; the burden is too heavy for me. <sup>15</sup> If this is how you are going to treat me, please go ahead and kill me—if I have found favor in your eyes—and do not let me face my own ruin."*

Whoa! The complaining spirit has even reached Moses! That's how powerful it can be! No longer does Moses cheerfully submit to God's call and faithfully intercede for them. The entire camp is gripped by grumbling. *Every family* is impacted! The nation is paralyzed. And if Moses is taken out of the picture, as he requests, this whole grand enterprise will come crashing down.

We can't be too hard on Moses. I suspect every leader has moments like this, when you are ready to throw in the towel and give up. Sometimes on a weekly basis! But when we fall into this pit there is usually a whole lot of self-pity, deception, and outright lies involved. The enemy is having a field day. Let's look carefully at what Moses says:

- *Why have you brought this trouble on your servant?* Well, in one sense God did, calling Moses out of his tranquil life herding sheep. But God didn't cause this! The people did! In your heart, are you blaming God for the result of someone else's sin?

- *What have I done to displease you that you put the burden of all these people on me?* When things don't go right in our church or family we may assume God is displeased with us: Certainly if we had his favor he would make things easier! God gives us the burden he knows we can carry, and no more. If the burden is heavy, it is because he *is* pleased with you. He is not out to get you!

- *Did I conceive all these people? Did I give them birth?* Sometimes leadership feels like parenting, and it may be as painful as childbirth! Moses is right - these are *God's* people. Of course he didn't conceive or give birth to them. But, like an adoptive parent, he agreed to be God's delegated authority, in effect becoming a father to them, with all the related struggles.

- *Why do you tell me to carry them in my arms, as a nurse carries an infant, to the land you promised on oath to their ancestors?* We don't know when God told him this; it is not recorded. But what a beautiful picture of the charge God gives spiritual leaders! Both of these are feminine images! Yes, there is definitely fathering involved in pastoring or leadership, but there is also mothering! Sometimes you get tired of dealing with a bunch of babies, but they need to be tenderly carried in your arms! At this point that is probably the last thing Moses wants to do! It might not come naturally to you, but along with the call, God will give you the ability to do it.

- *Where can I get meat for all these people? They keep wailing to me, 'Give us meat to eat!'* "I don't have what the people want! I don't have money to provide for them! They keep demanding – and there is no way I can supply it." Instead of focusing on your inability, realize the sinfulness of what they're asking for. If it is a legitimate request, God will provide. But when the request is obviously impossible, don't despair. You don't have to get them meat.

- *I cannot carry all these people by myself; the burden is too heavy for me.* He is right! If you felt you could carry them you wouldn't need God! You may be feeling that God's call on your life is too heavy a burden. That doesn't mean you are in the wrong place – or that you are in over your head. You may just be getting to the place where God can start doing miracles. When you get to the end of yourself, God will be there. Perhaps up to this point Moses had been valiantly trying to do everything and be a good leader. Now he can start learning about grace.

- *If this is how you are going to treat me, please go ahead and kill me—if I have found favor in your eyes—and do not let me face my own ruin.* Okay, be honest. You have probably said something similar at some point. Moses really is having a pity party. Again, it's not God who is mistreating him. And death – sometimes it can even be thoughts of suicide – is really an escape from dealing with what feels like more than you can bear. But now we see what may be at the heart of Moses' fears – and is very common among men: The fear of failure. In his case it's not ever the fear of what the people will say if he fails. He can't bear the thought of facing his own ruin. He couldn't live with himself. There probably will be failures along the way in your life. Some will be more devastating than others: A failed marriage, or getting fired from your church or job. It hurts. But it's not the end of the world. There's no need to kill yourself – or ask God to kill you.

God wants to set you free from that fear of failure. Ultimately it represents a lack of faith that God will see you through, that he is sovereign, and that he loves you and wants the best for you.

## GOD'S ANSWER

*16 The Lord said to Moses: "Bring me seventy of Israel's elders who are known to you as leaders and officials among the people. Have them come to the tent of meeting, that they may stand there with you. 17 I will come down and speak with you there, and I will take some of the power of the Spirit that is on you and put it on them. They will share the burden of the people with you so that you will not have to carry it alone.*

## GOD'S PROVISION: OTHERS TO SHARE THE BURDEN

Are you still trying to do everything yourself? Too many pastors do. Nobody else can do it as good as you. It can be hard to trust that others will come through – especially when you have been let down in the past. Most men try to make it by themselves as husbands and fathers. It is very hard for men to talk to other men about family problems. But God designed us to function in community, and you need the support of family members, friends, and brothers in Christ to share your burdens.

Moses was able to select the seventy, who were probably mostly already in place. Moses had learned about delegating authority when his father-in-law visited back in Exodus 18. Seventy elders had accompanied Moses up Mt. Sinai, but they hadn't entered God's glory with him. Now they will be standing with him and hearing God speak. It would be nice to know what he said; possibly he reaffirmed Moses' position and authority.

The people will have someone else to complain to, although Moses will have to train them to go to the elders. People like to go to the main man. It's important that these leaders be officially recognized, just as we need some kind of ceremony in church to confirm new leaders. One of the dangers of delegating leadership is giving them a position without the power. They need the Holy Spirit. Although these men held leadership positions prior to this, they had not been given the Spirit, which God now distributed to them from the Spirit that was on Moses.

## In their complaining they rejected the Lord

*[18]* *"Tell the people: 'Consecrate yourselves in preparation for tomorrow, when you will eat meat. The Lord heard you when you wailed, "If only we had meat to eat! We were better off in Egypt!" Now the Lord will give you meat, and you will eat it.* *[19]* *You will not eat it for just one day, or two days, or five, ten or twenty days,* *[20]* *but for a whole month—until it comes out of your nostrils and you loathe it—because you have rejected the Lord, who is among you, and have wailed before him, saying, "Why did we ever leave Egypt?"'"*

What an interesting glimpse of God's character! They want meat? He will give them meat, but they will be eating it until they loathe it. Do you think God does that with us? Have you pleaded with God for something – and gotten much more than you bargained for?

Three things made this so displeasing to God:

- We have already looked at the wailing. In itself there is nothing wrong with crying, but God isn't impressed with selfish wailing.

- Looking back, and regretting the decision to follow God and leave the world and slavery behind.

- They might be quick to say: "Oh no. We still want God. We just want him to do things the way we want him to," but they are essentially rejecting God.

When we look back and say we were better off without God, when we complain about what he has done in our lives and make an idol out of something (in this case, meat), we reject God. What's sad is it says he is *"among them."* God almighty is right in their midst - and they don't even realize it or care that they are hurting him! God's presence is far more rewarding than the juiciest steak!

Have you been tempted to look back? Have you pinned all your hopes on something that seems out of reach? Something God hasn't provided for you? Have you been wailing?

Because of their sin, they have to consecrate themselves before they can receive God's provision. That probably involved confession of sin, a renewed commitment to follow God, and an open heart to receive from him.

Uncharacteristically, Moses has also fallen into unbelief and must be reminded of who God is.

## Moses' Unbelief

*21 But Moses said, "Here I am among six hundred thousand men on foot, and you say, 'I will give them meat to eat for a whole month!' 22 Would they have enough if flocks and herds were slaughtered for them? Would they have enough if all the fish in the sea were caught for them?"*

This is the same man that witnessed the plagues in Egypt, the parting of the Red Sea, and God's glory on Mt. Sinai, to say nothing of water coming from a rock and manna from heaven! And now he can't believe God could provide meat?

Moses' despair and burn-out clouded his vision and made him unable to see God and his power. I have seen it happen to many people. They were walking in faith, but reach a point where that faith is stretched to the limit and they can't imagine how God could do anything more. Moses sounds remarkably like the disciples when Jesus asked them to feed the multitude!

Are you finding it hard to believe that God could do something major in your life? Have you looked at all the figures and statistics and it just seems there is no way? What has God done for you in the past? What is keeping him from doing something even greater in the future?

*²³ The Lord answered Moses, "Is the Lord's arm too short? Now you will see whether or not what I say will come true for you."*

God is much more gracious with Moses than with the people, but he obviously is not pleased. Moses is doubting his word and questioning his power! For Moses, seeing is believing, and God will prove himself.

Could God be saying the same thing to you? Are you questioning his ability to do something he has promised you or spoken in his Word? God's arm is not too short!

*²⁴ So Moses went out and told the people what the Lord had said. He brought together seventy of their elders and had them stand around the tent.*

Moses was definitely having a bad day, but he does two very important things which you also should do, no matter how much you are struggling:

- He trusted God's Word enough to go out and proclaim it to the people. If God doesn't come through, the Lord will also look bad! You can always feel confident preaching what God has said.

- He did what God told him to do. Aside from consecrating the people, there was nothing Moses had to do to provide the meat. He was only instructed to get the seventy elders together, and he did that immediately. When he did, there was a near-Pentecost experience.

## FILLED WITH THE HOLY SPIRIT

*²⁵ Then the Lord came down in the cloud and spoke with him, and he took some of the power of the Spirit that was on him and put it on the seventy elders. When the Spirit rested on them, they prophesied—but did not do so again.*

This is not the only Old Testament reference to people "prophesying" when God's Spirit came on them. It's almost certain that all seventy did not bring forth inspired messages from God at the same time. This was most likely ecstatic praise, very possibly in other tongues. In the Scriptures, when the Spirit comes on someone, often the immediate result is an unloosed tongue: in praise, or prophecy, or unknown tongues. This was a one-time event, but there was an interesting twist to it:

*²⁶ However, two men, whose names were Eldad and Medad, had remained in the camp. They were listed among the elders, but did not go out to the tent. Yet the Spirit also rested on them, and they prophesied in the camp. ²⁷ A young man ran and told Moses, "Eldad and Medad are prophesying in the camp."*

*²⁸ Joshua son of Nun, who had been Moses' aide since youth, spoke up and said, "Moses, my lord, stop them!"*

*²⁹ But Moses replied, "Are you jealous for my sake? I wish that all the Lord's people were prophets and that the Lord would put his Spirit on them!" ³⁰ Then Moses and the elders of Israel returned to the camp.*

In the midst of one of his weakest moments, Moses utters a prophecy that we have seen fulfilled! God now distributes his Spirit to every believer and gives them the ability to prophesy!

There are some Joshua's in the church today, who seek to maintain an aura around those with special giftings, and give the impression that others are less spiritual and can't have the same experience. That was especially true in the medieval church, where lay people were purposely kept ignorant.

God knew who the seventy were, and the Spirit also fell on these two, who may have scoffed at being part of this gathering. Don't think it always happens this way – if you had chosen to stay home the morning of Pentecost you would have missed out on the outpouring of the Spirit!

## THE QUAIL CAME

*$^{31}$ Now a wind went out from the Lord and drove quail in from the sea. It scattered them up to two cubits deep all around the camp, as far as a day's walk in any direction. $^{32}$ All that day and night and all the next day the people went out and gathered quail. No one gathered less than ten homers. Then they spread them out all around the camp. $^{33}$ But while the meat was still between their teeth and before it could be consumed, the anger of the Lord burned against the people, and he struck them with a severe plague.$^{34}$ Therefore the place was named Kibroth Hattaavah, because there they buried the people who had craved other food.*

That is a rough ending to a sad story. They got their meat. God miraculously provided it. Lots of it. But just as they were ready to enjoy it, God strikes them with a plague. We don't know how many died, but we are told the plague was severe.

Rejecting God and his provision is serious. Complaining and wailing arouse God's anger. Rebelling against his authority and not submitting to him invites judgment. Whether you are tempted to look back and complain about where God has you, or you are a Moses who has had as much as he can take, God has a powerful message for you today. May his Spirit rest on you and give you the faith to believe, and eyes to see that his arm is not too short, no matter what you are facing.

# 29

# THE DANGER OF UNDERMINING GOD'S LEADERS
## NUMBERS 12

There has been considerable discontent among the Israelites on this exodus journey, but so far very little was directed at Moses personally. When the attack comes, it's not from the general population, but from family: His sister and brother. Yes, Aaron, the one who stood with him before Pharaoh. Aaron, his mouthpiece. Aaron the high priest. And Miriam, who led the whole assembly in worship after crossing the Red Sea. Miriam, who witnessed her baby brother placed in a basket on the Nile and talked Pharaoh's daughter into allowing their mother to care for him.

It's sad, but all too often our fiercest opposition comes from those closest to us. Of course they know our weaknesses and how to get to us. They may also envy us. But Miriam and Aaron had a problem: They couldn't come up with any legitimate criticism, so they decide to focus on his wife. If you are in leadership, be prepared for people to talk about your family. Make sure you stand with your wife and children! Satan would love to use church politics to drive a wedge between you and your family.

## MOSES' WIFE
<sup>1</sup>*Miriam and Aaron began to talk against Moses because of his Cushite wife, for he had married a Cushite.*

We already discussed how some believe this "Cushite wife" was not Zipporah, and use this verse to justify divorce and remarriage, saying that when Moses sent Zipporah away (Exodus 18:2), he divorced her and then married this woman. Perhaps that is why Miriam and Aaron didn't like her. We do know his relationship with Zipporah wasn't the best, but to read a divorce into this Scripture is really stretching it. What was very common during most of the Old Testament period was men taking multiple wives. He might have married her in Egypt before he had to flee, or even met her when he returned to Egypt. Or this may well refer to Zipporah. Miriam may have had a problem with her not being Jewish. Indeed, considering Moses' stature in the Bible, it is a little surprising he didn't marry a Jew.

The rest of the Hebrews may not have known or cared about Moses' wife, but Miriam and Aaron tried to make a case out of it, hoping to create unrest among the people. Whatever the facts, their criticism was a smokescreen. We are about to see the real reason for their complaints.

## JEALOUSY
<sup>2</sup> *"Has the Lord spoken only through Moses?" they asked. "Hasn't he also spoken through us?" And the Lord heard this.*

Both Miriam and Aaron held significant positions; Aaron as a priest, and Miriam as worship leader and prophetess (Exodus 15:20). Apparently God did speak through her. Micah 6:4 says that God sent both of them, along with Moses, to lead the people. But that wasn't enough. They envied Moses' face-to-face meetings with God and the way God spoke through him. They were jealous that he was God's main man.

# THE DANGER OF UNDERMINING GOD'S LEADERS

Have you been jealous of someone else's gifting or anointing? Perhaps their preaching, gifts of healing, or notable prophetic abilities? Or maybe their charisma and "popularity" in the church? Are you aware of people who envy your position and gifts? Maybe even family members? The New Testament clearly teaches that God gives gifts according to his will – and everyone is equally important in the Body of Christ (1 Corinthians 12).

They didn't incite rebellion against Moses or try to take his position; they just wanted to be recognized as equally gifted, and share in his prophetic anointing. When God took the Spirit that was on Moses and distributed it among the seventy elders in the previous chapter, Aaron and Miriam were not among the recipients, which may have sparked their discontent. On the surface, what Aaron and Miriam did doesn't seem that serious. But it was to God.

## THE MOST HUMBLE MAN ON EARTH

*³ (Now Moses was a very humble man, more humble than anyone else on the face of the earth.)*

Wow. That is a strong statement, and one we must assume was inserted later. We believe Moses wrote Numbers, but it wouldn't be very humble for him to write this! It is remarkable that he stayed humble, given his authority and amazing spiritual experiences. He had been brought up in the palace. He left Egypt a young, proud, self-confident man. The forty years in Midian probably included considerable breaking, and witnessing God's glory helped keep him humble.

How about you? Would anyone say this about you? Pride is a real temptation for successful pastors – and any man. Humility is highly valued in God's eyes.

## GOD CONFRONTS THE REBELS

*⁴ At once the Lord said to Moses, Aaron and Miriam, "Come out to the tent of meeting, all three of you." So the three of them went out.*

God didn't waste any time. He couldn't let this talk continue and possibly undermine Moses' authority. He immediately called them out. We don't know if Moses knew what they had been saying. If he did, there is no record of him defending himself or rebuking them. He left that to God, and that may be the best course to follow if someone seeks to undermine you.

Challenges to pastoral authority are common. What starts as sowing doubt about a person's character or actions can quickly lead to church splits and significant wounding of the Body of Christ. Great wisdom is needed in responding to it – but God's example encourages us to deal with it quickly and decisively. If allowed to grow it can be extremely destructive. It may be necessary to call in someone with spiritual authority over the church, instead of the person who is under attack trying to resolve it.

*⁵ Then the Lord came down in a pillar of cloud; he stood at the entrance to the tent and summoned Aaron and Miriam.*

He may not be speaking *through* them, as they had hoped, but God definitely is speaking *to* them. If you picture this, it is awe-inspiring and terrifying. What were Aaron and Miriam thinking? Were they arrogant enough to believe God was going to give them a special commission and anointing? Or did they realize they were in trouble?

*When the two of them stepped forward, ⁶ he said, "Listen to my words:*

> "When there is a prophet among you,
>   I, the Lord, reveal myself to them in visions,
>   I speak to them in dreams.
> ⁷ But this is not true of my servant Moses;
>   he is faithful in all my house.
> ⁸ With him I speak face to face,
>   clearly and not in riddles;
>   he sees the form of the Lord.
> Why then were you not afraid
>   to speak against my servant Moses?"

Moses was more than a prophet: He was God's friend. Typically we receive prophetic words in dreams or visions, both of which Joel prophesies would be common after Pentecost. Now, as then, those prophetic revelations often come in riddles. Why God chooses to do this we don't really know; perhaps so that only those given discernment by the Holy Spirit can understand them.

How about you? Have you had dreams or visions? Are you open to them?

Moses' faithfulness was what really touched God. We have seen it repeatedly in his very challenging task. He was faithful in *all* God's house. And you? God obviously places a high value on faithfulness. Have you been faithful to your wife and family? To God's calling on your life? Faithful in God's house?

To speak against someone the Lord has placed in authority is very serious. It doesn't matter if there is some foundation to the criticism. Whether it be a husband, pastor, or someone else in authority, speak against them with fear and trembling. If you are doing it now, stop. Guard your heart, and honor those God has placed in authority over you. If others are speaking against you, trust God to deal with them and vindicate you. And don't be so prideful that you don't stop and examine yourself to see if there is some truth in what they are saying.

## GOD'S JUDGMENT
*⁹ The anger of the Lord burned against them, and he left them.*

When God is angry, he will leave. He doesn't like to stay around rebels. If you suddenly find him gone from your life or church, ask him why. You don't want God angry with you while you think everything is fine! We don't know what form the Lord's burning anger took. They must have been very aware he was angry, but it wasn't until he departed and the cloud lifted that they saw the evidence of his anger:

*¹⁰ When the cloud lifted from above the tent, Miriam's skin was leprous—it became as white as snow. Aaron turned toward her and saw that she had a defiling skin disease, ¹¹ and he said to Moses, "Please, my lord, I ask you not to hold against us the sin we have so foolishly committed. ¹² Do not let her be like a stillborn infant coming from its mother's womb with its flesh half eaten away."*

Why was Miriam afflicted and not Aaron? Why didn't Miriam ask forgiveness? Miriam may have been the ringleader of this rebellion. Aaron may be demonstrating the same weakness he showed with the golden calf: easily influenced and unable to resist being drawn into the situation. He calls Moses lord, and asks his forgiveness – although he doesn't ask God's forgiveness.

## MOSES INTERCEDES FOR HIS SISTER
*¹³ So Moses cried out to the Lord, "Please, God, heal her!"*

That takes grace and humility. Would you be tempted to say: "Hey, that's not my problem. Talk to God about it. Maybe if you both really repent, God will heal her." Would you have secretly been delighted that she was afflicted and had learned her lesson?

Not Moses. With the same compassion and depth of character we have seen repeatedly, he cries out to God, knowing that he has the power to heal her.

**[14]** *The Lord replied to Moses, "If her father had spit in her face, would she not have been in disgrace for seven days? Confine her outside the camp for seven days; after that she can be brought back."*

If it weren't for Moses' intercession, Miriam might have remained leprous the rest of her life. God will honor Moses' plea – but only after she spends seven days outside the camp. God may be saying, "I have spit in her face...now she needs to spend those days in disgrace." A public rebuke required a period of public shame.

**[15]** *So Miriam was confined outside the camp for seven days, and the people did not move on till she was brought back.*

That is humiliating. Everyone knew why they were staying in camp. Word quickly spread about what Miriam had done and God's judgment on her. It was a clear warning to everyone not to mess with God's anointed. Miriam was never mentioned again until her death is recorded in Numbers 20:1.

God expects honor, respect, and obedience to those he places in authority. Undermining that authority is a very offensive to him. That said, I have also seen abusive leaders use this passage to command unswerving allegiance. Any questioning of their decisions, or even suggestions on how to do things better, are taken as a challenge to their authority. The "rebel" may be beat into submission – or thrown out of the assembly. Perhaps verse three is the most important in this chapter. Moses was humble. You don't see him using strong-arm tactics to bring the people into line. A humble leader will have a servant's heart and be open to criticism and advice. We are never told we can't approach a leader and share our concerns with him. For serious matters, Jesus gave us a procedure to follow in Matthew 18:15-17. Moses now has the protection of the seventy elders. Plural leadership is healthy. When one person runs everything (as Miriam and Aaron hinted Moses did) there is a much greater chance for abuse.

Social media and the internet now provide a platform for all the Miriams and Aarons in our world, and there are plenty of them, especially with our culture's bias against authority. Be very careful of what you post online (and read, share, or believe) about God's leaders. And follow Moses' example of humility.

# 30

## INVITATION TO REBELLION
### NUMBERS 13

*¹The Lord said to Moses, ² "Send some men to explore the land of Canaan, which I am giving to the Israelites. From each ancestral tribe send one of its leaders." ³ So at the Lord's command Moses sent them out from the Desert of Paran. All of them were leaders of the Israelites.*

### WHO ASKED FOR THE SPIES?

The spies ended up being a nightmare for Israel, and they present a problem for us before we even get into the passage. Numbers clearly says they went at God's command, but the parallel account in Deuteronomy (1:22-23) seems to contradict that:

*Then all of you came to me and said, "Let us send men ahead to spy out the land for us and bring back a report about the route we are to take and the towns we will come to." The idea seemed good to me; so I selected twelve of you, one man from each tribe.*

So how do we explain the difference? God may speak to a leader – but have them wait to share it with everyone else. Just like you might do with your child, sometimes it is better to let them think *they* came up with the idea! God may have commanded this mission – and then put it in the hearts of the Israelites to request it. Or they may have made their request, and Moses sought the

Lord to discover his will. Deuteronomy suggests that Moses embarked on this very significant mission without consulting the Lord, but that seems very uncharacteristic of him.

## SOVEREIGNTY OR FREE WILL?

Just as parallel passages in the Gospels can give slightly different perspectives on the same event, Numbers focuses on God's sovereignty and his purpose in sending the spies. Did God need to know who was in the land? Of course not! Did he already know the outcome of their exploration? Of course! But despite his unchanging plan to get them into the land, man's free will can change details of how it works out. In this case it delayed their entrance into Canaan by forty years. Deuteronomy emphasizes their freedom by having the people request the spies. Just as in the age-old debate of sovereignty versus free will, both are probably true. The ultimate outcome is the same.

What doesn't change is in the first verse of Numbers 13: God is giving Israel the land. It is theirs, whether they claim all of it by faith, or refuse to go in and take it. What actually took place is similar to what often happens as we move into the fullness of God's plan: Their sin and rebellion caused significant delay as they learned some hard lessons. Eventually they did get into the land, but they did only a partial job of eliminating its inhabitants, resulting in constant warfare and struggles. They were able to enjoy its fruits, but they made life hard for themselves.

## SELECTION OF THE SPIES

Verses four through sixteen list the representatives of each tribe which were sent out. The only two names of real importance are Caleb, from Judah, and Hoshea (whom Moses renamed Joshua) from Efraim. Two other things are significant:

- Each tribe is carefully represented and had equal input. As with the selection of the seventy elders, representation of all the people is an important part Israel's government even at this point. Perhaps we could call it a representative theocracy.

- This is the first major task on this exodus journey which Moses has not led. He is trusting these men to do the job. There may be times when we are forced to delegate, and this is probably one of them. He had already been apart from the people for lengthy periods on Mt. Sinai, resulting in the golden calf disaster. His presence is needed with the people, plus his age made him unfit for spying and the extensive travel involved.

## MOSES' INSTRUCTIONS TO THE SPIES

[17] *When Moses sent them to explore Canaan, he said, "Go up through the Negev and on into the hill country.* [18] *See what the land is like and whether the people who live there are strong or weak, few or many.* [19] *What kind of land do they live in? Is it good or bad? What kind of towns do they live in? Are they unwalled or fortified?* [20] *How is the soil? Is it fertile or poor? Are there trees in it or not? Do your best to bring back some of the fruit of the land." (It was the season for the first ripe grapes.)*

Moses made their mission very clear, even telling them how to enter a land we can assume none of them had ever seen:

- What is the land like?
- Are the people strong or weak?
- How many people are there?
- What kind of land is it? Good or bad? Is the soil fertile or poor?
- Are there trees?
- What are the towns like? Do they have walls and fortifications?

For a people who have heard about this land flowing with milk and honey for so many years, the last instruction is touching: Do your best to bring back some fruit from the land. That would be visible encouragement to go for it!

I have moved many times, and it is always exciting to make that first trip to a new place and ask some of those same questions! They were finally on the brink of achieving what they have been waiting for so long! There are high expectations – and some anxiety. Positive as it could be, there is considerable risk involved. This will be a critical test of Moses' ability to manage his people.

## THE EXPLORATION
*²¹ So they went up and explored the land from the Desert of Zin as far as Rehob, toward Lebo Hamath. ²² They went up through the Negev and came to Hebron, where Ahiman, Sheshai and Talmai, the descendants of Anak, lived. (Hebron had been built seven years before Zoan in Egypt.) ²³ When they reached the Valley of Eshkol, they cut off a branch bearing a single cluster of grapes. Two of them carried it on a pole between them, along with some pomegranates and figs. ²⁴ That place was called the Valley of Eshkol because of the cluster of grapes the Israelites cut off there. ²⁵ At the end of forty days they returned from exploring the land.*

Important biblical events often last forty days. Aside from showing the significance of the exploration, it gave them plenty of time to get a feel of the land. It must have been some cluster of grapes, to require two men to carry it on a pole between them! They managed to get some pomegranates and figs as well. They all survived. So far everything looks good.

## REPORT ON THE EXPLORATION
*²⁶ They came back to Moses and Aaron and the whole Israelite community at Kadesh in the Desert of Paran. There they reported*

to them and to the whole assembly and showed them the fruit of the land. *²⁷ They gave Moses this account: "We went into the land to which you sent us, and it does flow with milk and honey! Here is its fruit.²⁸ But the people who live there are powerful, and the cities are fortified and very large. We even saw descendants of Anak there. ²⁹ The Amalekites live in the Negev; the Hittites, Jebusites and Amorites live in the hill country; and the Canaanites live near the sea and along the Jordan."*

First, the good news: The land really does flow with milk and honey. They have the fruit to prove it. Yet in this life there is usually a "but." And this is a big but: Big and powerful people seem to fill the land, and there are large, fortified cities.

Obviously, they were all anxious to hear what happened. It appears a general report was given to everyone, and then more specifics were given to Moses. It might have been wiser to brief Moses first and screen the information given to the whole assembly. Once the voice of doubt and fear is heard it will be almost impossible for him to counteract it.

## TWO RESPONSES TO THE EXPLORATION

*³⁰ Then Caleb silenced the people before Moses and said, "We should go up and take possession of the land, for we can certainly do it."*

*³¹ But the men who had gone up with him said, "We can't attack those people; they are stronger than we are." ³² And they spread among the Israelites a bad report about the land they had explored. They said, "The land we explored devours those living in it. All the people we saw there are of great size. ³³ We saw the Nephilim there (the descendants of Anak come from the Nephilim). We seemed like grasshoppers in our own eyes, and we looked the same to them."*

Now the people have a choice: To obey, or to rebel. To have faith, or allow fear to paralyze them and lead to sin. It is all a matter of perspective, isn't it?

There are good and bad aspects of almost everything we face in life. It would be great if they could just walk right into the land and the inhabitants would move out and let them take over. But life isn't like that; practically everything we get involves some kind of struggle. We have God's word and his promises. We know his purposes for us. We have to choose to press into what may be unknown and fearful, trusting him to come through for us. We can draw encouragement from the grapes, and the testimonies of others who have experienced God's faithfulness. Or we can listen to the negative reports and the grumblers. We can look at the obvious facts, and we can also acknowledge our tendency to exaggerate. So much of how we approach life involves how we look "in our own eyes." Do you see yourself as a grasshopper? Or as a mighty warrior armed with powerful spiritual weapons?

Only two men saw the situation with the eyes of faith. We are told that Caleb *"had a different spirit."* We already know about Joshua's faith. Those two men were countered by ten cowards. Only two out of twelve. That may be the typical ratio of those who move boldly ahead in faith, and those who sow doubt and fear. Which group do you tend to be part of? Are there opportunities for obedience and service before you? Are you tempted to play it safe? Do you see only the obstacles? Or can you trust that the obstacles allow God to glorify himself?

# 31

## ALL-OUT REBELLION
### *NUMBERS 14:1-19*

This has to be one of the saddest chapters in the Bible: To be so close to the land of your dreams, so close to God's miraculous provision – *and lose it*. Yes, our rebellion can cause us to miss the fullness of God's blessing. You may not lose your salvation. They were still God's people. They were walking with God and he was teaching them, but they would never make it to the Promised Land. Their children would inherit the land. Hopefully they could impress on those children the importance of obedience – and the dangers of rebellion.

This is a tragic - but powerful – chapter, which may have a special message for you:

- Are you facing a life-changing decision? Are you at a crossroads?

- Like the spies in Numbers 13, have you checked out the options?

- Are you facing things that put fear in your heart?

- Are you tempted to take what seems like an easier path? Even if it means wandering around in a wilderness for the next forty years?

- Are you living with regrets over a wrong choice you made years ago? Have you seen how parents' sins can be visited on their children – whether you were the child or the parent?

- Could it be that your main task now is helping your children follow Christ more closely and avoid your mistakes?

## "Where can we go?"

It has only been a few months. They left Egypt, crossed the Sinai, received the Law - and in God's eyes were ready to move into the land. That's a lot of change in a short time. God was wasting no time getting them into the land. The spies had explored it and were enthusiastic about its abundance, but ten of the twelve focused on the giants and difficulties of taking the land, sowing fear and unbelief in the peoples' hearts. The parallel passage in Deuteronomy 1:28 expresses their desperation: *Where can we go? Our brothers have made our hearts melt in fear.*

Have you ever felt your heart melt in fear? It is hard to strengthen a melted heart. A person who feels trapped and that fearful may act foolishly.

## Fear paves the way to an all-out rebellion

*[1]That night all the members of the community raised their voices and wept aloud. [2] All the Israelites grumbled against Moses and Aaron, and the whole assembly said to them, "If only we had died in Egypt! Or in this wilderness! [3] Why is the Lord bringing us to this land only to let us fall by the sword? Our wives and children will be taken as plunder. Wouldn't it be better for us to go back to Egypt?" [4] And they said to each other, "We should choose a leader and go back to Egypt."*

Read these verses again. How could something so good end up so ugly?

1. They hear words of faith - and words of fear. The unbelieving spies drown out the voices of faith, infecting everyone with their fear. Be careful of who you listen to! And watch for the infection of unbelief.

2. They gather together, not to worship God and seek his face, but to wallow in tears of self-pity. God and his Word are out of the picture. All they can think about is themselves. Have you ever witnessed a pity party like that?

3. They direct their fear and anger at their leaders, Moses and Aaron. They have gotten good at grumbling. Is there anyone you are grumbling about right now? Or are you the target of others' complaints – perhaps unfairly?

4. They prefer death over life. The fear of the unknown is so great that they wish they had died in Egypt or the desert. If you long for death or contemplate suicide, you know the devil is at work. God wants to give you life! It is Satan who wants to take your life! Yet it is surprisingly common for Christians to feel like the Israelites did.

5. They are spiritually deceived – acknowledging that God brought them to the land, but portraying him as a capricious, evil, God, who did it just to let them die. In fact, in Deuteronomy 1:27 they say *The Lord hates us*. Lies. Theological error leads to rebellion. Are there any lies you have come to believe about God? How does your picture of God line up with biblical truth? Are there some beliefs you need to challenge?

6. They picture the worst: their women and children taken as plunder. What would be your worst-case scenario?

7. The only option they can think of is going back to Egypt, where at least life was predictable and familiar. Beware when the past beckons and you become fearful or unsure about following God into the future. What are you tempted to return to? Is it really as rosy as you may be painting it? How realistic is it to even consider going back?

8. They are ready to reject God and his delegated authority, Moses, and choose their own leader, who would do what they want him to do. They are about to abandon God and the land he wants to give them to return to slavery – and probably death. Have you thought of ditching everything and looking for someone who could offer you a better life? A new woman, a new pastor – or even a new religion?

## WHAT CAN A LEADER DO IN THE FACE OF REBELLION?

*⁵Then Moses and Aaron fell facedown in front of the whole Israelite assembly gathered there.⁶ Joshua son of Nun and Caleb son of Jephunneh, who were among those who had explored the land, tore their clothes⁷ and said to the entire Israelite assembly, "The land we passed through and explored is exceedingly good. ⁸ If the Lord is pleased with us, he will lead us into that land, a land flowing with milk and honey, and will give it to us. ⁹ Only do not rebel against the Lord. And do not be afraid of the people of the land, because we will devour them. Their protection is gone, but the Lord is with us. Do not be afraid of them."*

Moses can't even think of anything to say. What could he do? What would you do? All he and Aaron can do is fall facedown

## All-out Rebellion

before the people. Joshua and Caleb apparently are the only two who join them, and they speak words of faith and reason to the assembly. God is giving them one more chance to wake up and repent before judgment. Their simple plea should have been enough to gain at least some hearers:

- They had seen the land - and it is wonderful. It is great to draw faith and encouragement from believers who have gone before us and experienced God's goodness.

- Remarkably, Joshua and Caleb understood the conditional nature of the promise for the land. God has said he will lead them into it and give it to them, but if they displease the Lord they can't count on his gracious blessing. If they persist in their grumbling and unbelief, they can't expect God to give them the land. It is popular to have "Promise Boxes" of Bible promises, or get a new promise every day on your phone. But do you take the time to study the conditions that come with them?

- The people may think they are rebelling against Moses, but they are really rebelling against the Lord. Rebellion will have dire consequences.

- Sure, there may be giants in the land, but we have no need to fear them. God will fight for us and defeat them. They had already seen God do that in Egypt, and on this journey. Are you facing some giants? Do you believe God can fight for you? Can you trust him to defeat your enemies?

- With great insight, they point out that whatever protection those people might have enjoyed is gone. God is with Israel. That is really all that matters. If God is with us who can be against us?

- For emphasis, twice Joshua and Caleb plead with them not to be afraid. What they should have been fearing is God, and the consequences of their rebellion.

We don't know exactly when Moses got up and spoke, but he may have been encouraged by Joshua and Caleb's words to speak what is recorded in Deuteronomy 1:29-31: *"Do not be terrified; do not be afraid of them. The Lord your God, who is going before you, will fight for you, as he did for you in Egypt, before your very eyes, and in the wilderness. There you saw how the Lord your God carried you, as a father carries his son, all the way you went until you reached this place."*

- God loves them!
- He has been faithful!
- He has carried them as a father carries a son.
- They can count on that to continue!
- Relax!
- Let your Father carry you!
- Let him fight for you!

Offering words of faith and encouragement like this doesn't come naturally to everyone. How about you? Are you able to step into situations of fear and discouragement in your home, church, or job and speak for God?

## GOD'S OFFER TO MOSES

[10] *But the whole assembly talked about stoning them. Then the glory of the Lord appeared at the tent of meeting to all the Israelites.* [11] *The Lord said to Moses, "How long will these people treat me with contempt? How long will they refuse to believe in me, in spite of all the signs I have performed among them?* [12] *I will strike them down with a plague and destroy them, but I will make you into a nation greater and stronger than they."*

Talk about your message falling on deaf ears! They are so wrapped up in fear and rebellion that they are ready to stone their leaders! And they very well might have, if God's glory hadn't shown up. This isn't the first time God made this offer. Remember the golden calf? God wanted to destroy them all right there and start over with Moses (Exodus 32:10).

This isn't just understandable fear on the part of poor ex-slaves who don't really know God. It is not kids acting up. They are treating God with contempt. The crux of the matter is their refusal to believe what he said. It has only been a few months, but he expects that they had seen enough to strengthen their faith. God has been patient with them, but there are limits to his patience.

How many Christians today treat God with contempt, refusing to believe what he has clearly spoken in his Word? You may not have seen the Red Sea opened, but haven't you seen enough of God's work to give you faith to press on?

We also see the extent to which God honors the man who stands firmly with him. He will basically do anything for that person – and is ready to eliminate the rest.

## Moses Makes His Case to Spare Them

It might be tempting to take God up on his offer, but we have already seen Moses' commitment to the people. He never even contemplates it, and he presents a case so solid you would think he spent hours preparing it. But he didn't have that kind of time; he had to move quickly if he was going to save the nation. It has nothing to do with their merits - or his own merits. It has everything to do with God. It is a great model of intercession for us.

¹³ Moses said to the Lord, "Then the Egyptians will hear about it! By your power you brought these people up from among them. ¹⁴ And they will tell the inhabitants of this land about it. They have already heard that you, Lord, are with these people and that you, Lord, have been seen face to face, that your cloud stays over them, and that you go before them in a pillar of cloud by day and a pillar of fire by night. ¹⁵ If you put all these people to death, leaving none alive, the nations who have heard this report about you will say, ¹⁶ 'The Lord was not able to bring these people into the land he promised them on oath, so he slaughtered them in the wilderness.'

¹⁷ "Now may the Lord's strength be displayed, just as you have declared: ¹⁸ 'The Lord is slow to anger, abounding in love and forgiving sin and rebellion. Yet he does not leave the guilty unpunished; he punishes the children for the sin of the parents to the third and fourth generation.'¹⁹ In accordance with your great love, forgive the sin of these people, just as you have pardoned them from the time they left Egypt until now."

There are three main components to his prayer:

1. Concern for God's reputation and honor. In the eyes of the world, God is identified with this nation. He has led them, done miracles among them, and talked with them. If God destroys them, word will get back to the Egyptians, who will tell the nations that God wasn't able to do what he said he would do. The result would be exactly opposite what God wanted: for Israel to be a testimony to all the nations of God's power and goodness. Of course, the real reason for God killing them would never be known.

2. He appeals to God's Word – what he has already spoken and revealed about his character. He said he is slow to

anger and forgiving of rebellion. It takes strength to continue loving and forgiving in the face of sin.

3. Moses asks for a pardon, appealing for love and mercy to outweigh judgment. God has already pardoned them several times; this would be in keeping with his past action.

What do you think? Will Moses' argument be enough to move God's heart? In the next chapter we will see how God responds to Israel's rebellion.

# 32

# THE DEVASTATING FRUIT OF REBELLION
## *NUMBERS 14:20-45*

Israel lacks the faith to trust God, obey him, and move into the Promised Land. Instead they want to choose a new leader and go back to Egypt. God is ready to destroy them all and start over with Moses. In the midst of this craziness, Moses, Joshua, and Caleb are the only men of strength and integrity. There isn't much Moses can do but plead for God's mercy. The survival of an entire nation depends on this one man. He asks nothing for himself – only forgiveness of his people's sin. How will God respond to his prayer? What will be the ultimate outcome of their rebellion?

### FORGIVENESS DOESN'T ELIMINATE CONSEQUENCES

*[20] The Lord replied, "I have forgiven them, as you asked. [21] Nevertheless, as surely as I live and as surely as the glory of the Lord fills the whole earth, [22] not one of those who saw my glory and the signs I performed in Egypt and in the wilderness but who disobeyed me and tested me ten times— [23] not one of them will ever see the land I promised on oath to their ancestors. No one who has treated me with contempt will ever see it. [24] But because my servant Caleb has a different spirit and follows me wholeheartedly, I will bring him into the land he went to, and his descendants will inherit it. [25] Since the Amalekites and the*

Canaanites are living in the valleys, turn back tomorrow and set out toward the desert along the route to the Red Sea."

Despite his inclination to wipe them all out and start over with Moses, God honors his servant's request and forgives them. Just like that. The sin of multitudes is wiped out. God has been patient. But there is a very important teaching here: forgiveness doesn't eliminate consequences. In this case the consequences are severe: none of that generation will ever see the Promised Land.

There are various ways to translate the Hebrew word describing Israel's actions in verse 23: "treat with contempt, provoke, spurn, despise, reject." You get the idea. They had deeply grieved and angered God, and will still have to pay for their sin.

Yes, the land was promised to them, but promises almost always come with conditions. Their children will still get the land, but only two adults will enter: Joshua and Caleb, the two spies who stood strong with the good, faith-filled report. Caleb was unique among the Israelites: he followed God wholeheartedly, with a different spirit than the rest.

Why is it so hard to follow God? Why do so many treat God with contempt: not believing his Word, grumbling and complaining, and disobeying him? How can we despise and provoke someone who has done so much for us? How can we reject the offer of eternal life? Are there really so few who have that different spirit? How about you? Are you more like Caleb – or the multitude?

I thank God that Jesus purchased our salvation on the cross. So many times, by his mercy, we are spared the consequences of our sin. But not always. There are often severe consequences:

losing a wife because of our unfaithfulness, doing hard time in prison, severely injuring ourselves, or contracting some disease.

They tasted the delicious fruit of the land. They heard the good report. It could have been theirs. But they lost it.

## TURN AROUND

*²⁶ The Lord said to Moses and Aaron: ²⁷ "How long will this wicked community grumble against me? I have heard the complaints of these grumbling Israelites. ²⁸ So tell them, 'As surely as I live, declares the Lord, I will do to you the very thing I heard you say: ²⁹ In this wilderness your bodies will fall—every one of you twenty years old or more who was counted in the census and who has grumbled against me.³⁰ Not one of you will enter the land I swore with uplifted hand to make your home, except Caleb son of Jephunneh and Joshua son of Nun. ³¹ As for your children that you said would be taken as plunder, I will bring them in to enjoy the land you have rejected. ³² But as for you, your bodies will fall in this wilderness.³³ Your children will be shepherds here for forty years, suffering for your unfaithfulness, until the last of your bodies lies in the wilderness. ³⁴ For forty years—one year for each of the forty days you explored the land—you will suffer for your sins and know what it is like to have me against you.' ³⁵ I, the Lord, have spoken, and I will surely do these things to this whole wicked community, which has banded together against me. They will meet their end in this wilderness; here they will die."*

More than their rebellion, God was angry with Israel's grumbling and complaining - a constant, annoying, expression of unbelief and discontent. It insults God and implies he doesn't know what he is doing. God hates it. Have you fallen into the same sin? God wanted to kill them on the spot, and in some ways that might have been better. This is almost a taste of hell. For the rest of their lives they will know what it is like to have God against them, as they suffer for their sin. Is it possible that God allows some who have sinned against him to live, experience the consequences of their sin, but still avoid the eternal punishment of hell?

God says the people *banded together* against him. It was a conspiracy. They claimed that one of their key concerns was their children being taken as plunder. Ironically, it is those very children who will possess the land. But for the next forty years the very children they claimed to care so much about will suffer because of their parents' sin, wandering around in the wilderness. I wonder what that did for the children's attitude toward their parents.

We have seen Aaron's weakness, but Moses has been exemplary. Yet in Deuteronomy 1:37 he says to the nation: *Because of you the Lord became angry with me also and said, "You shall not enter it, either.* We will see the act of disobedience that cost him so dearly when we get to Numbers 20. Out of the same frustration the Lord expresses here, Moses struck a rock instead of speaking to it, and even Moses suffered the consequences of dishonoring the Lord in front of the people. Joshua and Caleb were ready to go in. They had done nothing wrong, yet they too have to turn around and wander in the wilderness for forty years! We also are part of a body. When one part suffers, we all suffer. When part of the body refuses to move ahead with God's purposes, the whole body may pay for it.

*[36] So the men Moses had sent to explore the land, who returned and made the whole community grumble against him by spreading a bad report about it— [37] these men who were responsible for spreading the bad report about the land were struck down and died of a plague before the Lord. [38] Of the men*

## THE DEVASTATING FRUIT OF REBELLION

*who went to explore the land, only Joshua son of Nun and Caleb son of Jephunneh survived.*

The judgment on those responsible for the rebellion was swift. Don't play with God. If he has given you a position of leadership and authority, be careful not to make a little one stumble. Don't discourage the faith of your wife or child. God takes that very seriously.

## PRESUMPTION

*[39] When Moses reported this to all the Israelites, they mourned bitterly. [40] Early the next morning they set out for the highest point in the hill country, saying, "Now we are ready to go up to the land the Lord promised. Surely we have sinned!"*

I have seen this countless times among inmates: When they get arrested and convicted, suddenly they wake up and are repentant. They make deals with God. They recognize their sin and are ready to walk in obedience. But it's not only inmates. When the wife walks out, when we lose our job – when we start to experience the consequences – we tend to get serious about seeking God. However, there is a point at which it is too late to avoid the consequences, and we lose the blessings God planned for us.

*[41] But Moses said, "Why are you disobeying the Lord's command? This will not succeed! [42] Do not go up, because the Lord is not with you. You will be defeated by your enemies, [43] for the Amalekites and the Canaanites will face you there. Because you have turned away from the Lord, he will not be with you and you will fall by the sword."*

First they disobeyed by refusing to go up as God commanded them. Now that opportunity is gone, and God commands them to turn around. But they don't want to. Suddenly they are ready to go up and fight. But God is no longer with them, and without the Lord they face certain defeat. Even if they had a superior army, they would be defeated. God would make sure of that.

I shudder for those who turn away from the Lord today. They have lost their covering. They are vulnerable to the demons of hell and all the evil in the world. Unless they repent and get serious about obedience they will fall.

*$^{44}$ Nevertheless, in their presumption they went up toward the highest point in the hill country, though neither Moses nor the ark of the Lord's covenant moved from the camp. $^{45}$ Then the Amalekites and the Canaanites who lived in that hill country came down and attacked them and beat them down all the way to Hormah.*

Presumption is behavior that is arrogant, disrespectful, and transgressing the limits of what is permitted or appropriate. They arrogantly ignore God and his commands, and do what seems right to them, somehow thinking they can defeat their enemies without the Lord. The fact that neither Moses nor the ark accompanied them should have been a clue that the outcome would not be good. When we arrogantly step out from under God's covering in flagrant disobedience, the result is always disastrous.

Deuteronomy 1:45 says: *You came back and wept before the Lord, but he paid no attention to your weeping and turned a deaf ear to you.* How genuine were their tears? Were they truly repentant? Or just dismayed at their defeat? There may be times when God pays no attention to your cries, when you have acted in blatant rebellion. You won't feel his presence. You have missed out on your blessing. All you can do is humble yourself and turn around and do what he tells you to do.

## Psalm 78 recounts Israel's tragic history

Speaking of this time, verses 32 to 43 say:

*In spite of all this, they kept on sinning;*
  *in spite of his wonders, they did not believe.*
*So he ended their days in futility*
  *and their years in terror.*
*Whenever God slew them, they would seek him;*
  *they eagerly turned to him again.*
*They remembered that God was their Rock,*
  *that God Most High was their Redeemer.*
*But then they would flatter him with their mouths,*
  *lying to him with their tongues;*
*their hearts were not loyal to him,*
  *they were not faithful to his covenant.*
*Yet he was merciful;*
  *he forgave their iniquities*
  *and did not destroy them.*
*Time after time he restrained his anger*
  *and did not stir up his full wrath.*
*He remembered that they were but flesh,*
  *a passing breeze that does not return.*

*How often they rebelled against him in the wilderness*
  *and grieved him in the wasteland!*
*Again and again they put God to the test;*
  *they vexed the Holy One of Israel.*
*They did not remember his power—*
  *the day he redeemed them from the oppressor,*
*the day he displayed his signs in Egypt,*
  *his wonders in the region of Zoan.*

How about you? Are you putting God to the test? Vexing him?

## When your people don't want to move with God

On one hand it looks like Moses didn't save the day; he couldn't convince his people to move ahead in faith. It is tough when a pastor, leader, husband, or father knows what God desires to do and tries to get his people moving with God's plan, but they don't want to move. Moses provided an outstanding example of faith. He preached God's Word and interceded for the people. He obeyed God in everything, and repeatedly saw God rescue them. But ultimately there was nothing he could do to move them from fear and unbelief to joyful obedience. And there is nothing you can do to make your wife, your children, or your church be who you believe God wants them to be. They have to make that choice. They may decide to persist in their rebellion, and you will agonize as you see God's judgment on their lives, and all his blessings they are missing. And, despite your faithfulness, it just may disrupt your life as well. Instead of a nice retirement home in the land flowing milk and honey, Moses would spend the last forty years of his life wandering around the wilderness with a bunch of whiners. That doesn't seem like a great reward for one of the greatest men in history. Some men might be resentful of the people or even decide to chuck it all and take off on their own for the Promised Land, but that was never an option for Moses.

## God's message for you in this chapter

Are you struggling because you are suffering as a result of someone else's rebellion? Do you still feel responsible, like you should have been a better pastor, husband, or father? If there was failure on your part, ask God's forgiveness – and let it go. But chances are you have done what you could, and they are just exercising their free will. Endless "if only's" about what you could have or should have done really serve no purpose. I wish I could say it gets easier from here on, but it may not. You may be walking with some difficult people for the rest of your life. And don't think divorce or going to a new church will make everything alright.

You may be at a critical junction in your walk with Christ. You could be right on the edge of blessing and fruitfulness like you have never imagined. There may be plenty of naysayers, telling you it is too hard or too late. No one has ever done it before. Who do you think you are to attempt that? You may be aware that significant battles await you. The obstacles are great. You may be wavering. Your heart may melt in fear at times. Even your wife may not support you. But you have a deep confidence that God has told you to move ahead. What are you going to do?

Maybe the Lord offered you something, but, unfortunately, grumbling and rebellion ruled your heart. You missed that opportunity. Some may say to keep pressing on and claim it by faith, but God may be saying it is too late. Life may be harder, but it is critical not to be presumptuous or arrogant at this point. Humble yourself and get ready for some more training. Maybe your children or a young leader can learn from your mistakes, and inherit what you missed out on. That is tough – but it is way better to pick up the pieces and walk in obedience with the Lord now. That will bring you eternal benefits, although it may be hard going for a while. For Israel it would be almost forty years of death, as God made sure every single one of those adults died before they made it to the Promised Land.

## DON'T HARDEN YOUR HEART
It is far better to trust God and move ahead when he tells us to go. Battles may be tough, but it is amazing to see God fight them for you. Put aside your fear and walk in obedience, step by step. God will take care of the rest. We close this sobering chapter with a passage from the New Testament, Hebrews 3:15-4:2:

> *"Today, if you hear his voice,*
> *do not harden your hearts*
> *as you did in the rebellion."*
>
> *Who were they who heard and rebelled? Were they not all those Moses led out of Egypt? And with whom was he angry for forty years? Was it not with those who sinned, whose bodies perished in the wilderness? And to whom did God swear that they would never enter his rest if not to those who disobeyed? So we see that they were not able to enter, because of their unbelief. Therefore, since the promise of entering his rest still stands, let us be careful that none of you be found to have fallen short of it. For we also have had the good news proclaimed to us, just as they did; but the message they heard was of no value to them, because they did not share the faith of those who obeyed (they did not combine it with faith).*

The author of Hebrews clearly believes that we face the same danger as the Israelites. Our "Promised Land" is the rest that God offers us. What is God speaking to you today? Don't harden your heart. Determine to walk in obedience to him, no matter what that may mean. How is your faith? Confess any unbelief as sin. Take that step of obedience in faith. God will be right there with you.

# 33

## STRANGE FIRE
### LEVITICUS 10

Rebellion is the primary symptom of a disease we all have called sin. We have seen its devastating impact on every single Israelite who left Egypt. This case, which involved only two men, reminds us of how critical it is to do the Lord's work in the Lord's way.

*¹Aaron's sons Nadab and Abihu took their censers, put fire in them and added incense; and they offered unauthorized fire before the Lord, contrary to his command.*

What command did they violate? Exodus 30:1-10 states that only the high priest could offer incense, and only the specific incense God approved. Any other incense was prohibited.

### WHY DID THEY DO IT?
They never had a chance to say. They may have sincerely wanted to worship God, or been ignorant of his command. Or they may have purposely trespassed into an area they knew was forbidden. What is tragically clear is that they didn't pay close attention to God's instructions, or understand how serious and holy worship is. Once again, a rebellious, unsubmissive heart is exposed.

Many of us would be quick to defend them:

- They were ministering to the Lord.

- They were not worshipping any foreign god.
- They just slightly bent a rule which they didn't even understand.
- God was being too restrictive, and not inclusive enough.

We are probably used to compromising far more of what God's Word clearly says, like the man in Matthew 7:21-23: he does great things for God, but he does them his own way, and not explicitly according to God's will. It is a perfect example of customized religion, where we conveniently pick and choose from the Bible what we feel like doing – and ignore or write off the rest.

## GOD'S RESPONSE TO REBELLION

*² So fire came out from the presence of the Lord and consumed them, and they died before the Lord.*

There was no mercy, and no chance for Moses' intercession to save them. Don't play with God!

*³ Moses then said to Aaron, "This is what the Lord spoke of when he said:*

*"'Among those who approach me*
  *I will be proved holy;*
*in the sight of all the people*
  *I will be honored.'"*

*Aaron remained silent.*

It's not the first time Aaron was silent. He didn't know what to say. He may have been in shock, having just seen two of his sons burned up. But Moses' words were probably convicting; Aaron had failed to properly convey the seriousness of serving God, possibly an example of a father's sin visited on his children. Aaron had fashioned a golden calf and presented it as their God! It is amazing that lightning hadn't struck him! But that was before many of the guidelines for appropriate worship had been given.

God *will* be proved holy. If anyone approaches him incorrectly, he will pay for it. God *will* be honored before the people. If his ministers don't honor him, they will be dealt with accordingly, and he will somehow make sure people know who he is.

## HONORING GOD'S HOLINESS
This should put the fear of God in any worship leader or minister. It is serious enough when you are approaching God alone, but when you are leading hundreds of people into his presence, or he has given you the opportunity to honor him in front of a multitude, the responsibility is far greater.

- Do we adequately grasp and communicate God's holiness in our worship services today?

- Did people in imposing cathedrals with incense and all the trappings that went with worship actually get a better sense of his holiness? Were they more honoring to God?

- Do casually clothed, gyrating, and ear-splitting worship bands honor God and point to his holiness? Or draw more attention to the musicians and the good feelings the music elicits?

- Do flashing laser lights and smoke and all our other accoutrements really honor God?

I hope our leaders are not like Aaron. He never grasped the seriousness of God's command or instilled a fear of God in his sons, and they paid for it with their lives.

*⁴ Moses summoned Mishael and Elzaphan, sons of Aaron's uncle Uzziel, and said to them, "Come here; carry your cousins outside the camp, away from the front of the sanctuary." ⁵ So they came and carried them, still in their tunics, outside the camp, as Moses ordered.*

Since Aaron was silent, it was up to Moses to clear the sanctuary. These rebels needed to be taken out of the camp, and two of Moses' cousins were called on to do the job.

*⁶ Then Moses said to Aaron and his sons Eleazar and Ithamar, "Do not let your hair become unkempt and do not tear your clothes, or you will die and the Lord will be angry with the whole community. But your relatives, all the Israelites, may mourn for those the Lord has destroyed by fire. ⁷ Do not leave the entrance to the tent of meeting or you will die, because the Lord's anointing oil is on you." So they did as Moses said.*

God had their attention. There was no arguing; Aaron and his two remaining sons did exactly as Moses commanded. Otherwise they risked inciting God's anger against the whole community. When leaders fail to handle sensitive situations correctly, they can bring judgment on their whole church.

Since the Lord's anointing oil was on them, they were still "on duty," and were not allowed to mourn. That would be hard, but the alternative was to be killed by the Lord. The rest of the community – surely sobered by what happened - could mourn.

*⁸ Then the Lord said to Aaron, ⁹ "You and your sons are not to drink wine or other fermented drink whenever you go into the tent of meeting, or you will die. This is a lasting ordinance for the generations to come, ¹⁰ so that you can distinguish between the holy and the common, between the unclean and the clean, ¹¹ and* so you can teach the Israelites all the decrees the Lord has given them through Moses."

¹² Moses said to Aaron and his remaining sons, Eleazar and Ithamar, "Take the grain offering left over from the food offerings prepared without yeast and presented to the Lord and eat it beside the altar, for it is most holy. ¹³ Eat it in the sanctuary area, because it is your share and your sons' share of the food offerings presented to the Lord; for so I have been commanded. ¹⁴ But you and your sons and your daughters may eat the breast that was waved and the thigh that was presented. Eat them in a ceremonially clean place; they have been given to you and your children as your share of the Israelites' fellowship offerings. ¹⁵ The thigh that was presented and the breast that was waved must be brought with the fat portions of the food offerings, to be waved before the Lord as a wave offering. This will be the perpetual share for you and your children, as the Lord has commanded."

## WHAT WAS THE STRONG DRINK?

Moses took the opportunity to remind them of several other critical guidelines in serving God. One of them merits further explanation.

These priests were forbidden to drink "*wine or other fermented* (literally: *strong*) *drink*" when they went to serve in the tabernacle. God doesn't want drunk priests! It would hinder their ability to distinguish between clean and unclean, and they would be unable to clearly teach the people. It can be assumed that outside their tabernacle service, and for the general population, there was no prohibition on fermented drink.

I know many people who fondly hold onto the idea that wine in the Bible wasn't fermented. It is difficult to say with certainty what the alcoholic content might have been. Ancient peoples would boil grape juice at times, make a syrup, and later combine it with water to avoid the alcohol. Sometimes it would be boiled right before drinking to reduce the alcohol, or the juice of freshly squeezed grapes might be drunk. However it seems that none of those methods was widely used, and it wasn't until 1869 that a Methodist minister, Thomas Welch, discovered how to pasteurize grape juice so it wouldn't ferment, primarily so it could be used in the Lord's Supper. There are substantial arguments for biblical wine being fermented, not the least of them this prohibition on drinking it, and the coupling with "strong drink." When Paul commanded *"do not get drunk with wine"* (Ephesians 5:18), he was obviously thinking of wine with alcohol content. The Bible does clearly forbid excessive drinking or drunkenness, and there are many good reasons to avoid alcohol altogether.

## THE LORD'S WORK IN THE LORD'S WAY
*[16] When Moses inquired about the goat of the sin offering and found that it had been burned up, he was angry with Eleazar and Ithamar, Aaron's remaining sons, and asked, [17] "Why didn't you eat the sin offering in the sanctuary area? It is most holy; it was given to you to take away the guilt of the community by making atonement for them before the Lord. [18] Since its blood was not taken into the Holy Place, you should have eaten the goat in the sanctuary area, as I commanded."*

After the strange fire incident, Moses suspected other violations of the law. Indeed, a very significant part of the sacrifice for atonement had been overlooked. Someone needed to oversee the administration of sacrifices and offerings, and all that was involved in serving God. Aaron should have, but we already know he was not the strongest leader. It is only by God's mercy that Aaron's other two sons had not been burned up!

Too many pastors have no idea of what is going on in the various ministries in their churches. Not that they should micro-manage every detail, but they should make sure Scripture is not being violated and God is properly worshipped. Too many fathers have no idea what is going on in their homes. They are wrapped up in work - and even in church. Mom is left to run things in the home, or, even worse, kids are left by themselves with little oversight.

*[19] Then Aaron answered Moses, "Today my sons presented both their sin offering and their burnt offering to the Lord. And yet this tragedy has happened to me. If I had eaten the people's sin offering on such a tragic day as this, would the Lord have been pleased?" [20] And when Moses heard this, he was satisfied.*

The Hebrew here is difficult, but it had obviously been a very rough day for Aaron. It may seem he is making excuses for their failure, but the two remaining sons were probably afraid to touch the offering after what happened to their brothers. Aaron may have been wrestling with his own sin, and was in no condition to enter into something as significant as eating the sin offering. Moses understands that, and is satisfied with his explanation. God is serious about doing things his way, but he was still merciful.

Hopefully the message got through. The Lord's work must be done in the Lord's way. Over and over we have seen how slow the people were to learn that. Thousands died as a result.

We are not burdened with all the sacrifices and details of the Old Covenant – yet we seem to take the seriousness of serving God very lightly. How about you? Are you scrupulous in your service to God? Do you diligently study the Scriptures to make sure you are doing things according to God's will? We may not see many get consumed by fire today – but they certainly will have to give account on judgment day. Can you confidently say you are doing the Lord's work the Lord's way?

# 34

## KORAH'S REBELLION
### NUMBERS 16

After the disastrous experience with the spies you would think Israel might learn that rebellion doesn't pay. But they haven't.

¹*Korah son of Izhar, the son of Kohath, the son of Levi, and certain Reubenites—Dathan and Abiram, sons of Eliab, and On son of Peleth—became insolent* ² *and rose up against Moses. With them were 250 Israelite men, well-known community leaders who had been appointed members of the council.* ³ *They came as a group to oppose Moses and Aaron and said to them, "You have gone too far! The whole community is holy, every one of them, and the Lord is with them. Why then do you set yourselves above the Lord's assembly?"*

### ENVY

Does that sound familiar? It's not that long ago that Aaron, along with his sister Miriam, was making a similar accusation. Now the tables are turned and he is one of the targets of this rebellion. If you are in leadership, you may have heard similar criticisms:

- "Who do you think you are?"
- "Who made you God?"
- "Don't tell me what to do!"

It is jealousy; a direct challenge to God-ordained authority. Like most of the enemy's deceptions, there is truth in it. Indeed, Moses was no holier than anyone who was fully committed to the Lord, and God certainly is with all of them. One is not *better* than the other, but it is a stretch to say the whole community was holy. Korah certainly wasn't acting very holy at the moment, and it takes a lot of pride and boldness to put yourself on the level of a man like Moses. It is the same spirit that insists there is no difference between men and women and tries to undermine men's authority in the home. Certainly men are not better than women, but equality has nothing to do with function. The Father, Son and Holy Spirit are all God, but they have different functions. Jesus voluntarily submits to his Father, and the Spirit gladly does what the Father and Son direct him to do.

Ironically, Korah would almost certainly put himself above the assembly if he had the chance. It has happened over and over again. A common man, fighting a dictator, becomes the very dictator he condemned.

This was an interesting collection of rebels, led by Levites and Reubenites. Apparently they had been working on this for a while, gathering the support of 250 leaders. We're talking about a conspiracy, or even a coup. Korah may have hoped to be the leader who would take them back to Egypt. We know that elders had been appointed by Moses, but now we learn that a formal council had been established. That council should have been working closely with Moses, submitted to him, and operating under his authority. They should have publicly supported him and brought any concerns to him. Somehow that communication had broken down. Maybe Moses had been too busy wrestling with God so the Lord wouldn't destroy all the people after the incident with the spies. That affair was enough to distract anyone! If the

## KORAH'S REBELLION 299

leader is unaware of the discontent, there is usually a Korah ready to step in and take advantage of it.

The NIV translators provided the word *insolent* to describe the rebels. It means boldly rude, disrespectful, or insulting. Although not in the original Hebrew, it is a good description of these men.

### MOSES' RESPONSE
*⁴ When Moses heard this, he fell facedown.*

Moses had learned well. Instead of rising up in self-defense, he reflexively humbles himself. He knows God is the only one who can help. After all, it is him (and whatever help Aaron might provide) against 250 leaders, and Moses probably is not too popular with the rest of the people at this point.

*⁵ Then he said to Korah and all his followers: "In the morning the Lord will show who belongs to him and who is holy, and he will have that person come near him. The man he chooses he will cause to come near him. ⁶ You, Korah, and all your followers are to do this: Take censers ⁷ and tomorrow put burning coals and incense in them before the Lord. The man the Lord chooses will be the one who is holy. You Levites have gone too far!"*

Moses doesn't stay on his face. It is possible to hide behind God and not stand up like a man to confront the opposition. The difference between Moses and so many others is his total reliance on God. He issues a challenge and sets the parameters of how the issue will be resolved. Despite their rebellion, it is clear that Moses is the one in charge. He is confident God will back him up, and if for some reason he doesn't, Moses will probably be just as happy going back to his sheep and his family in Midian.

Moses is starting to lose his patience. He has dealt with lots of grumbling and complaining, but this challenge from his own leaders is too much. They have crossed the line, dishonoring those God has placed in authority.

## BE CONTENT WITH WHAT GOD HAS GIVEN YOU
*⁸ Moses also said to Korah, "Now listen, you Levites! ⁹ Isn't it enough for you that the God of Israel has separated you from the rest of the Israelite community and brought you near himself to do the work at the Lord's tabernacle and to stand before the community and minister to them? ¹⁰ He has brought you and all your fellow Levites near himself, but now you are trying to get the priesthood too. ¹¹ It is against the Lord that you and all your followers have banded together. Who is Aaron that you should grumble against him?"*

This is coveting: not being content with the gifts and position God has given you. It is not enough to be assistant pastor; you constantly find fault with the senior pastor and subtly try to undermine his authority, in hopes that you can get his position. Or you may have a seemingly insignificant role in the church and feel you deserve more. If you are faithful in little and humble yourself, God may lift you up and give you greater responsibility. Or not. He is the one in charge. This can apply at your job or other situations outside the church as well. And think about what you're coveting. Why would anyone want Moses' headaches? We see it in politics all the time. It is easy to criticize those in power and promise to do better, but usually, once they're in power, they quickly learn the challenges of leadership.

Be careful of envying others' gifts and calling. Are you coveting someone's position? Do you subtly criticize those in authority, trying to enhance your own popularity? Have you ever talked with your pastor or someone else in leadership about the challenges they face? Is there some way you could be supportive to them? Is there a Korah in your church or organization?

In this case the leaders were Levites, already set apart as a special tribe to minister to the Lord, with access to the holy places. As Moses correctly points out, they really are not rebelling against him, but against God. So he will allow God to settle the dispute.

## EGYPT: THE LAND OF MILK AND HONEY?

*¹² Then Moses summoned Dathan and Abiram, the sons of Eliab. But they said, "We will not come! ¹³ Isn't it enough that you have brought us up out of a land flowing with milk and honey to kill us in the wilderness? And now you also want to lord it over us! ¹⁴ Moreover, you haven't brought us into a land flowing with milk and honey or given us an inheritance of fields and vineyards. Do you want to treat these men like slaves? No, we will not come!"*

*¹⁵ Then Moses became very angry and said to the Lord, "Do not accept their offering. I have not taken so much as a donkey from them, nor have I wronged any of them."*

After dealing with the Levite leader, Moses turns to the two Reubenites. Apparently they weren't present when the others came with their complaint, and when Moses calls them, they refuse to come! Their contempt for him is obvious. Several things are fueling their angst:

- They had suffered as slaves in Egypt, and Moses reminds them of their Egyptian slave masters. They haven't overcome a general mistrust of authority or differentiated between God-ordained authority and the abusive Egyptian authority.
- Somehow they got the idea that Moses was mistreating the people and taking things from them for personal gain.
- They have conveniently forgotten why they failed to inherit the promised fields and vineyards. Instead, they

focus on Moses' failure to deliver a land flowing with milk and honey. On top of that, they have just been told they are embarking on a forty year journey in the wilderness, where they will die. They are determined to somehow make life better.

- As often happens when we are in rebellion, they totally confuse the facts, and the deceiver is always ready to help. Somehow they forget what life was like in Egypt, and amazingly call *it* a land flowing with milk and honey. Of course it is Moses' fault that they left that great life – and now it is Moses who is leading them to their deaths.

This was too much, even for Moses. He is angry, and asks God not to accept the offering they were planning to make in some hypocritical display of spirituality.

## THE CHALLENGE

*16 Moses said to Korah, "You and all your followers are to appear before the Lord tomorrow—you and they and Aaron. 17 Each man is to take his censer and put incense in it—250 censers in all—and present it before the Lord. You and Aaron are to present your censers also."*

I wonder what they expected. We don't know if God told Moses to set this up, or if Moses took the initiative to arrange it. Will they follow his instructions and come prepared with their censers?

*18 So each of them took his censer, put burning coals and incense in it, and stood with Moses and Aaron at the entrance to the tent of meeting. 19 When Korah had gathered all his followers in opposition to them at the entrance to the tent of meeting, the glory of the Lord appeared to the entire assembly. 20 The Lord said to Moses and Aaron, 21 "Separate yourselves from this assembly so I can put an end to them at once."*

Amazingly, they did exactly what Moses told them to do. Picture 254 men with their censers facing Moses and Aaron, as the glory of the Lord appears. This wasn't done quietly, behind the scenes. The entire assembly was waiting to see what happened. Many probably hoped Moses would be toppled from his lofty position. It's not clear if they all heard God's voice; it seems like he spoke only to Moses and Aaron, but he clearly is not happy. This is at least the third time he wanted to wipe out the entire nation. Only Moses and Aaron would be left – and they need to get away from the rest, or they might get struck down as well.

## MOSES INTERCEDES FOR THE ASSEMBLY

*[22] But Moses and Aaron fell facedown and cried out, "O God, the God who gives breath to all living things, will you be angry with the entire assembly when only one man sins?"*

Did you catch that? Moses and Aaron are back on their faces. This time it is in response to what *God* said. Why wouldn't he just let God wipe them out? How do you feel when you hear prophecies of judgment? Do you quietly smirk, happy that those "sinners" will finally get what is coming to them? Or do you fall on your face pleading for God's mercy on your nation?

No one would blame Moses for accepting God's offer and getting rid of the whole troublesome bunch. He was facing forty more years with them! How would you feel being stuck with your fiercest critics for the next forty years? But Moses is consistent – and very fair. He knew Korah was the ringleader, and he had seen how easily people can be led astray, so he begged God not to judge the whole assembly for one man's sin.

We should learn from his example, and avoid categorizing an entire church or group because of one person's sin. Ask for insight into who is responsible. Search your heart to see how much love you have for the lost. Are you more apt to call down judgment? Or plead for God's mercy? Could God be testing Moses to see how committed he was to his people? Could he be testing you?

## JUDGMENT

*[23]* *Then the Lord said to Moses,* *[24]* *"Say to the assembly, 'Move away from the tents of Korah, Dathan and Abiram.'"*

*[25]* *Moses got up and went to Dathan and Abiram, and the elders of Israel followed him.* *[26]* *He warned the assembly, "Move back from the tents of these wicked men! Do not touch anything belonging to them, or you will be swept away because of all their sins."* *[27]* *So they moved away from the tents of Korah, Dathan and Abiram. Dathan and Abiram had come out and were standing with their wives, children and little ones at the entrances to their tents.*

Dathan and Abiram finally show up. They may have purposely missed the censer challenge as a further sign of rebellion. The people were probably crowding around, wanting to see what would happen. That may be a natural reaction, but beware of curiosity. Have nothing to do with those caught up in rebellion. Don't touch anything they have been involved in, or you may be swept away with them in their sin. Tragically, the family doesn't have that option; when the head sins, the whole family suffers.

Are you hanging around people whom God is about to judge? Are you overly curious or fascinated about the lives of flagrant sinners? To the point of watching TV shows and using the internet to find out more about them?

## Korah's Rebellion

**²⁸** Then Moses said, "This is how you will know that the Lord has sent me to do all these things and that it was not my idea: **²⁹** If these men die a natural death and suffer the fate of all mankind, then the Lord has not sent me. **³⁰** But if the Lord brings about something totally new, and the earth opens its mouth and swallows them, with everything that belongs to them, and they go down alive into the realm of the dead, then you will know that these men have treated the Lord with contempt."

The stage is set, and it is dramatic. They were not just they treating Moses with contempt, they were provoking and despising God. We don't know if God told Moses what he was about to do, or if Moses knew God's heart from walking so close to him, and. Either way, in faith Moses boldly proclaims what God will do. If you make such a bold declaration, make sure it really is from God, and not just something you have thought up.

**³¹** As soon as he finished saying all this, the ground under them split apart **³²** and the earth opened its mouth and swallowed them and their households, and all those associated with Korah, together with their possessions. **³³** They went down alive into the realm of the dead, with everything they owned; the earth closed over them, and they perished and were gone from the community. **³⁴** At their cries, all the Israelites around them fled, shouting, "The earth is going to swallow us too!"

That should have been enough to convince the people that Moses was God's man, and make them think twice about rebelling against God's delegated authority. It did seem to put the fear of God in them!

When you contemplate doing something foolish, picture these men's wives and children (and dogs – and everything else they owned) being swallowed up. Listen to their cries. Even if you don't fear God, get right with God for your family's sake.

*35 And fire came out from the Lord and consumed the 250 men who were offering the incense.*

The slaughter was just starting; the fire that consumed all 250 men was almost as dramatic as the leaders being swallowed up.

*36 The Lord said to Moses, 37 "Tell Eleazar son of Aaron, the priest, to remove the censers from the charred remains and scatter the coals some distance away, for the censers are holy— 38 the censers of the men who sinned at the cost of their lives. Hammer the censers into sheets to overlay the altar, for they were presented before the Lord and have become holy. Let them be a sign to the Israelites."*

*39 So Eleazar the priest collected the bronze censers brought by those who had been burned to death, and he had them hammered out to overlay the altar, 40 as the Lord directed him through Moses. This was to remind the Israelites that no one except a descendant of Aaron should come to burn incense before the Lord, or he would become like Korah and his followers.*

The censers became a permanent reminder to Israel of how serious God is about doing things his way.

## MORE GRUMBLING!

*41 The next day the whole Israelite community grumbled against Moses and Aaron. "You have killed the Lord's people," they said.*

I am astounded that the people could actually do this! After God so convincingly vindicated Moses and Aaron and endorsed their leadership, how could they dare to grumble against them? How could they possibly accuse them of killing the people? Why is it so easy for us to doubt and disobey when we have seen God so clearly display his power, and we know what is right?

# KORAH'S REBELLION

*42 But when the assembly gathered in opposition to Moses and Aaron and turned toward the tent of meeting, suddenly the cloud covered it and the glory of the Lord appeared. 43 Then Moses and Aaron went to the front of the tent of meeting, 44 and the Lord said to Moses, 45 "Get away from this assembly so I can put an end to them at once." And they fell facedown.*

This is beginning to sound too familiar. Moses and Aaron are on their faces - again. God has had enough – again. But this time something is different. The killing has already started. This is an emergency. What will Moses do?

## ATONEMENT IS MADE FOR THE PEOPLE
*46 Then Moses said to Aaron, "Take your censer and put incense in it, along with burning coals from the altar, and hurry to the assembly to make atonement for them. Wrath has come out from the Lord; the plague has started." 47 So Aaron did as Moses said, and ran into the midst of the assembly. The plague had already started among the people, but Aaron offered the incense and made atonement for them.*

Somehow atonement had to be made for this sin. Moses knows that just praying for the people is not going to be enough this time. Exactly how the incense and burning coals from the altar provided atonement is not clear. Moses couldn't do it, but, as high priest, Aaron had the authority to intercede for the people. Aaron hasn't been too impressive so far, but he has seen enough to know he had better do what his brother tells him. He runs into the midst of the crowd that is already falling over dead, and atonement is made. This whole experience may have gone a long way in making a man of faith out of Aaron!

*48 He stood between the living and the dead, and the plague stopped. 49 But 14,700 people died from the plague, in addition to those who had died because of Korah. 50 Then Aaron returned to*

*Moses at the entrance to the tent of meeting, for the plague had stopped.*

Korah and all his men were already dead. Now, almost 15,000 more died of the plague. That should get their attention, but God isn't quite through showing his support for Moses and Aaron. In Numbers 17, an unusually short chapter for the Pentateuch (13 verses), the leader of each of the twelve tribes is told to place their staff, with their name written on it, in front of the ark, in the tabernacle. The one that sprouted would belong to the man God chose. God's purpose? *"I will rid myself of this constant grumbling against you by the Israelites."* (Verse 5)

Well, guess whose staff budded? Aaron's! Not only budded, but flowered and produced almonds! The staff was placed with the ark as a permanent reminder to the Israelites. And they seemed to get the message. For some reason this really scared them: *"We will die! We are lost, we are all lost! Anyone who even comes near the tabernacle of the Lord will die. Are we all going to die?"* (Numbers 17:12-13) There is no record of Moses' answer, but it did seem to do away with the grumbling for a while. In the following chapters God gives detailed instructions on the priesthood and its functions.

Rebellion has dealt a deadly blow to this young nation and deprived them of the Promised Land. It has touched almost everyone – except Moses, Joshua, and Caleb. In one last act of rebellion, it touches the great leader as well.

# 35

## MOSES' COSTLY MISTAKE
### NUMBERS 20

It is hard to find weaknesses in Moses. He has been an outstanding example of humility, faith, obedience, and sacrificial service. He stood firm while almost everyone around him rebelled. Such outstanding ministry should at the very least be rewarded with the chance to enjoy the Promised Land. Moses is the last one you would expect to miss out on that blessing because of his rebellion. But he does.

*¹In the first month the whole Israelite community arrived at the Desert of Zin, and they stayed at Kadesh. There Miriam died and was buried.*

Many years have gone by. Soon they will be entering the land. We know very little about the years of wilderness wanderings. The last time we heard about Miriam, she was leading a rebellion against her brother. Now she is dead. We don't know what her post-rebellion relationship with Moses had been like. Knowing Moses, he had probably forgiven her, so he is grieving her death. The last thing he needs this late in the journey is more problems from the Israelites.

### A FAMILIAR PROBLEM: NO WATER
*² Now there was no water for the community, and the people gathered in opposition to Moses and Aaron. ³ They quarreled with*

*Moses and said, "If only we had died when our brothers fell dead before the Lord! ⁴ Why did you bring the Lord's community into this wilderness, that we and our livestock should die here? ⁵ Why did you bring us up out of Egypt to this terrible place? It has no grain or figs, grapevines or pomegranates. And there is no water to drink!"*

Some things never change, especially in the desert: water shortages! Every other time, God had provided. No one died of thirst. But somehow that didn't translate into strong faith that God would supply water. And, after almost 40 years, they are still thinking about Egypt! So what do they do? Gather in opposition to Moses and Aaron. Quarrel with Moses. Blame him for being in this dry place. They are disillusioned, thirsty, and desperate. Death seems preferable.

We aren't all that different, are we? In desperate situations it is so easy to forget God's past faithfulness.

- Are you disillusioned with God because a pastor or leader has not delivered on his promises? Have you learned to differentiate between God's sure promises, and promises that men may flippantly make?

- Are you afraid of what may happen to you or your family?

- Have you lost the will to live – or even contemplated suicide?

- Are you in a terrible place at the moment?

- Can you still believe God will bring you to a place with figs, grapevines, and pomegranates, to say nothing of a necessity like water?

Desperate people tend to join with others who are suffering, and attack whoever is making life difficult. Is there someone you are blaming for your struggles? Have you unwittingly become part of a group of complainers?

## GOD'S PROVISION

*⁶ Moses and Aaron went from the assembly to the entrance to the tent of meeting and fell facedown, and the glory of the Lord appeared to them. ⁷ The Lord said to Moses, ⁸ "Take the staff, and you and your brother Aaron gather the assembly together. Speak to that rock before their eyes and it will pour out its water. You will bring water out of the rock for the community so they and their livestock can drink."*

Aaron has had his problems, particularly the golden calf and Miriam's rebellion. But in the end he got close to Moses, and they do everything together. They are about the only ones left from their generation. They have gotten good at falling on their faces. Instead of entering into the quarrelling, they did the right thing: They went to the Lord and humbled themselves in his presence. His glory reliably appeared, and he gave clear instructions to resolve the problem. Moses is to take his trustworthy staff, but he doesn't have to do anything with it this time: Just speak to the rock (with all Israel watching), and water will pour out. God wants the whole assembly present to witness this miracle. In Exodus 17, when Moses struck the rock with his staff, only the elders were present.

Wouldn't it be great if it were always that easy? Have you ever done what seemed to be the right thing -and God's glory was nowhere to be seen? Or pleaded for guidance, but the heavens were silent?

*⁹ So Moses took the staff from the Lord's presence, just as he commanded him. ¹⁰ He and Aaron gathered the assembly together in front of the rock.*

So far so good. Moses reliably does exactly what God told him to do. It almost becomes routine. You do all the right things. You have handled crises before and this doesn't seem that big. Water from a rock? No problem. Just one more day on the Exodus trail. But don't get too confident, because when you think you have it all together, you are liable to make what can seem like a minor mistake.

## MOSES' FOOLISH REBELLION

*And Moses said to them, "Listen, you rebels, must we bring you water out of this rock?" ¹¹ Then Moses raised his arm and struck the rock twice with his staff. Water gushed out, and the community and their livestock drank.*

Many times God had been ready to destroy them all. Moses has been very patient with them, although this is not the first time he has been irritated with them. He had saved their necks by his intercession so often, but they still weren't grateful! Maybe this had been bubbling under the surface for a while. The forty years were almost up, and Moses finally feels free to express his frustration and anger. He calls them rebels, which they were, but then he disobeys God's order and strikes the rock – twice – with the same staff God sanctified and used so many times. He strikes it in anger, and he strikes it hard. Speaking to it just seemed too tame.

At first it looks like it wasn't a big deal. Water gushed out. Everyone drank. The problem was solved. For some reason – maybe because Moses' sin had nothing to do with the community – God still does the miracle. But just because someone does miracles doesn't necessarily mean they are doing

God's will. God may honor their prayers for the sake of the person receiving the miracle.

True, in the past God did have Moses strike the rock to get water, but this wasn't the past. God likes to keep us alert by changing the way he does things. The community may not have known what Moses did wrong, but God catches up with him and Aaron, and the consequences are devastating.

## THE PENALTY FOR REBELLION

*12 But the Lord said to Moses and Aaron, "Because you did not trust in me enough to honor me as holy in the sight of the Israelites, you will not bring this community into the land I give them."*

God sees Moses' disobedience as a lack of trust, or faith. Did he not believe that speaking to the rock would produce water? Did he forget who was in charge? Anger is powerful, and probably played a key role in his sin.

Explicitly obeying God, and showing his love and care to the people, would have honored him as holy. Moses was very aware of how important that is. In the "strange fire" incident in Leviticus 10, he shared this word God had given him with Aaron:

*"'Among those who approach me*
  *I will be proved holy;*
*in the sight of all the people*
  *I will be honored.'"*

Moses had a responsibility to make God look good and accurately present him to the people. Instead, the whole nation saw him dishonor God. Leaders have a greater responsibility, and face a stiffer punishment for bringing disrepute to their Lord.

I still wince when I read this. How could God be so hard on a man who had done a nearly impossible job so incredibly well? If I couldn't step foot in the land I had been promising people for 40 years I would be devastated. Don't think you can get away with cutting corners on God just because you have been serving him for many years. Beware of anger or weariness clouding your discernment.

*13 These were the waters of Meribah, where the Israelites quarreled with the Lord and where he was proved holy among them.*

Earlier, they quarreled with Moses, but now it says they quarreled with the Lord. The two were apparently that closely linked together, making Moses' dishonoring God that much worse.

How was God proved holy? By displaying his power as he provided water, and by not allowing even a choice servant like Moses to get away with his rebellion. That would be a violation of God's holiness and justice. God doesn't play favorites.

## AARON'S DEATH

As if that wasn't a big enough blow, shortly after that, Aaron dies. Moses lost both siblings in the same chapter! Both Aaron and Moses were denied entrance to the Promised Land, but Aaron was more dispensable. His time came first.

*22 The whole Israelite community set out from Kadesh and came to Mount Hor. 23 At Mount Hor, near the border of Edom, the Lord said to Moses and Aaron, 24 "Aaron will be gathered to his people. He will not enter the land I give the Israelites, because both of you rebelled against my command at the waters of Meribah. 25 Get Aaron and his son Eleazar and take them up Mount Hor. 26 Remove Aaron's garments and put them* on his son Eleazar, for Aaron will be gathered to his people; he will die there."

It doesn't seem like a very fitting farewell for the first high priest and one of Israel's greatest leaders. It almost seems that Aaron is paying for Moses' sin. God addresses both of them, but speaks about Aaron in the third person. There is no thanks for what he has done, or words of reassurance that he had redeemed himself after a couple of major slip-ups. It is up to Moses to climb yet another mountain, take Aaron's clothes off, and put them on Aaron's son and successor as high priest.

*²⁷ Moses did as the Lord commanded: They went up Mount Hor in the sight of the whole community. ²⁸ Moses removed Aaron's garments and put them on his son Eleazar. And Aaron died there on top of the mountain. Then Moses and Eleazar came down from the mountain, ²⁹ and when the whole community learned that Aaron had died, all the Israelites mourned for him thirty days.*

This time Moses does exactly what God tells him to do. We don't know what final words were exchanged between these three men. After Aaron's death everything stops for thirty days of mourning. Moses must have known his time was approaching. There is this touching scene in Numbers 27 as Moses nears the end of his life:

*¹² Then the Lord said to Moses, "Go up this mountain in the Abarim Range and see the land I have given the Israelites. ¹³ After you have seen it, you too will be gathered to your people, as your brother Aaron was, ¹⁴ for when the community rebelled at the waters in the Desert of Zin, both of you disobeyed my command to honor me as holy before their eyes." (These were the waters of Meribah Kadesh, in the Desert of Zin.)*

Another mountain climb. In what must have been very bitter sweet, he gets to see the land flowing with milk and honey – but can't enter it. No mercy will be shown him. Moses doesn't argue with God, but seems to accept his fate. What else could he do? There may be times when we miss out on blessings the Lord intended for us because of our sin; a son or another leader may be the one who reaps the benefits of our hard labor.

## MOSES ANOINTS HIS SUCCESSOR

**15** *Moses said to the Lord,* **16** *"May the Lord, the God who gives breath to all living things, appoint someone over this community* **17** *to go out and come in before them, one who will lead them out and bring them in, so the Lord's people will not be like sheep without a shepherd."*

Like many elderly people, Moses may have had enough of this life and been ready to go and be with the Lord. His concern is for a shepherd to pick up the pastoring he had done so well all those years. Are you aware you won't be around forever? Are you preparing someone to pick up the work God has given you? Whether you die, or God moves you to another place, don't leave God's people without a shepherd.

**18** *So the Lord said to Moses, "Take Joshua son of Nun, a man in whom is the Spirit, and lay your hand on him.* **19** *Have him stand before Eleazar the priest and the entire assembly and commission him in their presence.* **20** *Give him some of your authority so the whole Israelite community will obey him.* **21** *He is to stand before Eleazar the priest, who will obtain decisions for him by inquiring of the Urim before the Lord. At his command he and the entire community of the Israelites will go out, and at his command they will come in."*

It seems obvious that Joshua would take over, but Moses wasn't about to take that for granted. He wanted confirmation from the

## MOSES' COSTLY MISTAKE

Lord, and there were specific steps to take in placing Joshua in as leader.

- The Holy Spirit indwelt very few people at that time. The Spirit's presence was essential for leadership; somehow Joshua was already Spirit-filled.

- Moses lays his hand on him, a practice still followed as we ordain and commission leaders.

- He is publicly commissioned in front of the high priest and all the people. It is important that leadership transitions be done publicly, and not sprung on people as a surprise.

- Moses was to pass on some (but not all) of his authority to Joshua. How that was done is not clear. God-given authority can be passed from one man to another, as long as God has ordained it. That authority was essential. Without it, there would be no need for Israel to obey him. With it, they are in sin if they don't.

- Moses had spoken directly with the Lord for guidance, but Joshua wouldn't have that privilege; now it would come through Eleazar, the high priest.

*22 Moses did as the Lord commanded him. He took Joshua and had him stand before Eleazar the priest and the whole assembly. 23 Then he laid his hands on him and commissioned him, as the Lord instructed through Moses.*

As he had done so many times, Moses did exactly as God instructed him. He will soon pay for the one time he didn't, but he is ready to go. He has seen the land, and his successor is in place. Soon he will hear those words we should all long to hear: "Well done, good and faithful servant."

## God's word to you

And you? This passage has important teaching that will help you be a good and faithful servant, and finish well:

- When you are in God's will and encounter a problem, he will provide a solution. Don't attempt to solve it on your own, or get into arguing with the people. Go straight to God, get on your face, and wait for his instructions.

- Moses seemed to doubt that at his word water could pour from a rock. When God gives you a word, there is tremendous power as you proclaim it. Trust him.

- Do exactly what he tells you to do. There is no room for your improvisations or "improvements" on his plan. This is why the ones doing great things in Matthew 7 were rejected by Jesus –they were not doing the Father's will.

- Watch out for anger or frustrations festering under the surface. They can cloud your judgment and get you in deep trouble.

- Be careful when you are almost home, almost to the Promised Land. It is easy to slack off a bit, and the consequences can be devastating.

- Honor God as holy in all you do. Never make him look bad or misrepresent him. Display your faith and trust in him by doing what he tells you to do.

If a great man like Moses missed out on the Promised Land because of what seems like a relatively minor disobedience, what will happen to those who flagrantly and consistently violate God's holiness and do ministry their own way?

# 36

## SALVATION THROUGH A SNAKE
### NUMBERS 21

Have you begun to wonder when – or if – Israel's rebellion will end? We have seen how it has angered, saddened, and wearied our God, and how deeply entrenched that rebellion remains in our fallen nature. Keep in mind, however, that we are talking about a period of forty years. Israel may have patiently endured the constant travel and same food for months on end. The scriptural record makes them seem frequent, but there may have been only one serious case of rebellion each year. You may have noticed the same phenomenon on your job or in your marriage: you can do great for months on end, but it is the one mistake that gets written up by your boss or endlessly recounted by your wife. Whatever the actual frequency, rebellion is serious, and the consequences severe. Even though we may not want to admit it, we are prone to the same pattern of unbelief, complaining, and disobedience. We try to justify our actions and attitudes, and downplay how serious they are, but at heart we are rebels as well. Have you examined your own heart for traces of rebellion?

### IMPATIENCE ON THE JOURNEY
*⁴ Then the people of Israel set out from Mount Hor, taking the road to the Red Sea to go around the land of Edom. But the people grew impatient with the long journey, ⁵ and they began to speak*

against God and Moses. *"Why have you brought us out of Egypt to die here in the wilderness?"* they complained. *"There is nothing to eat here and nothing to drink. And we hate this horrible manna!"*

It's the same complaint: nothing to drink and no food but manna (which they are sick of). They are correct lamenting that they will die in the wilderness; that was the punishment for their rebellion after the spies' report. With nothing to show for all those years in the wilderness, slavery in Egypt didn't look that bad. After all, by this point practically no one had actually experienced it; they had just heard romanticized versions of what life was like back there.

At first they had been hesitant to complain about God; their grumbling had been directed at Moses. Now they are emboldened to speak out against the Lord as well.

## "ARE WE THERE YET?"

Have you endured the endless "Are we there yet?" on family road trips, or do you remember asking that as a kid? We want to arrive! We want the promised blessings! But God uses the journey, the process, which shapes and prepares us for our destination, which, by the way, is not even here on earth. When we get impatient and start grumbling, we are vulnerable to all kinds of sin.

- Have you grown impatient with the long journey?
- Do you feel like you're getting nowhere?
- Do you long for the "good old days"?
- Does God's provision in the desert seem inadequate?
- Are you tired of his manna, especially when you see others enjoying choice food?
- Do you wonder if you will ever make it?
- Do you remember how God feels about grumbling?

## SNAKES!

*⁶ So the Lord sent poisonous snakes among the people, and many were bitten and died.*

This is a new punishment! It seems like the Lord enjoys keeping us on our toes. Too bad we have to get bitten and even die to get the message that we are displeasing God. How would you fare if God sent poisonous snakes after complainers today? The snakes didn't know who the offenders were; they bit everyone. Probably people who were perfectly content with their manna died because they happened to be in the wrong place. Watch the company you keep! Complaining is contagious – and dangerous!

*⁷ Then the people came to Moses and cried out, "We have sinned by speaking against the Lord and against you. Pray that the Lord will take away the snakes." So Moses prayed for the people.*

Do you remember someone else who called Moses in to ask God to stop the plagues? I wonder if Moses thought of Pharaoh repenting of his hard heart. It is interesting that the people never came to God directly. As usual, Moses faithfully prays for them – and then waits for God's solution. He never knows exactly what it will be.

*⁸ Then the Lord told him, "Make a replica of a poisonous snake and attach it to a pole. All who are bitten will live if they simply look at it!" ⁹ So Moses made a snake out of bronze and attached it to a pole. Then anyone who was bitten by a snake could look at the bronze snake and be healed!*

The solution God provided is as unique as the judgment.

The snakes weren't removed. The people got bit. But once they were bit, the Lord promises healing: They simply have to look at a replica of the very thing that afflicted them; healing would come from looking at a serpent, the creature that originally brought sin to our race!

Once again Moses' role is critical. He takes the brunt of the criticism. The whole crisis weighs heavily on him. Someone had to hear from God how to bring healing to a desperate situation. Moses was the only one who reliably heard from him. Then he had to obey an unusual command, make the snake, and raise it up on a pole. Can you imagine his haste in crafting the snake, as people were dying all around him?

## THE SON OF MAN MUST BE LIFTED UP

Jesus refers to this incident in his famous conversation with Nicodemus in John 3:14-15:

> *And as Moses lifted up the bronze snake on a pole in the wilderness, so the Son of Man must be lifted up, so that everyone who believes in him will have eternal life.*

With these words, the Son of God validates the biblical account of the exodus, and Moses' leadership.

At first it seems odd to compare Jesus with a bronze snake on a pole, but it is the idea of being lifted up, and the simple faith involved in looking to God's provision for salvation. Just as the snake bite was deadly, so the serpent's lasting legacy of sin in our race (as a result of listening to him) is deadly. One brings physical death, while the other brings spiritual death, yet in both cases God gives life and healing.

Finding salvation by looking at a snake may seem strange to us; finding salvation by looking at a bloodied man hanging on a cross may also seem strange to someone not familiar with the Gospel. But, as you agonize with your snakebite, you are probably willing to do anything that will heal you and save your life. When you understand the deadly impact of sin on your life, you may be ready to embrace the foolishness of the cross. If you have never looked to Jesus, read the Gospels (Matthew, Mark, Luke, or John) with the simple desire to see Jesus. If you are ready to believe that his death can pay for your sin and give you new life, tell him. Ask him to forgive you and heal you. If you have already done that, take some time to marvel at the preview of the cross way back in that wilderness, and how simple faith in Jesus can save you and give you eternal life.

Jesus made one more striking statement about the results of being lifted up on the cross, in John 12:32:

> "And I, when I am lifted up from the earth, will draw all people to myself."

In the wilderness Moses lifted up the serpent, but the people had to look at it to live. We still have to take that step of faith, but when Jesus was lifted up, supernatural power was unleashed. He is drawing people to himself. They can resist him, but he desires for everyone to come to him and live. Grab onto that and believe it for loved ones who are wandering far from him right now. Pray that he would draw people in your family and community to himself. When you speak to them about Jesus, trust that he is working with you to draw them in. Lift Jesus up in your words and actions, and present him with the urgency of Moses lifting up that bronze snake. They have been lethally bit by the serpent, and without Jesus they face a brutal future which only starts with death. You have the key to their salvation in your hands. It would be criminal for Moses not to lift up the serpent and offer healing. It is criminal for you to withhold Jesus from those who are perishing.

# 37

## SEX AS A WEAPON
## NUMBERS 25 AND 31

Sex: The number one snare for most men. When a man falls into sexual sin, his family and community suffer as well. So far sex hasn't been a big issue on this exodus journey, but now they are getting close to the Promised Land. They survived one rebellion after another, and God's threats to kill them. Satan knows he needs to act fast if he is going to derail God's plan for the nation. He knows that when all else fails, a woman will get to a man. Here he used the infamous Balaam to instigate this mess. The devil and his "prophet" were almost successful in getting God to destroy the nation one last time before entering the land.

### DON'T FLIRT WITH DISASTER
*[1]While the Israelites were camped at Acacia Grove, some of the men defiled themselves by having sexual relations with local Moabite women.*

Why is it so hard for a man to be satisfied with the woman God gave him? Why are ungodly women so attractive to many men? Adultery and relationships with pagan women were clearly prohibited in the law. God was very aware of the potential danger. That is why he commanded them to totally destroy the pagan nations in Canaan, just like you have to destroy any porn you have - and make sure you can't access it on the internet. If it is only a click away it will be a constant temptation. Cut off any relationship that could become adulterous, and demolish any idols. Don't flirt with disaster.

*² These women invited them to attend sacrifices to their gods, so the Israelites feasted with them and worshiped the gods of Moab. ³ In this way, Israel joined in the worship of Baal of Peor, causing the Lord's anger to blaze against his people.*

## SEXUAL SIN LEADS TO IDOLATRY

For God, the idolatry was worse than the sexual sin, although women and sex often become idols. Instead of helping the women meet the true God, the Israelite men quickly embraced their pagan religion. That seems to be the norm in relationships with unbelievers. They rarely come to the Lord. Of course, the effectiveness of your evangelism is limited when you are already in sin. In fact, once you fall into sexual sin, Satan has a foothold – and a strong one. It is often a slippery slope into drug or alcohol abuse, false religion, and any number of corrupt practices. To say nothing of the evil spirits that freely pass between the couple engaged in sexual intercourse.

If God's anger is blazing against you because of sexual sin or idolatry, don't wait to repent. Confess your sin and get back right with God. The sin may be pleasurable at the time and not seem like that big a deal, but it will destroy you.

*⁴ The Lord issued the following command to Moses: "Seize all the ringleaders and execute them before the Lord in broad daylight, so his fierce anger will turn away from the people of Israel."*

## DRASTIC ACTION REQUIRED

Poor Moses. One hundred twenty years old, and he has to round up and execute these men. The plague had already begun. Usually Moses would already be interceding for the people, but he is strangely silent. Instead, God comes to him and tells him how to stop the killing: execute all the ringleaders, but spare the men who followed them. Moses needs to act quickly to avoid a bigger slaughter.

*⁵ So Moses ordered Israel's judges, "Each of you must put to death the men under your authority who have joined in worshiping Baal of Peor."*

Moses had learned about delegation, and wisely tasks each judge with killing those men under his authority who had sinned. "Judge" is used here in the same sense as in the book of Judges: They were in authority, initially responsible for settling disputes, and thus called judges. Maybe executions were a new addition to their job description! To follow Moses' order they had to know the men under them, and where they were. It might take some time to find them all and kill them. Moses seems to expand the group from the ringleaders, to include everyone who joined in idol worship. But before they have a chance to act, an outrageous violation takes place.

## BOLD SIN, AND A MAN AS ZEALOUS AS GOD

*⁶ Just then one of the Israelite men brought a Midianite woman into his tent, right before the eyes of Moses and all the people, as everyone was weeping at the entrance of the Tabernacle. ⁷ When Phinehas son of Eleazar and grandson of Aaron the priest saw this, he jumped up and left the assembly. He took a spear ⁸ and rushed after the man into his tent. Phinehas thrust the spear all the way through the man's body and into the woman's stomach. So the plague against the Israelites was stopped, ⁹ but not before 24,000 people had died.*

As usual, our sin impacts those around us. The plague had already killed 24,000 people. It probably wasn't selective, so innocent people were dying. Everybody came weeping and joined Moses at the Tabernacle. And then, incredibly, in front of everyone, a man takes a Midianite woman into his tent! Is anyone going to do anything about it? Moses doesn't. Everybody is in shock! Except Phinehas. He was zealous for the Lord, and runs after them. Apparently his father, Eleazar the high priest, raised him right. Phinehas bursts in on an intimate embrace and plunges his spear through them both. There is no indication that any of the other ringleaders got killed in obedience to God's command, but that single bold act was enough to stop the plague.

*$^{10}$ Then the Lord said to Moses, $^{11}$ "Phinehas son of Eleazar and grandson of Aaron the priest has turned my anger away from the Israelites by being as zealous among them as I was. So I stopped destroying all Israel as I had intended to do in my zealous anger. $^{12}$ Now tell him that I am making my special covenant of peace with him. $^{13}$ In this covenant, I give him and his descendants a permanent right to the priesthood, for in his zeal for me, his God, he purified the people of Israel, making them right with me."*

We begin to sense that Moses' time is short. A new generation is doing the Lord's work. It is Phinehas who is zealous and purifies the people. He is already stepping into his role as priest, and interceding for the nation, as Moses had done so many times. He is willing to take a bold step to rid Israel of the sin and make them right with God. Once again, just one man willing to stand up and act saved the lives of multitudes.

Although his days are numbered, Moses is still the one who receives God's word, and now the truth comes out: God was ready to destroy the entire nation, but he found someone as zealous as he was. Someone needed to do something. Thank God for Phinehas.

This story doesn't justify killing a sinner, or other extreme acts, yet the underlying lesson is clear: Sin must be dealt with decisively, just like Jesus advocated cutting off your hand or gouging out your eye if it causes you to sin. Our lives, our families, and our churches must be kept pure.

Are you zealous for God and his holiness? Willing to take a bold stand? Are you aware of God's anger at his church, or at your nation? Do you think it is possible for you to turn away his anger, purify the people, and make them right with God? That is what Jesus did, isn't it? Do you think he could use you? He used Phinehas – and the young man was rewarded with a special covenant of peace. His descendants would inherit a permanent priesthood.

*14 The Israelite man killed with the Midianite woman was named Zimri son of Salu, the leader of a family from the tribe of Simeon. 15 The woman's name was Cozbi; she was the daughter of Zur, the leader of a Midianite clan.*

These were prominent people from both Israel and Midian. Israel's sin had been dealt with, but there was still much more killing to be done.

## MOSES' LAST BATTLE
*16 Then the Lord said to Moses, 17 "Attack the Midianites and destroy them, 18 because they assaulted you with deceit and tricked you into worshiping Baal of Peor, and because of Cozbi, the daughter of a Midianite leader, who was killed at the time of the plague because of what happened at Peor."*

Now the Midianites would pay. Israel had plenty of time for war games and preparing to take over the land those forty years in the wilderness, and had developed an efficient army. Word was getting out. Their sheer numbers that had everyone in their path terrified. Most important, God's favor was with them, and he blessed their efforts. The Midianites had used devious means to fight Israel. Now they will die because of their deceit and trickery.

## THE BATTLE AS RECORDED IN NUMBERS 31

*¹Then the Lord said to Moses, ² "On behalf of the people of Israel, take revenge on the Midianites for leading them into idolatry. After that, you will die and join your ancestors."*

God was determined to get revenge on Midian, and kept Moses around for the battle. This would be his last battle - and it might be extremely painful for him. His wife was a Midianite. His family was living in Midian. They may not have been in the same area, and they certainly weren't involved in Baal worship. But it is bitter irony that Moses' last major act was overseeing the devastation of a people he had been intimately connected with.

*³ So Moses said to the people, "Choose some men, and arm them to fight the Lord's war of revenge against Midian.⁴ From each tribe of Israel, send 1,000 men into battle." ⁵ So they chose 1,000 men from each tribe of Israel, a total of 12,000 men armed for battle.⁶ Then Moses sent them out, 1,000 men from each tribe, and Phinehas son of Eleazar the priest led them into battle. They carried along the holy objects of the sanctuary and the trumpets for sounding the charge.*

Look who is leading the battle! Moses is too old, but Phinehas is definitely up for a fight! The one who is notably missing in this whole story is Joshua, who shortly would assume Moses' leadership and take them into the Promised Land. We have no idea where he might have been.

*⁷ They attacked Midian as the Lord had commanded Moses, and they killed all the men. ⁸ All five of the Midianite kings—Evi, Rekem, Zur, Hur, and Reba—died in the battle. They also killed Balaam son of Beor with the sword.*

## BALAAM
So, that is the end of Balaam. You can read about his troubled life in Numbers 22-24, where we get a glimpse of this conflicted man:

*Now when Balaam saw that it pleased the Lord to bless Israel, he did not resort to divination (or sorcery) as at other times, but turned his face toward the wilderness. When Balaam looked out and saw Israel encamped tribe by tribe, the Spirit of God came on him and he spoke his message* (Numbers 24:1-3).

Now we finally learn who was responsible for this whole fiasco! A man who initially seemed to be serving God, but is soundly condemned throughout the Bible. Moab and Midian had joined together in fear of Israel. They hired Balaam to curse God's people. When that didn't work, they used sex to get to them. That almost worked. Their problem would have been solved if God had destroyed the whole nation as he wanted to!

Balaam's story reminds us of the vigilance needed with "prophets." Just because someone sounds good doesn't necessarily mean they are from the Lord. Jesus warned of many false prophets in the last days (Matthew 7:15; 24:24). Watch for Balaams in your midst. Apparently even someone who speaks the word of God, and has the Spirit come on him, can be into sorcery.

## SPARE THE WOMEN!
*[9] Then the Israelite army captured the Midianite women and children and seized their cattle and flocks and all their wealth as plunder. [10] They burned all the towns and villages where the Midianites had lived. [11] After they had gathered the plunder and captives, both people and animals, [12] they brought them all to Moses and Eleazar the priest, and to the whole community of Israel, which was camped on the plains of Moab beside the Jordan River, across from Jericho.*

Israel was about to enter the Promised Land. They were at the end of their journey. It sounds like the army was on target and did a great job, but when Moses goes out to meet them, he is in for a big surprise.

*[13] Moses, Eleazar the priest, and all the leaders of the community went to meet them outside the camp. [14] But Moses was furious with all the generals and captains who had returned from the battle. [15] "Why have you let all the women live?" he demanded. [16] "These are the very ones who followed Balaam's advice and caused the people of Israel to rebel against the Lord at Mount Peor. They are the ones who caused the plague to strike the Lord's people. [17] So kill all the boys and all the women who have had intercourse with a man. [18] Only the young girls who are virgins may live; you may keep them for yourselves.*

## KEEP THE VIRGINS!

What? Kill the women and boys - but keep the young virgins? Verse 35 tells us there were 35,000 of them! That would be a lot to integrate into the Jewish community. Do you suppose they caused some jealousy among the Jewish women - and made a lot of Jewish men very happy? It seems like a strange accommodation for men who have just come out of sexual sin and idolatry, almost like rewarding them for their sin!

The rest of the chapter outlines the purification needed, and the spoils of battle. It was a great start on the livestock and supplies needed in the Promised Land: 675,000 sheep! Amazingly, verse 49 states that not a single Israelite died in this major battle. God truly was with that army! And that is the last we hear about this whole strange affair!

It is a tragic and ominous end to a journey that has been plagued with grumbling and rebellion. After so much time walking with Moses, it is sad to see his evident decline. There is no question he has done an amazing job, and it is encouraging that someone zealous like Phinehas is on the scene. Yet it seems like the devil, idolatry, and our own sinful nature – especially sexual temptation – are always lurking, eager to destroy us. Is there some sin you are involved in that will eventually devastate your family? Or result in your own death? Are you aware of sin around you that needs to be challenged? May God give you the zeal and strength of Phinehas to stand up and make things right!

# PART 6

## *DEUTERONOMY*

*MOSES REFLECTS ON HIS 40 YEARS LEADING ISRAEL AND GIVES HIS FINAL ADDRESS TO THE NATION*

# 38

## Highlights of the Journey
### Deuteronomy 2 & 3

Moses' task is almost done. He has led the people to the border of the Promised Land – twice. Almost forty years earlier, their rebellion kept them from entering in. Did Moses ever regret taking a job that consumed the rest of his life? Did he resent the people for robbing him of retirement with his family in that land flowing with milk and honey? He didn't seem to. He has faithfully completed his task. With Moab and Midian destroyed, his last battle is behind him. Now the nation is camped out on the plains of Moab, waiting to cross the Jordan. But before they do, Moses has one last chance to address them. He recounts some of their journey, shares his urgent concerns that they walk in obedience to God, and finally ascends Mount Nebo - to die.

Deuteronomy is the account of his last words. In chapter two he recalls some of the highlights of the journey.

### God's faithfulness
*2:7* The Lord your God has blessed you in all the work of your hands. He has watched over your journey through this vast wilderness. These forty years the Lord your God has been with you, and you have not lacked anything.

It was only Moses' intercession that kept God from destroying them because of their constant complaining and rebellion. They certainly were not deserving of his favor, yet they were still his people. And in spite of our sin and its consequences, God is good. Look at all he did for them:

- He blessed them in everything they did, prospering whatever they put their hand to.

- He watched over their travels throughout the journey. He has *"guarded you"* (Message), *"taken care of you"* (GNB), and *"watched your every step"* (NLT). Literally, he has *"known your goings"* (NASB).

- For forty years he has been with them, night and day, without fail. He has never left them, even though he wanted to at times.

- They have lacked nothing, at least nothing they needed to survive. They would say they lacked the choice food of Egypt and many of life's comforts. They went days without water. But God always provided what was truly needed.

If God did that for these grumbling, rebellious Israelites, don't you think he will do that - and more - for you? He has adopted you as a son through your faith in Jesus. God wants to bless the work of your hands! He will watch over you – and your journey probably won't be half as rough as those wilderness wanderings! He has promised to never leave you or forsake you, and to provide everything you truly need. As you think back on your life in Christ, has he ever let you down?

Israel's struggles those forty years serve as an example to us. They made it to the Promised Land! That should be a tremendous encouragement to you. You will make it too!

## TAKE POSSESSION OF WHAT GOD HAS GIVEN YOU

*⁹ Then the Lord said to me, "Do not harass the Moabites or provoke them to war, for I will not give you any part of their land. I have given Ar to the descendants of Lot as a possession."*

They were charged with eliminating the pagan nations from the land and promised God's help in battle, but they had to listen to him, and fight when he told them to fight.

Even though Lot was not necessarily godly, God set land aside for his descendants because of his covenant with Abraham. The Moabites were just outside the Promised Land, so Israel might be tempted to covet some of their land. Actually, as we saw in Numbers 31, the Moabites brought destruction on themselves. The essential lesson was to do everything in God's time and his way.

What is the "land" God has given you? What is yours to possess? Don't attempt to take what belongs to another man, especially his wife. If God has given you "territory" for a church or ministry, don't covet someone else's gifting and ministry. Mind your own business, and listen closely for what God directs you to do. If you attempt to move in on something he hasn't given you, you will find yourself frustrated and on the losing end! On the other hand, be confident that God will jealousy guard what is yours. If someone messes with your wife or territory, God will rise up, and they will pay dearly.

*¹⁴ Thirty-eight years passed from the time we left Kadesh Barnea until we crossed the Zered Valley. By then, that entire generation of fighting men had perished from the camp, as the Lord had sworn to them. ¹⁵ The Lord's hand was against them until he had completely eliminated them from the camp.*

*16* Now when the last of these fighting men among the people had died, *17* the Lord said to me, *18* "Today you are to pass by the region of Moab at Ar. *19* When you come to the Ammonites, do not harass them or provoke them to war, for I will not give you possession of any land belonging to the Ammonites. I have given it as a possession to the descendants of Lot."

It seems contradictory: Moses just said God was with them and watched over them, but the Lord's hand was also against an entire generation. Nothing more would happen until they all died. Would it have been easier to kill them all at once? Probably – but that would leave no one to raise the next generation!

There may be things that have to happen in your life or family before you can move on to the next place God has for you. That can be frustrating, as you see others who are not even walking with God enjoying their land. Trust God that he knows what he is doing, even though it will probably take longer than you think it should. Be careful to follow his plan. If God's hand is against you for some reason, plead for mercy, accept the judgment, and help your children and other believers avoid your mistakes. Don't get resentful with God, but continue to praise him and seek him even in the difficulties.

## GOD PUTS THE TERROR OF YOU ON YOUR ENEMIES

*24* "Set out now and cross the Arnon Gorge. See, I have given into your hand Sihon the Amorite, king of Heshbon, and his country. Begin to take possession of it and engage him in battle. *25* This very day I will begin to put the terror and fear of you on all the nations under heaven. They will hear reports of you and will tremble and be in anguish because of you.

Now they are released to do warfare. There is a time to pass by your enemy, and a time to engage them in battle. God is sovereign over the battles of your life! When it's his time, he will give your enemies into your hand. Even before they crossed the gorge and set foot in Sihon's territory, God had determined the outcome! But they still had to fight and take possession of it. It probably won't be with swords or guns, but is there something you need to fight for or take possession of?

God is good at psychological warfare! The nations would be in fear and terror of Israel. There may be times when it is appropriate to pray that those opposed to the Gospel would tremble and be in anguish of us. Too often they scoff at us and think we're a joke! God doesn't want that!

Our warfare is usually against principalities and powers, against the devil. When we are walking in holiness and the power of the Spirit, demons will tremble; they fear the prayer of a godly man and tremble at the name of Jesus. They also know when our spirituality is a show, and can harm us if we are battling in the flesh. When God leads us, we can do damage to the kingdom of darkness and take territory for the King of kings.

## DEUTERONOMY 3 – BE CONTENT WITH WHAT GOD HAS GIVEN YOU

*3:12 Of the land that we took over at that time, I gave the Reubenites and the Gadites the territory north of Aroer by the Arnon Gorge, including half the hill country of Gilead, together with its towns. 13 The rest of Gilead and also all of Bashan, the kingdom of Og, I gave to the half-tribe of Manasseh.*

Moses couldn't cross into the Promised Land, but, after the army took the land, several tribes settled in Trans-Jordan, the area east of the Jordan River.

Hopefully they had learned on the Exodus to be content with what God gave them, but I could imagine their complaints:

- We're separated from our relatives by the river.

- The best land is on the other side.
- We don't want to live in the hill country.
- The distribution should have been more democratic.
- Everyone should be able to live where they want.

Do you remember the pillar of cloud and fire? We go where God tells us to go, and accept what he gives us, with joy and thanksgiving. Learn to be content with what God has given you.

## WORK TOGETHER UNTIL EVERYONE RECEIVES WHAT BELONGS TO THEM

*[18]  I commanded you at that time: "The Lord your God has given you this land to take possession of it. But all your able-bodied men, armed for battle, must cross over ahead of the other Israelites. [19] However, your wives, your children and your livestock (I know you have much livestock) may stay in the towns I have given you, [20] until the Lord gives rest to your fellow Israelites as he has to you, and they too have taken over the land that the Lord your God is giving them across the Jordan. After that, each of you may go back to the possession I have given you."*

Some tribes already had their land. Women, children, and livestock could stay in their new towns and begin to establish homes there, but there would be no rest for able-bodied men until everyone had their territory. Apparently there were no men to guard the families (except perhaps some disabled men who couldn't fight), but God would protect them. Most men would find it hard to leave their families in a strange land, but no one could rest until they all had what God allotted them.

This is a principle for the body of Christ as well: Before we can sit back and take it easy, we are responsible to our brothers to ensure they have what God has given them. We all fight together and work together to gain possession of what he has promised us. It is wrong for those who have been privileged to "make it" to ignore those who are still struggling. There is a strong tendency for each person to strike out on their own to find their place, but God works through his body. We are in this together. That has been a key lesson of the exodus, and it is a principle which can be applied on a global scale as well: We need to be truly concerned that our brothers and sisters around the world have received what God has planned for them before we rest. That may mean there will be no rest until we get to heaven!

Moses has much more to share with them, but it must be received from the perspective of what they have already learned and experienced. All too often we repeat our mistakes and fail to learn from history. Despite our determination not to be like our parents, we fail just as they did.

- What are the major lessons God has taught you?
- What mistakes have you made? Are you falling back into the same destructive patterns?
- Are you content with what God has given you?

Don't settle for less than he has planned for you. Keep fighting to take possession of it. And beware the dangers of going it alone.

# 39

## OUT OF THE IRON-SMELTING FURNACE
### *DEUTERONOMY 4:1-40*

Every Christian has probably endured what seemed like a never-ending sermon. On the other hand, some preachers are so good you're not even aware of the time. We don't know the time frame of Moses' final messages, but he obviously has a lot to say. His biggest concern was the importance of obeying God and the dire consequences of disobedience. That is understandable after putting up with forty years of their complaints and rebellion.

Think back on this great man whom we have followed through so many experiences. He is old now, and knows death is near. Listen to his heart:

*¹Now, Israel, hear the decrees and laws I am about to teach you. Follow them so that you may live and may go in and take possession of the land the Lord, the God of your ancestors, is giving you. ² Do not add to what I command you and do not subtract from it, but keep the commands of the Lord your God that I give you.*

### FOLLOW GOD'S LAWS SO YOU MAY LIVE
- Listen to the Word of God. Someone needs to hear from God and then teach that word to the people. Moses is sharing commands from God, not his opinion.

- It is interesting that he says "I'm about to teach you" these laws; he has been teaching them for almost forty years!

- Be careful not to add to or subtract from anything God has said. Every word is important. It is extremely presumptuous for us to think we can change God's Word.

- The next step is simple, but very hard: Do it. Follow God's heart as revealed in his Word. Keep all his commands.

- When we do, God rewards us; he has something to give us. The result of following him is life.

- He has plans for us. If we walk with him, we can move into those plans and take possession of all God has prepared for us.

*³You saw with your own eyes what the Lord did at Baal Peor. The Lord your God destroyed from among you everyone who followed the Baal of Peor, ⁴but all of you who held fast to the Lord your God are still alive today.*

They're not getting his commands in some kind of vacuum. They have experienced miracles (like the daily manna), and have seen how serious God is about what he says. Idolatry brings devastation. The vivid memory of all the people who died at Baal Peor (Numbers 25) should encourage obedience and instill a healthy fear of God.

## A TESTIMONY TO THE NATIONS
*⁵See, I have taught you decrees and laws as the Lord my God commanded me, so that you may follow them in the land you are entering to take possession of it. ⁶Observe them carefully, for this will show your wisdom and understanding to the nations, who will hear about all these decrees and say, "Surely this great nation*

*is a wise and understanding people." ⁷ What other nation is so great as to have their gods near them the way the Lord our God is near us whenever we pray to him? ⁸ And what other nation is so great as to have such righteous decrees and laws as this body of laws I am setting before you today?*

Moses has done his part; he has been obedient to teach what God has given him. Those commands were not just for the exodus; that was training for following God in the Promised Land. But God has a greater purpose than blessing them. Even though the Old Testament seems focused on Israel, God's purpose from the start was to reach all nations. Israel was the vehicle God intended to use to display his greatness.

- Others who have never heard of the true God should be impressed with the wisdom and understanding that comes from living his Word.
- God's people should have a reputation for being wise and understanding. It will be so evident that news about how blessed they are will spread throughout the earth.
- God also answers prayer so others will be impressed at how alive and close he is to his people.
- Nobody else at that time had the great privilege of this teaching, and the blessing of God almighty on their lives as they live it out.

When was the last time you heard people marveling at Christians because they had been shown a simple, wise, way of living that really works? Do we live in such a way that people are impressed that God has entrusted us with his Word?

It may seem contradictory that God's intention was a witness to the nations when he was about to have them destroy all the people in the Promised Land, but that was part of ensuring a pure testimony to the rest of the world, untainted by idolatry or other sin.

## REMEMBER WHAT GOD HAS DONE
*⁹ Only be careful, and watch yourselves closely so that you do not forget the things your eyes have seen or let them fade from your heart as long as you live. Teach them to your children and to their children after them. ¹⁰ Remember the day you stood before the Lord your God at Horeb, when he said to me, "Assemble the people before me to hear my words so that they may learn to revere me as long as they live in the land and may teach them to their children."¹¹ You came near and stood at the foot of the mountain while it blazed with fire to the very heavens, with black clouds and deep darkness.¹² Then the Lord spoke to you out of the fire. You heard the sound of words but saw no form; there was only a voice. ¹³ He declared to you his covenant, the Ten Commandments, which he commanded you to follow and then wrote them on two stone tablets. ¹⁴ And the Lord directed me at that time to teach you the decrees and laws you are to follow in the land that you are crossing the Jordan to possess.*

What memorable experiences have you had in the Lord?

- The amazing sense of being loved and forgiven when you asked Jesus into your life?
- Your baptism? Or baptism in the Spirit?
- The first time you led someone to the Lord or were used by God to bring healing to someone?

Most of what Moses is calling them to remember would have taken place when they were children; all the adults who left Egypt had died by this time, but the memory of God speaking out of fire amidst the darkness would be unforgettable. Moses' instruction to the Israelites also applies to you:

- Be careful
- Watch yourself closely
- Don't forget what you have seen
- Don't let it fade from your heart
- Teach it to your children and grandchildren

Why does Moses make such a point of this? We have short memories! Without a conscious effort, what was so real to you that day you accepted Christ can get hazy. That is why holidays like Passover were so important; they are an everlasting reminder of God's great works. That is why altars and monuments were so common. What a loss that many believers today downplay traditional celebrations of the birth, death, and resurrection of Jesus. We need to be reminded of all Jesus did for us!

- Do you keep a journal?
- Do you have pictures of important events in your Christian life posted on Facebook or around your house?
- Do you talk about those earlier experiences with your family and Christian brothers and sisters?
- Do you make a conscious effort to teach your children and grandchildren what God has taught you?

## OUT OF THE IRON-SMELTING FURNACE

*[15] You saw no form of any kind the day the Lord spoke to you at Horeb out of the fire. Therefore watch yourselves very carefully, [16] so that you do not become corrupt and make for yourselves an idol, an image of any shape, whether formed like a man or a woman, [17] or like any animal on earth or any bird that flies in the air, [18] or like any creature that moves along the ground or any fish in the waters below. [19] And when you look up to the sky and see the sun, the moon and the stars—all the heavenly array—do not be enticed into bowing down to them and*

worshiping things the Lord your God has apportioned to all the nations under heaven. [20] But as for you, the Lord took you and brought you out of the iron-smelting furnace, out of Egypt, to be the people of his inheritance, as you now are.

What kind of "iron-smelting furnace" were you in? What did God have to do to get you out? Israel spent more time in the furnace, in slavery, than they thought they could bear. It took mighty displays of God's power for Pharaoh to let them go, but God took them and brought them out. He has probably done that for you. If he hasn't yet, there is a purpose in you reading this. Don't stay in the furnace any longer than you have to! Start seeking God! If you have loved ones in the furnace, pray, and trust that the same God who brought you out will bring them out as well. God does all that so he will have heirs! We are the people of his inheritance! Or, as the NLT says, *his very own people and his special possession*.

Idolatry, and sun and moon worship, were very common at that time. Men like to have something tangible to worship. They are quick to put aside a relationship with the living God to follow a man-made idol. We may look down on idol worshippers, but remember, anything that takes center stage in our lives and occupies more of our time, energy, and affection than God is an idol: The cell phone, computer, sports – even your kids and the woman you love – can become idols.

## GOD IS A CONSUMING FIRE

[21] *The Lord was angry with me because of you, and he solemnly swore that I would not cross the Jordan and enter the good land the Lord your God is giving you as your inheritance.* [22] *I will die in this land; I will not cross the Jordan; but you are about to cross over and take possession of that good land.* [23] *Be careful not to forget the covenant of the Lord your God that he made with you;*

do not make for yourselves an idol in the form of anything the Lord your God has forbidden. <sup>24</sup> For the Lord your God is a consuming fire, a jealous God.

After so many faith-filled years, Moses learned the hard lesson his people had learned earlier: You can't play with God. In a moment of anger he struck the rock instead of speaking to it, and was kept from entering the land. We focus on God's love and blessings, but he is still just as much a consuming fire as he was back then, and he is jealous. Don't do anything to arouse his jealousy.

## SEEK GOD WITH ALL YOUR HEART AND SOUL
[25] *After you have had children and grandchildren and have lived in the land a long time—if you then become corrupt and make any kind of idol, doing evil in the eyes of the Lord your God and arousing his anger,* [26] *I call the heavens and the earth as witnesses against you this day that you will quickly perish from the land that you are crossing the Jordan to possess. You will not live there long but will certainly be destroyed.* [27] *The Lord will scatter you among the peoples, and only a few of you will survive among the nations to which the Lord will drive you.* [28] *There you will worship man-made gods of wood and stone, which cannot see or hear or eat or smell.* [29] *But if from there you seek the Lord your God, you will find him if you seek him with all your heart and with all your soul.* [30] *When you are in distress and all these things have happened to you, then in later days you will return to the Lord your God and obey him.* [31] *For the Lord your God is a merciful God; he will not abandon or destroy you or forget the covenant with your ancestors, which he confirmed to them by oath.*

Over time we tend to get complacent. They might enthusiastically affirm the covenant while Moses was still with them, but when they are comfortably settled in their homes and life is good, they could easily become corrupt. Can they just rest on the assurance of past promises and live however they want? No!

- God will make sure they perish from the land and are destroyed.
- They will be scattered among the nations with only a few survivors.
- There they will have their fill of idol worship.

Moses is speaking prophetically. That is precisely what happened. So often we go through the same cycle: God blesses, and we get complacent and forget about him. Judgment brings great loss. God may let us pursue the "idol" that was so important to us, but often we reach bottom and do what Moses prophesied: Seek the Lord and obey him once again.

Have you drifted from the Lord? Are you experiencing his discipline? Are you beginning to seek him again? Are you wondering why you haven't found him? The promise to find is for those who seek him with *all* their heart and *all* their soul. That means nothing else is more important. It is more than just praying for relief from hardship; it is devoting yourself to soak in his word and his presence, and take advantage of every opportunity to draw close to him. I have seen too many people get discouraged and give up seeking God because they half-heartedly go about it, and then wonder when he doesn't fix everything right away.

God is a consuming fire – but he is also merciful, and he is faithful to his covenant. Even in the midst of our sin he doesn't abandon us. You have a covenant with God sealed with the blood of Jesus, which you reaffirm every time you share in the Lord's Supper. How are you doing on your part of that covenant?

In verse 27 Moses said they *would* be destroyed – in 31 he says they will *not* be destroyed. A contradiction? Which is it? I believe *individuals* would be destroyed – but God will not destroy his people. He remembers his covenant and will always have a remnant.

## THE ONLY TRUE GOD
*[32] Ask now about the former days, long before your time, from the day God created human beings on the earth; ask from one end of the heavens to the other. Has anything so great as this ever happened, or has anything like it ever been heard of?[33] Has any other people heard the voice of God speaking out of fire, as you have, and lived? [34] Has any god ever tried to take for himself one nation out of another nation, by testings, by signs and wonders, by war, by a mighty hand and an outstretched arm, or by great and awesome deeds, like all the things the Lord your God did for you in Egypt before your very eyes?*

We are part of what is called salvation history: the story of God's work with us since creation. Today there is an appalling ignorance of church history, and even less knowledge of all God did in the centuries before Christ. There are many competing religions out there, and many who believe they are all valid paths to God. But think about the amazing things that happened in the Old Testament, and the life and sacrificial death of Jesus. These are utterly unique. Let your faith be strengthened by the consistent testimony of the Bible, and stay informed about how God continues to work in his people.

## THE BOTTOM LINE: OBEDIENCE
*[35] You were shown these things so that you might know that the Lord is God; besides him there is no other.[36] From heaven he*

made you hear his voice to discipline you. On earth he showed you his great fire, and you heard his words from out of the fire. [37] Because he loved your ancestors and chose their descendants after them, he brought you out of Egypt by his Presence and his great strength,* [38] to drive out before you nations greater and stronger than you and to bring you into their land to give it to you for your inheritance, as it is today.*

[39] *Acknowledge and take to heart this day that the Lord is God in heaven above and on the earth below. There is no other.* [40] *Keep his decrees and commands, which I am giving you today, so that it may go well with you and your children after you and that you may live long in the land the Lord your God gives you for all time.*

The bottom line of reflecting on all these mighty acts should be a solid faith that the Lord alone is God. He has loved and chosen us, delivered us from bondage, and disciplined us as a father. He has blessed us and given us an inheritance. He desires that everything would go well for us and we would enjoy a long life. That blessing will then flow down to your children. What is your part?

- Acknowledge who he is and worship him. Take it to heart. Let it move from head knowledge down to your heart in a living relationship.

- Keep his decrees and commands. Obey him.

We have followed Israel through forty long years. They are finally poised to actually take possession of the long-promised land flowing with milk and honey. Moses has done everything he can to prepare them. God has provided everything they need to make it. If you know the story, things didn't turn out so great. Whatever furnace you have been in, however you have suffered because of your rebellion and sin, you have the opportunity now to move ahead in faith and live in the abundance God has for you. Moses is sharing his heart with them. Think carefully about what he is saying.

# 40

# THE *SHEMA* – HEART OF THE JEWISH RELIGION
## *DEUTERONOMY 6:4-19*

Moses may not have been aware of it, but this is the heart of the Jewish religion. If you ignore the chapter divisions (which were inserted much later), verse four clearly starts a new message in his series of final discourses. Verses 4-9 are the famous *Shema* (Hebrew for *hear*). Devout Jews still recite verse four every morning and evening, as an oath of allegiance to God and often say the *Shema* as death approaches. Jesus was very familiar with the *Shema*, quoting it as the most important commandment.

### GOD IS ONE
*4 Hear, O Israel: The Lord our God, the Lord is one.*

As the only monotheistic religion in the world at that time, Judaism stood in stark contrast to the multitude of pagan idols and gods. God is one, the *only* one. He is not one option among many, but the *only* true God. Polytheism and syncretism (combining worship of God with another religion) is also prohibited. He is *our* God – making it personal, and focusing on Israel's special place as God's chosen people. Now, by his grace, all believers can say he is *our* God.

In a tantalizing reference to the trinity, the Hebrew word used for *one* (*echad*) can imply unity in diversity. The various parts of the tabernacle made *one* tent (Exodus 26:6), and husband and wife are *one* flesh (Genesis 2:24). God said *"Let **us** make man in **our** image"* (Genesis 1:26). Indeed, the very word used for God here (Elohim) is the plural from of El. He exists in three distinct persons – but is clearly one God, not three. The trinity is a mystery that is affirmed by the Scriptures, and, unknowingly, by Jews, every time they say the *Shema*!

After that clear statement of who God is, Moses gives our required response, the command that summarizes the law:

⁵ *Love the Lord your God with all your heart and with all your soul and with all your strength.*

## GOD A LOVING FATHER

Relationship comes before legalistic obedience. The greatest was love, even under the law! We don't tend to think of love as a significant part of the Old Covenant, but God was just as much a god of love back then. As a loving father he led them in the pillar of cloud and fire. He provided manna and water. He protected them. He promised amazing blessings if they would only be faithful to him and his commands.

> *The Lord your God, who is going before you, will fight for you, as he did for you in Egypt, before your very eyes, and in the wilderness. There you saw how **the Lord your God carried you, as a father carries his son**, all the way you went until you reached this place."*
>
> *In spite of this, you did not trust in the Lord your God, who went ahead of you on your journey, in fire by night and in a cloud by day, to search out*

> *places for you to camp and to show you the way you should go.* (Deuteronomy 1:30-33)

God wanted a people for himself, a bride, much like a man courts a lady and longs for her love in return. He expected them to respond to his care with love and trust, but we haven't seen much evidence of Israel's love for God these forty years in the wilderness; it has been mostly complaining about him and walking in fear of his judgment. Making it long-term in the Promised Land will take more than grudging obedience. Many "Christians" have found that legalistic obedience doesn't last: resentment builds, and eventually rebellion. Our obedience should flow out of our love.

## TOTAL, UNCONDITIONAL, LOVE

The Hebrew word used for love (*'ahebh*) refers to the duty to care for and cherish someone, typically in the context of a husband/wife or parent/child relationship. There is no sense of sexual or even romantic love. When the Old Testament was translated into Greek (the Septuagint) they used a form of *agape* (God's unconditional love) in this verse.

God calls for total love on our part:

- Spirit: *With all our heart,* our emotions, the very depth of who we are. Our devotion must be undivided.

- Soul: *With all our soul*. The will.

- Body: *With all our strength*. Love expressed in obedience and actions. Not just words, but total dedication in all we do.

The importance of this command was strongly affirmed by Jesus:

> *One of the teachers of the law came and heard them debating. Noticing that Jesus had given them a good answer, he asked him, "Of all the commandments, which is the most important?"*
>
> *"The most important one," answered Jesus, "is this: 'Hear, O Israel: The Lord our God, the Lord is one. Love the Lord your God with all your heart and with all your soul and with all your mind and with all your strength.' The second is this: 'Love your neighbor as yourself.' There is no commandment greater than these."*
>
> *"Well said, teacher," the man replied. "You are right in saying that God is one and there is no other but him. To love him with all your heart, with all your understanding and with all your strength, and to love your neighbor as yourself is more important than all burnt offerings and sacrifices."*
>
> *When Jesus saw that he had answered wisely, he said to him, "You are not far from the kingdom of God." And from then on no one dared ask him any more questions* (Mark 12:28-34).

Jesus directly quotes the *Shema*, adding *"with all your mind."* For the second command (love your neighbor), Jesus cites Leviticus 19:18. In the parallel passage (Matthew 22:40) Jesus makes the remarkable statement: *"All the Law and the Prophets hang on these two commandments."* In the parable of the Good Samaritan, when the teacher of the law cited them as the summary of the law, Jesus said: *"Do this and you will live."*

How are you doing on your love for God? Do you even have a concept of what it means to love him? If it is that important, I believe he will help you understand and live out that love if you sincerely ask him. By nature we are self-centered, so one of the key lessons of life is learning to love with agape love, not the romantic, erotic love as portrayed in movies and on TV. To teach us, God will often bring people who are difficult to love into our lives. Marriage and family, along with the close relationships within the body of Christ, are great places to learn love.

## THE CENTRAL PLACE OF THE WORD

*[6] These commandments that I give you today are to be on your hearts.*

The first essential step to success is love for God. The second is to move God's word from the head to the heart; to meditate on it and have it before us continually, central in our thoughts, so it will shape our lives and instruct our daily decisions.

*[7] Impress them on your children. Talk about them when you sit at home and when you walk along the road, when you lie down and when you get up. [8] Tie them as symbols on your hands and bind them on your foreheads. [9] Write them on the doorframes of your houses and on your gates.*

If you know any observant Jews, you have probably seen the *mezuzah* (Hebrew for doorframe) next to the front door. That little box contains a parchment copy of the *Shema*. To bind the law to their hands and forehead, phylacteries (little boxes of scriptures, Hebrew: *tefillin*), are tied on with leather straps. They are typically used by devout Jews only in prayer, so you may not have seen them. Is that effective? Honestly, I don't think so, and I don't think it was what God intended in this command. It keeps the law external – in a box! Not that different from us having a beautiful Bible on the coffee table or shelf. Jesus addressed the dangers of external display in Matthew 23:5, in his condemnation of the Pharisees and teachers of the law: *Everything they do is done for people to see: They make their phylacteries wide and the tassels on their garments long.* Instead, the Word should guide everything we do with our hands, and be a filter for everything that comes into our heads.

God's word is to hold a prominent place in our homes and families. It should be a central topic of conversation with our children. Impressing it on them means much more than just reading them the Bible; it is explaining the Scripture and living it out. They should see us giving the word priority in our daily lives. When we get together with other believers, much of our fellowship should be around the word.

How about you? What part does Scripture play in your family life? With the omnipresent smart phone and endless entertainment, does the word of God get more than a few minutes? If we are serious about loving God we are going to be serious about what he has to say.

That is the end of the *Shema*, but not the end of Moses' message.

## THE DANGER OF ABUNDANCE

*[10] When the Lord your God brings you into the land he swore to your fathers, to Abraham, Isaac and Jacob, to give you—a land with large, flourishing cities you did not build, [11] houses filled with all kinds of good things you did not provide, wells you did not dig, and vineyards and olive groves you did not plant—then when you eat and are satisfied, [12] be careful that you do not forget the Lord, who brought you out of Egypt, out of the land of slavery.*

They had never known that kind of abundance. They had suffered in slavery under the Egyptians for hundreds of years, and spent the last forty years in subsistence living, as nomads in the wilderness. Imagine thinking about large, flourishing cities! It's like someone from a small village in the developing world about to go to New York City! Houses filled with good things! Something other than manna to eat! God has a good life prepared for them!

People often move out of poverty when they come to Christ. I have known many people who endured great hardship to find a better life in the United States, and many inmates thinking about life after release. There is nothing wrong with that! God wants to bless us – not in the greedy, excessive way that prosperity preachers promise, but providing a good life for us. He even longs to plunder things of the world for us; nothing he promised Israel here came by the work of their hands. They would fight for them, but others had done the work; others had built the cities, furnished lovely houses, dug wells, and planted all kinds of fruit-bearing plants. Now Israel would come in and reap the benefits.

## DON'T FORGET GOD IN THE GOOD TIMES!

There is a huge danger in the things of the world. It is so easy to forget who gave them to us, and forget where we came from. We begin to think we got them by the work of our hands, become proud, and so engrossed in enjoying them that we forget the first two things Moses just talked about: loving God, and keeping his word central, which keeps the good things he gives us in perspective. It is a constant struggle to resist getting caught up in the "stuff." Singing about loving God, fervently proclaiming "I love you Lord" in church, and reading the Bible for fifteen minutes with our family won't do it. I fear this is where much of American Christianity is at: God has blessed us – and we have forgotten him.

## SOME COUNSEL TO KEEP US ON TRACK

*¹³ Fear the Lord your God, serve him only and take your oaths in his name.*

- Do you have a healthy fear of God?
- Do you realize he could take away all your goodies if he wanted to?
- Do you serve him? Are you actively involved in his work, even if you have a full-time secular job? *Serve* can also be translated worship. Our service to God *is* worship, perhaps more important than the worship bands that fill our churches today.

*¹⁴ Do not follow other gods, the gods of the peoples around you; ¹⁵ for the Lord your God, who is among you, is a jealous God and his anger will burn against you, and he will destroy you from the face of the land.*

- What are the gods of the people around you?
- What would be involved in following them?
- Have you done anything to arouse God's jealousy by running after one of those gods?

We may think the threat of being destroyed was only for Israel. We certainly see it happening in the Old Testament, but we seem comfortably insulated from his anger by Jesus' love. Don't be deceived – it may be delayed, but we still face judgment, where we will have to account for all we have done.

*¹⁶ Do not put the Lord your God to the test as you did at Massah.*

Israel tested God at Massah by complaining about the lack of water. Grumbling and complaining are one way of testing God, and he doesn't like it. Seeing how much we can get away with while maintaining his favor is another way. Jesus cited this verse in resisting Satan's temptation. Is the devil tempting you to test God? Are you putting God to the test in some way right now?

*$^{17}$ Be sure to keep the commands of the Lord your God and the stipulations and decrees he has given you. $^{18}$ Do what is right and good in the Lord's sight, so that it may go well with you and you may go in and take over the good land the Lord promised on oath to your ancestors, $^{19}$ thrusting out all your enemies before you, as the Lord said.*

It is so important that Moses will keep repeating it: Obey God's commands. When we do, it will go well with us. We will experience the blessings of God's promises, take over what previously belonged to the devil, and thrust out all our enemies through God's power.

Following Christ is remarkably simple, though incredibly hard. So many people prefer a religion of works. If we can check off the right boxes (went to church, read the Bible every day, prayed fifteen minutes each morning), and avoid the worst sins (no porn, no booze, no cursing) we feel we are doing okay. It is so much harder to deal with our heart and learn what it means to love God and those around us, but it is infinitely more rewarding. For thousands of years the *Shema* has daily reminded Jews of what is most important. Follow it, so that it will go well with you.

# 41

## WHEN...NOT IF
### *DEUTERONOMY 7*

Which is it? God's absolute sovereignty? Or man's free will? Or both? The Bible clearly shows God powerfully working on our behalf, but also our need to respond to him. God has chosen to work in partnership with us, which is an awesome and humbling thought in itself! Prayer is one of the clearest expressions of the part we have to play, but it is great to know that God has plans which nothing will change. For example, despite all the unbelief and opposition Jesus experienced, nothing could stop God's plan of salvation. And despite Israel's persistent rebellion on the exodus, God *will* bring a people into the Promised Land. This portion of Moses' final messages to Israel starts with an encouraging and dramatic affirmation of that.

### WHEN – NOT IF
*¹When the Lord your God brings you into the land you are entering to possess and drives out before you many nations— the Hittites, Girgashites, Amorites, Canaanites, Perizzites, Hivites and Jebusites, seven nations larger and stronger than you— ² and when the Lord your God has delivered them over to you and you have defeated them...*

The word *if* appears nowhere in these verses. Instead we see the word *when* – twice.

God didn't deliver them from Egypt and bring them forty long years through the wilderness to leave them on the other side of the Jordan. The land was promised them, and he will make sure they get it. He *will* bring them into it. He *will* deliver the inhabitants over to them. He *will* drive out those pagan nations. He *will* fight for Israel and defeat the enemy.

It's all about God. On their own, the task would be daunting. Each of these seven nations was larger and stronger than Israel, but that's no problem. I can picture God smiling as he says that, because it will be obvious to everyone that the only possible way to overcome them is through God's power.

Are there things God has clearly promised that you have put in the "if" category? Get rid of the uncertainty! If God says "when," he means it! It will happen! What are you facing that is bigger and stronger than you? Have you let it intimidate you? Start praising God and anticipating his awesome work on your behalf. Expect him to deliver those enemies into your hand! It's not a question of if – but when! Just make sure you are moving into the right land and confronting the right enemy. God sets the agenda. It's his plan. We don't decide what we want to possess and then declare that God is going to give it to us.

Isn't it encouraging to be reminded of God's sovereign power and plans? But there is more. Now we get to our part.

## A CALL TO HOLINESS

*Then you must destroy them totally. Make no treaty with them, and show them no mercy. ³ Do not intermarry with them. Do not give your daughters to their sons or take their daughters for your sons, ⁴ for they will turn your children away from following me to serve other gods, and the Lord's anger will burn against you and will quickly destroy you. ⁵ This is what you are to do to them: Break down their altars, smash their sacred stones, cut down their Asherah poles and burn their idols in the fire. ⁶ For you are a people holy to the Lord your God. The Lord your God has chosen you out of all the peoples on the face of the earth to be his people, his treasured possession.*

God has done his part. He died on the cross to forgive your sins, and gave you his Holy Spirit to empower you to obey him. That is awesome. Now it is time for you to step up and do your part. Compared with what he has done, it doesn't seem that hard.

- The enemy has been defeated. Now every trace of him must be destroyed, like mopping up every single cancer cell: Just one could kill you. Nothing can be left that could allow a foothold for the devil. His power has been destroyed on the cross; now we must choose to clean house and destroy everything that belonged to him. Is there anything you can think of that needs to go?

- This is not the time for love and mercy. We can't make compromises with sin or the devil. He will take advantage of the slightest hesitation on your part. Watch for some of these typical excuses:
    - "Just one drink won't hurt."
    - "I can watch "R" rated movies without sinning."
    - "This girl is so nice. I may be able to lead her to Christ if we're dating!"
    - "Just once I can "borrow" this from my job."

- Marrying an unbeliever is prohibited. Period. Don't date them, no matter how wonderful they are. Don't get taken in by someone who is "spiritually open." Don't even think about it. Do everything you can to encourage your children to date and marry believers. Unbelievers will turn their hearts away from the Lord.

- Clean house. Remove every trace of idolatry or false religion. Has the TV become an idol to you? Are you unable to resist the sensuality of the internet? Are there movies, books, magazines, or pictures you need to get rid of? Be ruthless.

You may be saved, but you can still incite the Lord's wrath by making compromises with the world and failing to live in holiness:

> *You adulterous people, don't you know that friendship with the world means enmity against God? Therefore, anyone who chooses to be a friend of the world becomes an enemy of God* (James 4:4).

> *"No one can serve two masters. Either you will hate the one and love the other, or you will be devoted to the one and despise the other. You cannot serve both God and money"* (Jesus – Matthew 6:24).

If you fail to take God seriously, he may become your enemy and destroy you. Don't think it can't happen. Just look at Israel's history. Too often the devil gets blamed for the destruction, when it is actually God's judgment on our sin.

We smile at the archaic KJV translation of 1 Peter 2:9 that says we are a "peculiar" people. We don't want to be different! We want to be like everyone else! But you are not like everyone else! You are a Christian! You are part of God's holy people! He purchased you by his blood, and you belong to him – assuming you have given him your life.

## GOD CHOSE YOU

Many Christians struggle with the idea of election, but there it is, in verse six. God chose them. They didn't choose God. He came to them. He chose them to be his treasured possession! Does that sound too controlling to you? Does it make you squirm a little? Do you want to bring up the arguments against election? Wait a minute! What could be better than being God's treasured possession! Why on earth wouldn't you want to be chosen by God? You should be praising him for it!

But election isn't a source of smugness or pride. Look at what he says next:

*⁷ The Lord did not set his affection on you and choose you because you were more numerous than other peoples, for you were the fewest of all peoples. ⁸ But it was because the Lord loved you and kept the oath he swore to your ancestors that he brought you out with a mighty hand and redeemed you from the land of slavery, from the power of Pharaoh king of Egypt. ⁹ Know therefore that the Lord your God is God; he is the faithful God, keeping his covenant of love to a thousand generations of those who love him and keep his commandments. ¹⁰ But*

*those who hate him he will repay to their face by destruction;*
  *he will not be slow to repay to their face those who hate him.*

*¹¹ Therefore, take care to follow the commands, decrees and laws I give you today.*

Did God choose you, call you, and save you because you were so special? Nope. There was nothing special about Israel, either. They were a small, insignificant tribe. Their most recent occupation had been "slave." The lives of the patriarchs – Abraham, Jacob, and his sons – were far from perfect. It is about

God's love and faithfulness to Abraham, who, despite his flaws, believed God and walked with him.

Isn't it great to think of God *"setting his affection"* on you? If you love him and keep his commands, those blessings will flow down to your children and their descendants. But if you hate God by snubbing him and doing your own thing, you will bring a curse on your children, and experience devastation in your life now.

## NOT BECAUSE OF YOUR RIGHTEOUSNESS

Later on in another message Moses returns to the same theme of why God chose them (9:4-6):

*After the Lord your God has driven them out before you, do not say to yourself, "The Lord has brought me here to take possession of this land because of my righteousness." No, it is on account of the wickedness of these nations that the Lord is going to drive them out before you. It is not because of your righteousness or your integrity that you are going in to take possession of their land; but on account of the wickedness of these nations, the Lord your God will drive them out before you, to accomplish what he swore to your fathers, to Abraham, Isaac and Jacob. Understand, then, that it is not because of your righteousness that the Lord your God is giving you this good land to possess, for you are a stiff-necked people.*

Do you think repeating three times *"It is not because of your righteousness"* should get the message across? Election is not based on works. God chooses us and saves us, and then we respond with good works. Our righteousness is as filthy rags. We are not much better than the stiff-necked Israelites.

God wasn't being arbitrary in destroying the nations in the Promised Land. They were fully deserving of his judgment. It was their wickedness – rather than Israel's righteousness – that resulted in their destruction. Just in case they were getting too smug, in the following verses (in Deuteronomy 7) Moses reminds them of what happened with the golden calf.

## CONDITIONAL BLESSINGS

*<sup>12</sup> If you pay attention to these laws and are careful to follow them, then the Lord your God will keep his covenant of love with you, as he swore to your ancestors. <sup>13</sup> He will love you and bless you and increase your numbers. He will bless the fruit of your womb, the crops of your land—your grain, new wine and olive oil—the calves of your herds and the lambs of your flocks in the land he swore to your ancestors to give you. <sup>14</sup> You will be blessed more than any other people; none of your men or women will be childless, nor will any of your livestock be without young. <sup>15</sup> The Lord will keep you free from every disease. He will not inflict on you the horrible diseases you knew in Egypt, but he will inflict them on all who hate you. <sup>16</sup> You must destroy all the peoples the Lord your God gives over to you. Do not look on them with pity and do not serve their gods, for that will be a snare to you.*

IF...they carefully follow God's word and obey him, destroying all the pagans and any trace of their religion, they are assured of tremendous blessing. But they are conditional on their obedience. Most covenants are conditional. God will always be faithful to his part, but failure to follow God fully will result in snares in their lives. Far too many Christians live with those snares because of their incomplete obedience.

Is it really worth holding on to those things of the world? If Israel does things God's way, they are promised:

- His love.
- His blessings.
- Increased numbers.

- No infertility; the fruit of the womb will be blessed - both human and animal!
- Crops and herds will be exceedingly productive.
- God will keep them free from every disease! Not just healing; this is true preventative care! God has the ability to keep us disease-free!

On the other hand, he will afflict their enemies with disease. What?! God can bring about sickness? That's what it says – as a judgment on those who hate him.

These are the kinds of scriptures prosperity preachers love to grab on to. Unfortunately, they overlook the need to live according to God's word, which precludes greed and a self-centered life. Yes, like a good father, God delights to bless those who are faithful to him, but let's stay balanced.

## DON'T BE AFRAID!

*[17] You may say to yourselves, "These nations are stronger than we are. How can we drive them out?" [18] But do not be afraid of them; remember well what the Lord your God did to Pharaoh and to all Egypt. [19] You saw with your own eyes the great trials, the signs and wonders, the mighty hand and outstretched arm, with which the Lord your God brought you out. The Lord your God will do the same to all the peoples you now fear.[20] Moreover, the Lord your God will send the hornet among them until even the survivors who hide from you have perished. [21] Do not be terrified by them, for the Lord your God, who is among you, is a great and awesome God.*

Does the enemy dwelling in your "land" seem too strong to drive out? Have you failed repeatedly as you tried psychotherapy, medicine, and self-help programs? Do you live in fear of the enemy? Is the alcohol overpowering? The drugs too addicting?

The pornography too gratifying? The money too seductive? The women too enticing?

Don't think about yourself and your ability to overcome that sin. Think about God. He not only is *among* you, as he was with Israel – he dwells *within* you! Think about how great and awesome he is! Think about his love for you, and let his perfect love cast out all fear. Trust him to come in and cast out that enemy who has enslaved you. Read the Bible again to see all he has done in the past. Read testimonies, and feed your soul with deep fellowship and solid teaching in a good church. What he has done for others, he will do for you!

## SANCTIFICATION TAKES TIME – AND EFFORT

*22 The Lord your God will drive out those nations before you, little by little. You will not be allowed to eliminate them all at once, or the wild animals will multiply around you. 23 But the Lord your God will deliver them over to you, throwing them into great confusion until they are destroyed. 24 He will give their kings into your hand, and you will wipe out their names from under heaven. No one will be able to stand up against you; you will destroy them. 25 The images of their gods you are to burn in the fire. Do not covet the silver and gold on them, and do not take it for yourselves, or you will be ensnared by it, for it is detestable to the Lord your God. 26 Do not bring a detestable thing into your house or you, like it, will be set apart for destruction. Regard it as vile and utterly detest it, for it is set apart for destruction.*

It would be great if God instantly removed all sinful desire and gave us complete victory. It would have been nice if Israel could wake up one morning to find all the inhabitants of the land gone, and fields overflowing with produce. But there would be many battles, and hard work planting and harvesting crops.

God reveals an important principle of sanctification here: He frees us from sin little by little. It keeps us humble and dependent on him, but it also allows us to develop new habits and deepen our understanding of who he is and what he wants for us. In their case, if the land was instantly cleared, it could be taken over by wild animals. In your life, if every trace of the enemy were instantly removed, you probably wouldn't be ready to walk in that level of holiness. It could open a door to the devil.

Trust God's timing. Work with him. Watch for his hand. Is there confusion in some area of your life? Maybe God is working to clean that up. Trust him that no one will be able to stand against you. What a tremendous promise!

Two important warnings are given about things that can easily trip us up:

- Watch out for gold and silver; especially money that has been tainted by sin. Beware of coveting other peoples' money. Notice that God didn't promise them riches. Good crops and herds, yes. Silver and gold, no. Don't get caught up in money.

- Be careful about what you bring into your house. Today, that especially means what comes in over the TV or internet; I am amazed at the filth that comes into many homes unchecked. But it could be other things as well: watch *who* you let into your home, especially how they relate to your young children. Watch the kinds of food you let in. Be vigilant. Be a watchman over your family.

## IS THIS THE TIME?

It was just about time for Israel. Years of preparation were about to pay off. God longed for a people who would bring him glory and be his treasured possession. The road had not been easy. The one man he could really count on all those years was about to die. But God had done his part. Soon it will become apparent how it will all work out.

Is this your time? Has the road been rocky? Can you see God's hand faithfully at work through the years? Is this the time to bring it all together, get serious about obedience, and start to experience God's blessings? God's word is full of promises for you. It's not a question of if...but when. Maybe that time is now.

# 42

# THE DANGER OF PROSPERITY
## *DEUTERONOMY 8*

With all the great blessings God promised, how could Israel ever forget him? And we have much more than they did! How could a Christian ever forget about God? Yet I have seen it countless times: When life is tough and there is no way we can make it on our own, we are in church, reading the Bible, and on our knees. Often our richest fellowship with Jesus is during the hardest times. And God comes through in amazing ways and delivers us, heals us, and pours out his blessings. But then everything is good, and suddenly we don't have time for him anymore. We don't feel the urgency of being in church or drawing on his strength. We wouldn't say we forget about him, but we coast...until the next crisis.

Moses was very aware of that danger, and warns them about it in this chapter. It's not just about getting the blessing, the money, or the wife. It's what you do with your marriage, how you manage your money, and how you walk with God in the hard times - and the good times. It's not so much about how you start, but how you finish.

## OBEDIENCE!
*[1]Be careful to follow every command I am giving you today, so that you may live and increase and may enter and possess the land the Lord promised on oath to your ancestors.*

There it is again. The priority is obedience: having Christ as Lord, submitting your will to his, and putting the Word into practice. It's the foundation of the Christian life. Even though we are under grace now, obedience is every bit as important for us as it was for Israel. Our great advantage is the power of the Holy Spirit enabling us to obey.

## HUMBLING AND TESTING IN THE WILDERNESS
*² Remember how the Lord your God led you all the way in the wilderness these forty years, to humble and test you in order to know what was in your heart, whether or not you would keep his commands.*

As we have already seen, Israel didn't do too well on the test. They said they would keep his commands – but then failed miserably. Moses knows that if this pattern continues, they are doomed.

- Have you been in a wilderness?
- Has it been much longer than you think necessary?
- Can you accept that it is God who led you into that wilderness – and has kept you there?
- Have you sensed his leading in that desert?
- Can you see how he has humbled you in the trials?
- How has he tested you? What has it shown about your heart?

If we are honest, most of us have some pretty dark corners in our hearts. The prouder you are, and the more important your assignment from the Lord, the more he will probably need to humble you.

Have you kept obeying him even when it seemed like nothing was happening? Can you be faithful to your wife - and to God - when it seems your marriage is dying? When all the feeling is gone? Or when she is seriously ill? Can you continue to trust him when you keep getting turned down for jobs and the money is running out? How about when one door for ministry after another gets slammed in your face and you feel misunderstood by everybody?

## MAN DOES NOT LIVE ON BREAD ALONE

*³ He humbled you, causing you to hunger and then feeding you with manna, which neither you nor your ancestors had known, to teach you that man does not live on bread alone but on every word that comes from the mouth of the Lord.*

God caused them to hunger. He purposely put them in a place where there was no food. It was part of his humbling. If there is always plenty to eat, there is no need for God to supply manna. It is humbling when a man can't feed his own family and has to rely on handouts. Or go out and collect manna each morning.

This is a verse Jesus used as he resisted Satan's temptation to change stones into bread. Don't get caught up in the bread. Food has become an idol for many people; they live to eat instead of eating to live. There are almost infinite varieties of food. We have well-stocked grocery stores where we live in Costa Rica, but I find it almost overwhelming when I visit the States and there are dozens of coffee creamers and a case full of every imaginable type and flavor of yogurt.

The true bread for our souls, what really feeds us, is the Word of God. Every word he has spoken is important; not just the highlighted verses we like to quote, but every word that has come out of his mouth. Don't settle for the bread Satan will try to give you, for the world's materialism, or for the spectacular. Go deep, and learn to feed on the Word of God.

Has God caused you to hunger lately? Has he put you in a place of scarcity so you can get your priorities straight and realize that physical provision is not most important? He won't let you starve! Have you been willing to go out and get the manna to sustain you? These trials may be intended to humble you. The sooner you get that message and stop trying to lift yourself up and do it on your own, the sooner the humbling can stop.

*[4] Your clothes did not wear out and your feet did not swell during these forty years.*

That is miraculous. Somehow God kept their clothes intact for forty years! They were walking around in the desert – and didn't have Nikes or hiking boots! Yet their feet didn't swell. Those little things should have been signs of God's love and instilled a deep trust in his provision.

Have you experienced God miraculously keeping an old car running? Or protecting you from illness? I have repeatedly seen Christians get years of service from appliances that break down for everyone else. Part of his blessing is making what we have last; not necessarily giving us the latest fashion all the time. Fashions surely changed a lot in forty years – but we are not slaves to fashion, are we? We don't throw away good clothes just because they are a little dated. We don't get a new car or refrigerator just because ours doesn't have the latest features. That would be an insult to God, who has graciously given us an extended warranty – free!

## IS GOD DISCIPLINING YOU?

*[5] Know then in your heart that as a man disciplines his son, so the Lord your God disciplines you.*

Are you a father? What has been your experience disciplining your son? Unfortunately, that is a challenge for many men. We tend to go overboard on harshness – or back off and let his mother handle it. Discipline is different than correction or punishment; it is drawing alongside him, counseling him, gently correcting him, and, yes, administering consequences when he doesn't get the message. Many of us lacked loving discipline from our fathers, so we have no idea how to discipline our own children. God intended us to learn how he works from the experience with our parents. If you didn't have that, now you can reflect on how God disciplines you, and apply those principles to your children.

Could some of what you have been experiencing recently be the Lord disciplining you? It is one thing to mentally agree with that, but Moses directs them to know it *"in your heart."* That allows God's love and his father heart to touch you. Discipline is rarely fun, but it helps to understand what is going on, and to know that your loving Father's hand is behind it:

> *In your struggle against sin, you have not yet resisted to the point of shedding your blood. And have you completely forgotten this word of encouragement that addresses you as a father addresses his son? It says,*
>
> *"My son, do not make light of the Lord's discipline,*
> *and do not lose heart when he rebukes you, because the Lord disciplines the one he loves, and he chastens everyone he accepts as his son."*
>
> *Endure hardship as discipline; God is treating you as his children. For what children are not disciplined by their father? If you are not disciplined—and everyone undergoes discipline—then you are not legitimate, not true sons and daughters at all. Moreover, we have all*

> had human fathers who disciplined us and we respected them for it. How much more should we submit to the Father of spirits and live! They disciplined us for a little while as they thought best; but God disciplines us for our good, in order that we may share in his holiness. No discipline seems pleasant at the time, but painful. Later on, however, it produces a harvest of righteousness and peace for those who have been trained by it (Hebrews 12:4-11).

Be encouraged that God is doing it out of love. Submit to it, and let him do the deep work he longs for in your life.

## BLESSINGS ARE ON THE WAY!

> [6] Observe the commands of the Lord your God, walking in obedience to him and revering him. [7] For the Lord your God is bringing you into a good land—a land with brooks, streams, and deep springs gushing out into the valleys and hills; [8] a land with wheat and barley, vines and fig trees, pomegranates, olive oil and honey; [9] a land where bread will not be scarce and you will lack nothing; a land where the rocks are iron and you can dig copper out of the hills.

That sounds good! After forty years in the desert, eating manna, this is truly something to look forward to. It is an incentive to keep walking in obedience. God doesn't delight in withholding these blessings from us – but he wants to make sure we are ready to handle them.

You may be in a desert place right now, and more than ready for some relief. Keep on walking in obedience to the Lord and in reverence of him. God wants to bring *you* into a good land as well.

Believe it or not, the hardest part comes once you are in the midst of those blessings.

## DON'T FORGET GOD
*10 When you have eaten and are satisfied, praise the Lord your God for the good land he has given you.*

First, realize that the blessings are a gift from God. Worship him. Thank him for them. Praise him for his goodness. Keep your eyes on him.

*11 Be careful that you do not forget the Lord your God, failing to observe his commands, his laws and his decrees that I am giving you this day. 12 Otherwise, when you eat and are satisfied, when you build fine houses and settle down, 13 and when your herds and flocks grow large and your silver and gold increase and all you have is multiplied, 14 then your heart will become proud and you will forget the Lord your God, who brought you out of Egypt, out of the land of slavery.*

Wealth and success dull our spiritual senses. When we start experiencing material blessings, we want more. We get so caught up with the goodies that we forget where *we* came from, and where *they* come from. We forget all that God has done for us, and our hearts become proud. We get lax on obedience. We were anxious to do things right so we would get God's favor, and experience his help and blessings. But now that we have them, it just doesn't seem that important any more.

If you are in that place of abundant blessing right now, have you slacked off on your walk with God? Has pride subtly come into your heart? If you are honest, is God one of the last things on your mind? Oh, of course you go to church and pay your tithe and do what is required. But are you feeling self-satisfied? Be careful!

## Humbling and testing

*[15]He led you through the vast and dreadful wilderness, that thirsty and waterless land, with its venomous snakes and scorpions. He brought you water out of hard rock. [16]He gave you manna to eat in the wilderness, something your ancestors had never known, to humble and test you so that in the end it might go well with you.*

There it is again. The hard times are allowed to humble and test you. You may pass the test and experience God's blessings — but if you forget about him, it will probably be another round of humbling. Prosperity can be a bigger test than scarcity.

Look at the words Moses uses to remind them of how bad things were: *vast, dreadful, thirsty, venomous snakes, scorpions, hard rock.* When you think back on your life, are there some ugly words that would describe it? We tend to forget how bad it was, and start taking God's blessings for granted.

If you are being humbled and tested right now, remember that God has a long-range perspective on your life. He knows that in the end the discipline will have a good result. It will go well with you. And he cares enough about you that he allows the discomfort for a while.

## Pride

*[17]You may say to yourself, "My power and the strength of my hands have produced this wealth for me." [18]But remember the Lord your God, for it is he who gives you the ability to produce wealth, and so confirms his covenant, which he swore to your ancestors, as it is today.*

The delusion is that good things come to us because of our intelligence, hard work, cleverness, and strength. But whatever smarts and physical abilities you may have, God gave them to you. Don't get puffed up! Give him the glory and thank him for those blessings. When we forget about him and start claiming all the glory for ourselves, we are getting into very dangerous territory.

*[19] If you ever forget the Lord your God and follow other gods and worship and bow down to them, I testify against you today that you will surely be destroyed. [20] Like the nations the Lord destroyed before you, so you will be destroyed for not obeying the Lord your God.*

The end result of becoming prideful and forgetting God is destruction. Once we forget him we tend to replace him with other gods, usually gods of pleasure, sensuality, and materialism. Israel would become just like the nations God threw out of the land. They would follow the natural path of fallen man in a sinful world.

Are there any other gods you have let into your life? Can you remember what it was like when Jesus first saved you and your life was transformed?

- He poured out his blessings on you.
- Obedience was a joy.
- You couldn't get enough of the Bible and fellowship with God's people.

Is that a distant memory now? Is it just possible that if you are honest you would have to say you have forgotten God, and really are no different than the unsaved people around you?

Maybe you are just starting on this journey and Jesus is very real to you. Take these warnings seriously. Receive whatever testing and humbling and discipline God may have for you. You can avoid a whole lot of heartache.

Beware of prosperity and the good life. It requires maturity to manage it, and stay humble and God-focused. Don't forget God.

# 43

# Why would God command you to kill "the wife whom you love"?
## Deuteronomy 13 & 18

Our world is full of prophets. But who are you to believe? Sometimes they directly contradict each other. They can claim impressive signs and wonders. But things are not always as they appear. Moses gives us one sure sign of a false prophet in Deuteronomy 13, and raises the alarming possibility of having to choose between God and those we love the most. Then, probably in another message on another day, he gives additional teaching in chapter 18.

### The dangerous allure of prophecy and miracles

*¹If a prophet, or one who foretells by dreams, appears among you and announces to you a sign or wonder, ² and if the sign or wonder spoken of takes place, and the prophet says, "Let us follow other gods" (gods you have not known) "and let us worship them," ³ you must not listen to the words of that prophet or dreamer. The Lord your God is testing you to find out whether you love him with all your heart and with all your soul.*

God has yet another test for Israel: Do you truly love me, as the greatest commandment requires?

Could you imagine a test of your wife's love for you? Another man offers her all she is dreaming of. He is everything you are not. But if she loves you she won't pay attention to him. She knows she already has the real thing – and she has chosen to follow you. For Israel, that had meant following God when it didn't make sense and miracles were in short supply. The desert wanderings seemed endless.

Today it is often a person who claims to be a prophet, or predicts the future based on his dreams. What makes the test more difficult is the signs and wonders - yet here we see that they are no proof of authenticity. Many of us are suckers. Someone simply claims to be a prophet or receive visions, and we put aside our common sense. And if their predictions come true, especially if there are signs and wonders, we believe they must be of God. The Apostle Paul tried to open the eyes of the Corinthians who had been taken in by false apostles: *In fact, you even put up with anyone who enslaves you or exploits you or takes advantage of you or puts on airs or slaps you in the face* (2 Corinthians 11:20).

These counterfeits can be very convincing, but then they start leading you away from God in the pursuit of other gods. Back then it might have been one of the multitude of local deities. We are much too sophisticated for that, although we might be tempted by some questionable new "Christian" movement. Our other gods tend to be much more subtle. It could be the prophet himself, or some doctrine he teaches. It could be a church which has lost its first love and is caught up in its own success. Get suspicious when you start wondering where Jesus is. In these last days the deceitfulness of these gods will be greater than ever:

- *For false messiahs and false prophets will appear and perform great signs and wonders to deceive, if possible, even the elect* (Jesus, Matthew 24:24).

- *Dear friends, do not believe every spirit, but test the spirits to see whether they are from God, because many false prophets have gone out into the world* (1 John 4:1).

- *I urge you, brothers and sisters, to watch out for those who cause divisions and put obstacles in your way that are contrary to the teaching you have learned. Keep away from them. For such people are not serving our Lord Christ, but their own appetites. By smooth talk and flattery they deceive the minds of naive people* (Romans 16:17-18).

## DECEPTION PROTECTION

*⁴It is the Lord your God you must follow, and him you must revere. Keep his commands and obey him; serve him and hold fast to him.*

What is the remedy? Do we have to become detectives, ready to expose these charlatans? Not really, although there may be a place for that. But better than focusing on the negative is a vigorous and whole-hearted focus on Jesus. Now more than ever that is critical. Moses offers six ways to protect us from deception:

- **Follow the Lord.** Don't follow any man or doctrine. Don't follow a TV show or web site. Follow Jesus. Look at the Gospels to see what that meant for the early disciples – and follow their example. Make sure you're not leading the way. Don't run ahead of Jesus. Always keep your eyes on him as you walk behind him. He will prepare the way. You can't go wrong if you are following him. The apostle John echoed the need to deal decisively with anyone not following Jesus: *Anyone who runs ahead and does not continue in the teaching of Christ does not have God; whoever continues in the teaching has both the Father* *and the Son. If anyone comes to you and does not bring this teaching, do not take them into your house or welcome them. Anyone who welcomes them shares in their wicked work* (2 John 9-11).

- **Revere (or fear) him.** Have a wholesome respect for his lordship and power. Remember, he is also judge. Those who lead others astray will be judged more harshly. It is great that Jesus is our friend, but he is also God almighty. Don't lose that awe for him. Too many church services today are a casual hangout: texting on the cellphone, sipping coffee purchased at the lobby coffee bar, chatting with friends, and walking in and out as we feel like it. Where is the reverence for God?

- **Keep his commands.** That requires knowing what they are, which means spending significant time in the Bible, and regularly reminding ourselves (and others) of them. Examine your daily walk to see how you are doing. It's not a matter of how much Bible knowledge you have, but how much you are putting into practice. Do you fear you will scare people away from church if you start preaching that God requires something of us?

- **Obey him.** Obedience is far more than legalistic bondage to every word in the Bible. As Jesus taught when he spoke about the deeper implications of commands against adultery and murder (Matthew 5), we must obey the continual promptings of the Holy Spirit. Some who proudly point to their legalistic obedience to Scripture are actually the worst sinners. Just talk to a Pharisee.

- **Serve him.** We are not talking about a cloistered religion that is consumed with religious ritual. One of the best protections from sin – and deception – is actively serving the Lord. That is when the Holy Spirit most freely flows through you. Of course, if you are really following Jesus, you can't help but be busy serving him. That doesn't have to be full-time Christian service; even in a secular job we should work as unto the Lord, and be available for him to use.

- **Hold fast to him.** For dear life, and out of a deep love. That means staying in fellowship with him, knowing his presence, and not letting anything come between you.

How would you say your church is doing? What is your impression of Christians in general? Are we leaving ourselves wide open to deception? How are you doing in each of those areas? What steps can you take to put things in order?

## PURGE THE EVIL

*[5] That prophet or dreamer must be put to death for inciting rebellion against the Lord your God, who brought you out of Egypt and redeemed you from the land of slavery. That prophet or dreamer tried to turn you from the way the Lord your God commanded you to follow. You must purge the evil from among you.*

Here is where the judging part comes in. In the context of properly exercised authority in the Body of Christ, there needs to be scrupulous examination of prophets and others who claim special gifting from the Lord. That is happening on a very limited scale, but the internet has opened floodgates of error. We need to purge our libraries, apps, and internet bookmarks of anyone who is questionable. And, as the Body of Christ, we need to establish some kind of accountability for the proliferation of prophets in our midst.

We're not talking about killing anyone here. That has happened too often in the history of the church– and often godly men died at the hands of the very deceivers. We rightfully hesitate to say someone is inciting rebellion just because their teaching is a little off. But Moses clarifies rebellion as anything that *"turns you away from the way the Lord your God commanded you to follow."* That means any deviation from the six points we just looked at, or from the "straight and narrow" path.

Although the purging here refers to false prophets, God wants all evil purged, and I think there is a lot that needs to go. But doing that often puts us in some very uncomfortable situations with Christian brothers, friends – and even our closest family members.

## STONE YOUR WIFE?
*⁶ If your very own brother, or your son or daughter, or the wife you love, or your closest friend secretly entices you, saying, "Let us go and worship other gods" (gods that neither you nor your ancestors have known, ⁷ gods of the peoples around you, whether near or far, from one end of the land to the other), ⁸ do not yield to them or listen to them. Show them no pity. Do not spare them or shield them. ⁹ You must certainly put them to death. Your hand must be the first in putting them to death, and then the hands of all the people. ¹⁰ Stone them to death, because they tried to turn you away from the Lord your God, who brought you out of Egypt, out of the land of slavery. ¹¹ Then all Israel will hear and be afraid, and no one among you will do such an evil thing again.*

To me, this is one of the harshest passages in Scripture; worse than plucking out our offending eye or Israel wiping out the pagan nations in Canaan. God commands me to be the first to pick up the stone to kill my wife or son if they try to pull me away from the Lord! There is no time allowed for them to come back to their senses. No mercy. No tolerance, as we accept that they have chosen another path to follow. Nope. Kill them. Don't shield them. Don't listen to them. Be the first to cast the stone. An example must be given. Appropriate fear of the Lord must be maintained.

Jesus predicted family strife for his followers: *You will be betrayed even by parents, brothers and sisters, relatives and friends, and they will put some of you to death* (Luke 21:16). Notice he doesn't say to kill them, but we must stand firm and not let them pull us away from Jesus. Hold fast to him, even if your wife threatens to leave you – or kill you.

When was the last time you heard balanced teaching on handling children who are running after other gods? The church needs to provide clear guidance, since these situations are likely to increase.

## ONE REBELLIOUS TOWN BRINGS GOD'S WRATH ON EVERYONE

*¹² If you hear it said about one of the towns the Lord your God is giving you to live in ¹³ that troublemakers have arisen among you and have led the people of their town astray, saying, "Let us go and worship other gods" (gods you have not known), ¹⁴ then you must inquire, probe and investigate it thoroughly. And if it is true and it has been proved that this detestable thing has been done among you, ¹⁵ you must certainly put to the sword all who live in that town. You must destroy it completely, both its people and its livestock.¹⁶ You are to gather all the plunder of the town into the middle of the public square and completely burn the town and all its plunder as a whole burnt offering to the Lord your God. That town is to remain a ruin forever, never to be rebuilt, ¹⁷ and none of the condemned things are to be found in your hands. Then the Lord will turn from his fierce anger, will show you mercy, and will have compassion on you. He will increase your numbers, as he promised on oath to your ancestors— [18] because you obey the Lord your God by keeping all his commands that I am giving you today and doing what is right in his eyes.*

It could be one town out of the entire nation, or one church out of a whole denomination. Under the law, if they have turned away from the God of the Bible and his teachings, they were to be killed. Obviously we wouldn't go in and put an entire church to the sword, but we would publicly break fellowship with them. Before doing anything, though, we need to carefully examine the situation and have proof of the offense. All it takes to get the process started is *"if you hear it said."* Hear say. A rumor. If we are faithful to the Word we have got to get far more serious about church discipline.

Notice how extensive the cleansing had to be: No weeding out of the faithful. Everybody dies, even the livestock. Then burn everything as an offering to the Lord. It doesn't matter how beautiful the religious artifacts are. Nothing can be taken. And it must remain a ruin forever, as an example to others who might be tempted to depart from the Lord.

Failure to carefully maintain the purity of the nation by allowing even one rebellious city (or church) would result in God's anger toward everyone, and withdrawal of his mercy and compassion. They all suffer because leaders were unwilling to scrupulously follow God's commands.

## ANOTHER DAY, ANOTHER MESSAGE ON PROPHETS: CHAPTER 18

If you have spent much time in the Old Testament, you know how important prophets were in Israel's history. Great men like Samuel and Elijah and Isaiah and Jeremiah. And even though their function changed after Christ, there is no indication that prophets would disappear. Thankfully, the office of prophet has been restored in today's church, after being ignored for centuries. Of course there have always been prophets, they just weren't called that. Today it seems like everyone wants to be a prophet. Jesus' warning about false prophets in the last days needs to be taken very seriously, because the real thing seems hard to find.

## GOD WILL RAISE UP A PROPHET LIKE MOSES
*14 The nations you will dispossess listen to those who practice sorcery or divination. But as for you, the Lord your God has not permitted you to do so. 15 The Lord your God will raise up for you a prophet like me from among you, from your fellow Israelites. You must listen to him. 16 For this is what you asked of the Lord your God at Horeb on the day of the assembly when you said, "Let us not hear the voice of the Lord our God nor see this great fire anymore, or we will die."*

The one who speaks forth words that are not from God is practicing sorcery or divination. We must be careful not to listen to them, because they will surely lead us astray. Study the false prophets of the Old Testament and you will find they could sound very convincing. They were in the majority. They usually spoke what people wanted to hear, while the true prophet was persecuted.

Israel, even at this early point in their walk with God, was aware of how serious it was to hear from the Lord. They had been terrified at his awesome presence at Horeb. They begged him not to speak directly to them, because they felt they would die. It sounds like that is why God decided to use prophets; because of their request we may have missed out on hearing directly from God! But he wants to speak to us. He is not silent. He loves revealing himself. He wants to communicate with you.

Some see the Messiah prophesied here. Ultimately Christ would most fully proclaim God's word and reveal him, but this prophet is *from among their fellow Israelites*. In the church today God often raises up prophets from fellow brothers in the church. Don't be too quick to run after the celebrity prophet from outside.

*[17] The Lord said to me: "What they say is good. [18] I will raise up for them a prophet like you from among their fellow Israelites, and I will put my words in his mouth. He will tell them everything I command him. [19] I myself will call to account anyone who does not listen to my words that the prophet speaks in my name. [20] But a prophet who presumes to speak in my name anything I have not commanded, or a prophet who speaks in the name of other gods, is to be put to death."*

## TEACHING ABOUT PROPHETS

- God puts his words in the mouth of the prophet. That doesn't necessarily mean dictation. The person's background can influence how he speaks, but we don't prepare prophetic messages. The prophet waits on God and learns how to discern the words God puts in his mouth.

- The prophet must say *everything* God commands him to say. Woe to anyone who would hold back on what God has spoken to him for fear of a negative response!

- When a true prophet speaks in God's name we are obligated to listen to his words. God calls to account anyone who doesn't. That makes it very important to discern who is true and who is false. Then listen carefully, and act on what they speak. The internet is full of supposed prophetic words. Many people scan them and grab onto what they like, believing it is God's word to them. That is dangerous.

- Being a prophet is an awesome responsibility. The penalty for messing up was death. We don't kill prophets today, but we must deal with false prophets severely. Woe to the prophet who may have been used by God in the past who gets presumptuous and speaks forth something God has not commanded! If God uses you prophetically, be careful!

- Less common today is the prophet who speaks in the name of other gods, but the death penalty applied there as well. Read Jeremiah 23 for more of God's perspectives on false prophets.

*[21] You may say to yourselves, "How can we know when a message has not been spoken by the Lord?" [22] If what a prophet proclaims in the name of the Lord does not take place or come true, that is a message the Lord has not spoken. That prophet has spoken presumptuously, so do not be alarmed.*

You can find some very alarming messages on the internet. There may be need for alarm, if they are from God, but some of them may have been spoken presumptuously. How do you know? Does it come true? Moses already gave the penalty for proclaiming something that is not from the Lord. Somehow, all these words about economic and natural disasters need to be archived and carefully checked for accuracy in their fulfillment. For example, be careful of justifying predictions of earthquakes by pointing to a recent tremor. There will always be earthquakes. But if it is prophesied that California is going to be destroyed by an earthquake, that needs to happen if indeed the word is from God. Of course, there are times when a prophecy is given so we can repent and pray, and the disaster will be avoided. The only way to be really sure is the proper functioning of the gift of discerning of spirits. It would be great if the entire Body of Christ could agree on an appropriate response to false prophets. I almost hate to suggest it, but if you have seen the "Fact check" website about politicians, some similar site recognized by the entire church to catalog and check all these prophecies would seem helpful.

## JESUS' TEST OF A PROPHET

Things are not always as they seem. We need to look beyond the surface and know something about the person giving the prophecy:

> *"Watch out for false prophets. They come to you in sheep's clothing, but inwardly they are ferocious wolves. By their fruit you will recognize them. Do people pick grapes from thornbushes, or figs from thistles? Likewise, every good tree bears good fruit, but a bad tree bears bad fruit. A good tree cannot bear bad fruit, and a bad tree cannot bear good fruit. Every tree that does not bear good fruit is cut down and thrown into the fire. Thus, by their fruit you will recognize them* (Matthew 7:15-20).

Yes, serving God and speaking for him is an awesome responsibility, and privilege. He is a holy, jealous God. His word is to be taken very seriously. We must be careful to keep our lives and churches free from evil. Moses' ancient teaching needs to be carefully studied and applied, according to God's leading, in the church of Jesus Christ today.

# PART 7

*THE END OF THE ROAD*

# 44

## I WILL NEVER LEAVE YOU OR FORSAKE YOU
### *DEUTERONOMY 31*

Moses' sermons are finished. He will pass the leadership to Joshua, sing a song, and bless the tribes. Then he will be ready to go and meet his Lord.

### THE SUCCESSOR ANNOUNCED
Moses saved them from destruction and faithfully led them through some of the hardest times of their lives. We naturally get attached to a pastor who has walked through the valley with us. God may have to do something drastic to get our attention and remind us that the one we need to trust and follow is the Lord. I am alarmed at the way we have made superstars out of pastors, prophets, singers, and other Christian celebrities. It is so easy to become man-centered.

There will never be another man like Moses. Joshua would be an effective military leader, but now the priests and elders will play an increasingly important role. The people have heard God's word and had a chance to learn how to walk with him. Their focus will be more on the Lord and less on the man leading them. It is time for Moses to move aside and let them take over.

¹*Then Moses went out and spoke these words to all Israel:* ² *"I am now a hundred and twenty years old and I am no longer able to lead you. The Lord has said to me, 'You shall not cross the Jordan.'* ³ *The Lord your God himself will cross over ahead of you. He will destroy these nations before you, and you will take possession of their land. Joshua also will cross over ahead of you, as the Lord said.* ⁴ *And the Lord will do to them what he did to Sihon and Og, the kings of the Amorites, whom he destroyed along with their land.* ⁵ *The Lord will deliver them to you, and you must do to them all that I have commanded you.* ⁶ *Be strong and courageous. Do not be afraid or terrified because of them, for the Lord your God goes with you; he will never leave you nor forsake you."*

Each of us eventually reach the end of the road. It is helpful if we recognize when it is time to quit. Hopefully we go out gracefully, and in the Lord's presence. It is beautiful to see a godly man or woman make that transition to eternal life, but I have also seen the torment and terror of the unsaved as death approaches. Moses is old. Aside from the fact that God said his time was up, he is not capable of leading them anymore. It still was hard for him to accept that he couldn't enter the land, but at least he knows he is leaving his people in good hands; first and foremost, the Lord's hands. God has brought them this far, and will cross the river with them, where he will continue to display his awesome power.

## IN DELIVERING THEM FROM THEIR ENEMIES, GOD WILL:

- **Cross over ahead of them.** Whether you are crossing over into a new stage in your life (marriage, baby, new job), a new country (sent by God as a missionary), or the final crossing into death, it's great to know that God crosses over ahead of you. He prepares the way.

- **Destroy the nations before them:** The enemies awaiting them, the strongholds, the strong man. What enemy are you facing today? Do you believe God can destroy it?

- **Speak.** If you have had times when God seemed silent, you know how terrifying that can be. Especially with Moses' imminent departure, they might fear they would no longer hear from God, but twice Moses mentions what God has said. There is no reason to think he would stop speaking to them.

- **Do as he has done in the past.** They had seen his power: in Egypt, and more recently with Sihon and Og. You can be confident he doesn't change. How have you seen God's power in the past? He still does mighty deeds.

- **Go with them.** If God is for me, who can be against me? If he is with me, I have nothing to fear.

- **Never leave them or forsake them.** You may not always feel his presence, but he is always with you. Jesus is at your side, and his Spirit dwells within you! Do you fear that God may have left you? Maybe your sin has created a barrier. Confess it and seek the Lord. He is waiting for you! He has not forsaken you!

- **Provide someone to lead them.** God said Joshua would take Moses' place. He will provide a pastor and leadership for his church. In leadership transitions it is critical to wait on the Lord for his choice.

They can count on God to do his part; now it is time for the people to rise up and do their part.

### ISRAEL MUST:

- **Take possession of their land.** It is given to them. God will destroy the inhabitants, but they still must move in and take possession of it. Is there something God has given you that you need to take possession of by faith? Don't just sit there, thinking that somehow it will come to you! You may need to fight for it. Sometimes you just need to get up and, by faith, grab hold of what is yours!

- **Destroy the enemies that God delivers into their hand.** They needed to remove every trace of them. You may have experienced deliverance – or need to be delivered. God can deliver you from an evil spirit of pornography that has kept you in bondage, but you need to make sure your internet has filters you can't overrule, to keep you from accessing those sites. You need to destroy any magazines or DVDs you may have.

- **Be strong and courageous.** The weak and cowardly will have it rough. There are many weakling Christians who have not fed themselves on the Word or strengthened their faith in fellowship. Courageous men seem in short supply today, but, more than ever, we need strength to face the challenges coming our way, and courage in the face of persecution and intimidation. God will back you up.

- **Not be afraid or terrified.** That is a strong word: Terrified. Have you felt it? Is there something you are terrified of right now? Does fear grip your heart when you wake up in the middle of the night and think of some challenge facing you? That fear will destroy your faith and paralyze you. Fight it. Meditate on all God has promised to do for you and let his love surround you and cast out the fear. You can cast it out in the Name of Jesus!

## THE CHARGE TO JOSHUA

*⁷ Then Moses summoned Joshua and said to him in the presence of all Israel, "Be strong and courageous, for you must go with this people into the land that the Lord swore to their ancestors to give them, and you must divide it among them as their inheritance. ⁸ The Lord himself goes before you and will be with you; he will never leave you nor forsake you. Do not be afraid; do not be discouraged."*

A fearful, wimpy, leader is especially dangerous! If Joshua loses his courage, the nation won't make it. Moses just said it to everyone; now he repeats it specifically to Joshua, as he calls him and gives him this charge in the presence of all Israel. Joshua must:

- **Be strong and courageous.** God repeats this command in Joshua chapter one. We need to be reminded of it regularly. This isn't optional. It is a command. It may be a word you need to grab onto today.

- **Go with them into the land.** That seems pretty obvious, but sometimes, when we face a difficult task, we feel like running the other way! Joshua had seen plenty of their rebellion and the headaches Moses endured. It can be tempting to look for another church to pastor, or just give up on dealing with God's people at all. But we must do all God has commanded us to do. You may not like going any further with the people God has entrusted to you – whether it be your wife, family, or church. Stick with them.

- **Divide up their inheritance.** Give each tribe their portion. Make sure the people in your care have received all God wants for them. Rightly divide the Word of truth for them. Teach on how God distributes his gifts, and help each person find and operate in their gift.

- **Not be afraid.** Fear of man is especially debilitating; there is no need to fear with God backing him up.

- **Not be discouraged.** Discouragement seems especially common among pastors. Ministry is tough. People are sinful. Things rarely happen as quickly or easily as we think they should. You see the great things others are doing on the internet and your little ministry seems so insignificant. You feel you can never measure up to them. You don't have to. Fight discouragement.

With all the challenges facing him, Joshua needs to know deep down that God will go before him, be with him, and never leave him or forsake him. That word is for you, too.

## THE CENTRAL PLACE OF GOD'S WORD

Moses is leaving Joshua with something very valuable: God's Word.

*⁹ So Moses wrote down this law and gave it to the Levitical priests, who carried the ark of the covenant of the Lord, and to all the elders of Israel.¹⁰ Then Moses commanded them: "At the end of every seven years, in the year for canceling debts, during the Festival of Tabernacles, ¹¹ when all Israel comes to appear before the Lord your God at the place he will choose, you shall read this law before them in their hearing. ¹² Assemble the people—men, women and children, and the foreigners residing in your towns—so they can listen and learn to fear the Lord your God and follow carefully all the words of this law.¹³ Their children, who do not know this law, must hear it and learn to fear the Lord your God as long as you live in the land you are crossing the Jordan to possess."*

Joshua has two great resources as he assumes leadership:

## THE BIBLE

God instructed Moses to write down everything he told him. Thank God he did! We still have it today! The Bible has stood up to more scrutiny than any other book. It has faithfully guided millions of people. You probably have it on your phone, and may have numerous study Bibles and translations. Get into it – and let it get into your heart and guide your life!

## GOD'S APPOINTED LEADERS

Joshua's job will be infinitely easier if the people know that Word and are living by it. If the nation is to survive, children must learn the Word and follow it. Fortunately, Joshua doesn't have to do that work. The responsibility lies primarily with the family, but God also provided priests and elders to ensure that the Word was regularly taught and worship was conducted in accordance with it.

That would happen locally, but every seven years they were all required to gather and, in essence, have a revival service. They would have a chance to evaluate how they were doing, hear the Word again, and be challenged to live it out. Any foreigners living among them were to be included. And, unusual for that time, women and children had to be present.

Do we lack the fear of the Lord today? Moses says we learn to fear him by hearing his Word. Are we failing to adequately teach the Bible? The purpose of hearing the Word and teaching it is to *follow carefully **all** the words of this law*. That has been repeated many times by Moses. We tend to think we are doing great if we obey 50%. The standard is 100%.

## ISRAEL'S REBELLION PREDICTED

Moses has shared his heart; now it is time for God to speak to him one more time.

*¹⁴ The Lord said to Moses, "Now the day of your death is near. Call Joshua and present yourselves at the tent of meeting, where I will commission him." So Moses and Joshua came and presented themselves at the tent of meeting.*

Joshua's commissioning seems to have been a private affair; just him and Moses at the tent of meeting. In stark contrast to the optimistic picture just painted before the entire congregation, God is upfront in telling Joshua that he would eventually destroy Israel for breaking his covenant.

*¹⁵ Then the Lord appeared at the tent in a pillar of cloud, and the cloud stood over the entrance to the tent. ¹⁶ And the Lord said to Moses: "You are going to rest with your ancestors, and these people will soon prostitute themselves to the foreign gods of the land they are entering. They will forsake me and break the covenant I made with them. ¹⁷ And in that day I will become angry with them and forsake them; I will hide my face from them, and they will be destroyed. Many disasters and calamities will come on them, and in that day they will ask, 'Have not these disasters come on us because our God is not with us?' ¹⁸ And I will certainly hide my face in that day because of all their wickedness in turning to other gods.*

That is a discouraging word to hear after you have given most of your life to getting the people to this point. Not that it would surprise Moses, but it seems contradictory. God has just given them a new leader, his Word, and priests to help them obey it.

Yet there is something so deeply rebellious within us that they were already destined for failure. God just said he would never leave them or forsake them; now he specifically says he *will* forsake them! Apparently it is conditional: They forsake him and break his covenant first, and he has no choice but to forsake them. For a time. He will hide his face from them. His anger will be kindled. Like an unfaithful wife, they will prostitute themselves to other gods. God can't stand to look on their sin, so he will allow disasters and calamities to come on them, and they will be destroyed. And they will tend to put the blame on God, instead of repenting and recognizing the role they played in angering him.

## WHY WOULD GOD TALK SO NEGATIVELY?
I have to confess that at times I struggle with the Word of God. That is normal, and it's okay if you do too. The tone changes so quickly in this chapter, from the upbeat assurance that God is with them and they are headed into a great place, to the dire prediction that they will forsake God and he will forsake them. The same depressing tone fills the song in the next chapter. I consulted a number of evangelical commentaries and not one mentioned any concern about that. Apparently they weren't thinking about how it sounded to the people hearing it; they all were applauding how accurately Israel's sin was predicted. Of course, liberal commentators say this was a later addition which Moses never wrote. I can't take that kind of liberty with God's Word – especially when it just stated the importance of *every* word God speaks. Who am I decide what is and what isn't authentic? I have to accept the whole Bible as true.

So that leaves me to figure out why God would do this. Frankly, if I were one of those Jews who had just spent forty years trying to get it together while walking through the wilderness, I would be tempted to give up. Why go through the battles to get the land knowing that God was going to destroy you? These just aren't the motivational techniques we are taught today. It certainly doesn't fit in with "positive confession," positive mental attitude, and all those common approaches. Perhaps God is letting us know that it is important to face the reality of our sin and its consequences?

## THE SONG

*19 "Now write down this song and teach it to the Israelites and have them sing it, so that it may be a witness for me against them. 20 When I have brought them into the land flowing with milk and honey, the land I promised on oath to their ancestors, and when they eat their fill and thrive, they will turn to other gods and worship them, rejecting me and breaking my covenant. 21 And when many disasters and calamities come on them, this song will testify against them, because it will not be forgotten by their descendants. I know what they are disposed to do, even before I bring them into the land I promised them on oath." 22 So Moses wrote down this song that day and taught it to the Israelites.*

The song is written in Deuteronomy 32. We will study it in the next chapter. It's kind of depressing. It's not the kind of song usually taught in churches today. But God wants them to know why disaster befalls them. He wants them to be aware of the consequences of sin. God never tries to sugar coat things to give an unrealistic picture of the future.

Songs have always been a great way of remembering a message. I wish we knew what tune it was sung to! Music can elicit strong emotions and bring back vivid memories. Maybe God wanted them to remember what it was like having their great, aged, leader teach them this song. I am surprised that even conservative commentaries talk about Moses' ability in writing it. God clearly says here that Moses' job was to write it down and teach it – not write it. God was the author of this song. Maybe you should include it in the worship set next Sunday?

## God's Command to Joshua

*²³ The Lord gave this command to Joshua son of Nun: "Be strong and courageous, for you will bring the Israelites into the land I promised them on oath, and I myself will be with you."*

There it is again: Be strong and courageous. But that assurance of God's presence sounds a little weak after he was just told they would turn away from God and be destroyed. The need for strength and courage is more urgent knowing the kind of people he was dealing with!

*²⁴ After Moses finished writing in a book the words of this law from beginning to end, ²⁵ he gave this command to the Levites who carried the ark of the covenant of the Lord: ²⁶ "Take this Book of the Law and place it beside the ark of the covenant of the Lord your God. There it will remain as a witness against you. ²⁷ For I know how rebellious and stiff-necked you are. If you have been rebellious against the Lord while I am still alive and with you, how much more will you rebel after I die! ²⁸ Assemble before me all the elders of your tribes and all your officials, so that I can speak these words in their hearing and call the heavens and the earth to testify against them. ²⁹ For I know that after my death you are sure to become utterly corrupt and to turn from the way I have commanded you. In days to come, disaster will fall on you because you will do evil in the sight of the Lord and arouse his anger by what your hands have made."*

## The Song Summarizes the Book

The song wasn't the only witness against them, and maybe that is why it's not that big a deal that Moses would sing this depressing song. It just summarizes what they have already been told in his final messages! There is nothing new there! Have you noticed your own tendency to skim over the many sections on sin and judgment in the Bible and grab onto the promises? Most people know Jeremiah from the famous verse in 29:11 about the great plans he has for us. They barely read the majority of the book, which is very depressing! To say nothing of Lamentations, which Jeremiah also wrote. When was the last time you heard a sermon on that? If you did, it was probably the section on God's faithfulness (3:21-24).

The Book Moses wrote (the first five books of our Bible) would be placed in the ark as a permanent reminder of all God had said. Moses echoes God's depressing picture of Israel as they are about to embark on conquering the Promised Land:

- They are rebellious and stiff-necked. Moses expects them to get even worse after his death.
- He is going to call heaven and earth to testify against them.
- He knows they will become utterly corrupt and turn away from what he has taught.
- Disaster will befall them. They will do evil in God's sight and arouse his anger by their idols.

So what can we say about the depressing conclusion to this chapter? How would you feel taking over a church if these were the kind of people in it? What would be your reaction as one of the leaders – or a member of the congregation?

To experience God's grace and power, an honest recognition of our utter sinfulness and helplessness before him is essential. Are we downplaying that, and giving our people sugar-coated pep talks?

As I have reflected on what to take away from this chapter, I am reminded of the importance of living faithfully for God each day. I could get wrapped up in thoughts about aging and regrets I have, or all the talk about the tribulation and the impending disasters coming on the world. But God calls me to live for the moment. There is still plenty he has for me to do right now. I don't just stop evangelizing because he could come back any time. The priests back then don't stop encouraging people to live the law, just because ultimately they probably won't. It is that much more impetus to share the law and help them obey it, and grab onto God's power! Israel was still going to see God's power and enter the land! What does God have for you to do – right now?

# 45

## MOSES' SONG
### *DEUTERONOMY 32*

Here it is: The song God gave Moses. It is the *parshat* (portion) *ha'azinu* (Hebrew for "listen", the first word of the song). Jews read it on a Sabbath between the holy days of Rosh Hashanah and Sukkot, generally in September or October. The five books of Moses are broken down into weekly portions and read every year, similar to the lectionary some churches follow, and this is the 53rd *parshat*. It has been honored for millennia as one of the great portions of Scripture.

### INTRODUCTION

God gave this song to Moses, but, like much of inspired Scripture, that doesn't mean it was dictated. As God begins to fill Moses' mind with thoughts, he writes this introduction:

*¹Listen, you heavens, and I will speak;*
  *hear, you earth, the words of my mouth.*
*² Let my teaching fall like rain*
  *and my words descend like dew,*
*like showers on new grass,*
  *like abundant rain on tender plants.*

When you speak, does your teaching fall like rain? Not driving rain, but gently descending dew, showers which don't harm new grass, and rain abundant enough to provide all the water tender plants need -without breaking them. When you open the Bible, picture God's Word falling on you like refreshing showers for your thirsty soul. Let his rain revive you, as a tender plant that may have wilted in the heat of battle.

## THE ROCK
*³ I will proclaim the name of the Lord.*
  *Oh, praise the greatness of our God!*
*⁴ He is the Rock, his works are perfect,*
  *and all his ways are just.*
*A faithful God who does no wrong,*
  *upright and just is he.*

God was first called the Rock of Israel by Jacob (Genesis 49:24), but the name doesn't appear again until this song, where it is used six times. We also find it frequently in Psalms and Isaiah. 1 Corinthians 10:3-4 says: *They all ate the same spiritual food and drank the same spiritual drink; for they drank from the spiritual rock that accompanied them, and that rock was Christ.* Israel survived the desert because of the rocks that gave them water. Ironically, Jesus' dead body was placed in a tomb cut out of the rock. Grab onto the solid Rock today and trust his goodness in the midst of trials.

God can do no wrong. Everything he does is perfect. He is fully reliable, faithful, upright and just. We must proclaim this God to the nations! We must bow down and praise him!

You are one of his works! Whatever is happening in your life right now, he is working to perfect you. And if you are hurting because your children aren't serving him, be encouraged that even this great God reared warped and crooked children:

*⁵ They are corrupt and not his children;*
  *to their shame they are a warped and crooked generation.*

> *⁶ Is this the way you repay the Lord,*
>   *you foolish and unwise people?*
> *Is he not your Father, your Creator,*
>   *who made you and formed you?*

He is our Creator and Father. He intended for us to be one of his perfect works, but we have repaid his goodness and gracious work on our behalf with sin and rebellion. Have you felt that way about your children, and how they have repaid you for all you did for them?

So much for the common belief that we are all God's children! When we choose sin, we give up our rights as sons and daughters. As I look at the words that describe them, it reminds me of the world today:

- Corrupt
- Warped
- Crooked
- Foolish
- Unwise

Instead of thanking and praising God and willingly obeying him, they have brought shame on themselves by the foolish paths they have chosen. Paul describes them fully in the first two chapters of Romans!

## BOUNDARIES

> *⁷ Remember the days of old;*
>   *consider the generations long past.*
> *Ask your father and he will tell you,*
>   *your elders, and they will explain to you.*
> *⁸ When the Most High gave the nations their inheritance,*
>   *when he divided all mankind,*
> *he set up boundaries for the peoples*

> according to the number of the sons of Israel.
> ⁹ For the Lord's portion is his people,
>   Jacob his allotted inheritance.

Do we consider the generations long past? Some older folks are into *Ancestry.com*, but my guess is that most people barely think about their ancestors. With so much technology and so much grabbing our attention, they seem irrelevant. Have you sat down with your father (or other elderly people) and asked about their lives and experiences? Americans have largely lost respect and honor for the aged. Living in Costa Rica, I find the contrast striking. Here, young people still respect and speak with the elderly. So different from the US! We pay little attention to history. We are so much more "enlightened" than the "ignorant" biblical writers. Yet we ignore history at our own peril: We will find ourselves repeating it.

God has set up boundaries in his Word— not just physical boundaries for the tribes of Israel, but boundaries of what is acceptable and unacceptable; boundaries of who will and who will not enter his Kingdom. He has a great inheritance for us! He is not concerned about houses and land; his portion is his people! He is doing everything he can to ensure that we will receive all he has planned for us. Are you aware of his boundaries? Do you respect them? Do you follow his example and establish appropriate boundaries for your life and home?

## AN EAGLE!

> ¹⁰ In a desert land he found him,
>   in a barren and howling waste.
> He shielded him and cared for him;
>   he guarded him as the apple of his eye,
> ¹¹ like an eagle that stirs up its nest
>   and hovers over its young,

*that spreads its wings to catch them*
  *and carries them aloft.*
*¹² The Lord alone led him;*
  *no foreign god was with him.*

We have already seen God as Creator, Father, and Rock. Now he is an eagle. The next time you feel vulnerable and alone, picture God hovering over you as a mighty eagle. He delights in you! You are the apple of his eye! He wants to take you to the heights and train you to fly! And if you start to fall, he spreads his wings to catch you, like Jesus rescued Peter from sinking as he walked on water. What a beautiful image!

There is nothing impressive about a newborn bird. A young eagle gives no hint of the majestic adult bird. There was nothing impressive about Jacob that made God choose him. He didn't go looking for God. In fact, he was out in a barren and howling waste. God went looking for him in that desert, and found him. From that moment, Jacob's life was transformed, and his family changed forever. Are you grateful he reached out and chose you in that barren and howling wasteland of sin? Now God is actively involved in your life, shielding and protecting you, leading you, and caring for you.

If you are still out in that barren, howling, dangerous wilderness, if you are passing through what seems an endless desert, God is looking for you. That's why you are reading this. Let him be your Father, your Rock, and the eagle who will raise you up to overcome whatever is pulling you down.

## HONEY FROM THE ROCK
*¹³ He made him ride on the heights of the land*
  *and fed him with the fruit of the fields.*
*He nourished him with honey from the rock,*
  *and with oil from the flinty crag,*

*¹⁴ with curds and milk from herd and flock*
  *and with fattened lambs and goats,*
*with choice rams of Bashan*
  *and the finest kernels of wheat.*
*You drank the foaming blood of the grape.*

As we come to the Lord he lavishes us with his abundance. He is not a withholding God, but a generous Father who loves to bless his children. And he gives the best: *fattened* lambs, *choice* rams, *finest* wheat. Can you think of ways God has made you ride the heights of the land? How has he brought honey from a rock to bless you? When is the last time you thanked him for those blessings, acknowledging that every good and perfect gift comes from the Father of lights?

## ISRAEL'S RESPONSE TO GOD'S GOODNESS
*¹⁵ Jeshurun grew fat and kicked;*
  *filled with food, they became heavy and sleek.*
*They abandoned the God who made them*
  *and rejected the Rock their Savior.*
*¹⁶ They made him jealous with their foreign gods*
  *and angered him with their detestable idols.*
*¹⁷ They sacrificed to false gods, which are not God—*
  *gods they had not known,*
  *gods that recently appeared,*
  *gods your ancestors did not fear.*
*¹⁸ You deserted the Rock, who fathered you;*
  *you forgot the God who gave you birth.*

*Jeshurun,* a poetic name for Israel, comes from the Hebrew word for *upright, just,* or *straight.* Under Moses' leadership they proved themselves to be anything but. They are not even in the land flowing with milk and honey, and they are already self-satisfied, lazy, and focused on their own pleasure. As their situation improved and they enjoyed God's goodness, instead of responding with thanksgiving and faithfulness, they:

- **Abandoned their creator** – denying his obvious right of ownership as the one who made them. They forgot him. He is their father, but in Scripture he is also portrayed as a mother. After all, man and woman together were made in God's image. Here he is the one who "*gave you birth*." But like a rebellious teen, Israel wants nothing to do with mom and dad.

- **Rejected and deserted the Rock**. It is hard to ignore a rock. The Rock is their father and savior, and they have consciously and purposefully rejected him.

- **Angered him and made him jealous** with their idols and false gods. God loves them! He was mother and father to them! He provided for them. He is hurt, jealous, and angry. They have chosen man-made images and other gods over the living God!

- **Rejected the God of their fathers**. They broke tradition with hundreds of years of ancestors who worshipped God, all through the long years of slavery, to run after new gods. They sound like many young people today! No one even taught them these gods, but now, despite no evidence that they are real, they run headlong after them and sacrifice to them.

Do you know someone who is rejecting God's goodness, as Israel did? Too many Christians have become fat and sleek, kicking against God's restraints. Are there other gods beckoning you? Have you made God angry or jealous in the past? Could you imagine rejecting your mother, the one who gave you birth? Why would you even consider abandoning the God who fathered you?

Be careful of the subtle false gods you may be tempted to run after. Don't reject the only true Rock!

## God's Judgment
*<sup>19</sup> The Lord saw this and rejected them*
  *because he was angered by his sons and daughters.*
*<sup>20</sup> "I will hide my face from them," he said,*
  *"and see what their end will be;*
*for they are a perverse generation,*
  *children who are unfaithful.*
*<sup>21</sup> They made me jealous by what is no god*
  *and angered me with their worthless idols.*
*I will make them envious by those who are not a people;*
  *I will make them angry by a nation that has no understanding.*
*<sup>22</sup> For a fire will be kindled by my wrath,*
  *one that burns down to the realm of the dead below.*
*It will devour the earth and its harvests*
  *and set afire the foundations of the mountains.*

God can't just sit back and let them go. He may reject them (because they first rejected him) and hide his face from them, but he is still their Father, and they are his sons and daughters. He won't just forget about them; he will try to make them envious by embracing a people who had never known him - exactly what Paul said God did by including the Gentiles in the Gospel. But even that hasn't worked very well in drawing the Jews to their Messiah!

Don't make God angry! His wrath is hot enough to kindle a fire, which will devour the earth and its harvests. And that is only the beginning of his judgment.

## What Saves Them from Total Destruction?
*<sup>23</sup> "I will heap calamities on them*
  *and spend my arrows against them.*

> **²⁴** I will send wasting famine against them,
>     consuming pestilence and deadly plague;
> I will send against them the fangs of wild beasts,
>     the venom of vipers that glide in the dust.
> **²⁵** In the street the sword will make them childless;
>     in their homes terror will reign.
> The young men and young women will perish,
>     the infants and those with gray hair.
> **²⁶** I said I would scatter them
>     and erase their name from human memory,
> **²⁷** but I dreaded the taunt of the enemy,
>     lest the adversary misunderstand
> and say, 'Our hand has triumphed;
>     the Lord has not done all this.'"

Look at the words God uses to describe the coming judgments:

- Heaping calamities
- Spent arrows
- Wasting famine
- Consuming pestilence
- Deadly plague
- Fangs of wild beasts
- Venom of vipers gliding in the dust
- Made childless by the sword
- Terror reigning in their homes
- Scattered
- Names erased from human memory

This isn't the first time they heard about this judgment; Moses already predicted these calamities. The song simply repeats them. Wouldn't they be enough to make you think twice about running after other gods? Are you aware that similar judgments can come on those who reject God and his Word today?

So what keeps God from simply erasing their names from human memory? The taunts of the devil, or Israel's worldly enemies. God dreads those taunts! He is concerned that the enemy will misunderstand what he is doing! Since terror is the devil's specialty, Satan might take credit for it! He would see their destruction as a great triumph for his side! Unbelievers would also embrace that lie, but God won't give the devil that satisfaction, and that will save Israel. Just to rub it in, God will raise them up again.

This can apply to the sinful church today. God will not allow us to get so devastated that Satan thinks he has triumphed over us!

> 28 *They are a nation without sense,*
>   *there is no discernment in them.*
> 29 *If only they were wise and would understand this*
>   *and discern what their end will be!*
> 30 *How could one man chase a thousand,*
>   *or two put ten thousand to flight,*
> *unless their Rock had sold them,*
>   *unless the Lord had given them up?*
> 31 *For their rock is not like our Rock,*
>   *as even our enemies concede.*
> 32 *Their vine comes from the vine of Sodom*
>   *and from the fields of Gomorrah.*
> *Their grapes are filled with poison,*
>   *and their clusters with bitterness.*
> 33 *Their wine is the venom of serpents,*
>   *the deadly poison of cobras.*

Have you thought about how your life might end? Does it matter to you? Do you think it would make a difference in how you spend your time if you could see it?

God is trying to get a message to them: Wake up! Israel has only begun to enter their inheritance, and they are already blowing it! They are blind! When crazy things start to happen in your life it is time to ask "why?" God is probably trying to get your attention. Things like one man chasing a thousand. How can anyone ignore such clear signs? Even God's enemies know there is no one like him! But they are too caught up with the sin of Sodom and Gomorrah to notice! They eerily remind me of the United States!

Do you have spiritual discernment? Can you see where you are heading? Where does your "wine" come from? Is it full of poison and bitterness?

## VENGEANCE IS MINE
*34 "Have I not kept this in reserve*
*and sealed it in my vaults?*
*35 It is mine to avenge; I will repay.*
*In due time their foot will slip;*
*their day of disaster is near*
*and their doom rushes upon them."*

You reap what you sow. God will repay them. This is the first time the well-known saying "*It is mine to avenge*" appears in the Bible. God will let them follow their broad road of sin – until their foot slips. Doom and disaster is much closer than they imagine.

*36 The Lord will vindicate his people*
*and relent concerning his servants*
*when he sees their strength is gone*
*and no one is left, slave or free.*
*37 He will say: "Now where are their gods,*
*the rock they took refuge in,*
*38 the gods who ate the fat of their sacrifices*
*and drank the wine of their drink offerings?*

> Let them rise up to help you!
>   Let them give you shelter!

God may sound vindictive, but his heart is also moved to compassion as he sees their strength gone and everyone destroyed. Have you suffered under God's chastening hand? Be encouraged! He will relent when he sees you can't take any more. He will wait until you have exhausted your strength running after other gods, and you finally realize they have nothing to offer. I pray you won't hear him say: "You thought those gods were so great? Where are they now? You put your trust in your money, your position, or your worldly friends. Where are they now? Let them help you! They can't?" When you get to the end of your rope, God is there. And if you are waiting for your vindication, take heart! God will vindicate his people!

## THE GREAT I AM

> [39] "See now that I myself am he!
>   There is no god besides me.
> I put to death and I bring to life,
>   I have wounded and I will heal,
>   and no one can deliver out of my hand.
> [40] I lift my hand to heaven and solemnly swear:
>   As surely as I live forever,
> [41] when I sharpen my flashing sword
>   and my hand grasps it in judgment,
> I will take vengeance on my adversaries
>   and repay those who hate me.
> [42] I will make my arrows drunk with blood,
>   while my sword devours flesh:
> the blood of the slain and the captives,
>   the heads of the enemy leaders."

This is the song's crescendo. I picture extra instruments and loud voices, as God declares himself the great I AM (somewhat hidden in our English translation of verse 39). God will avenge himself and repay his enemies, and it will be ugly. This has become a major theme in the song. To emphasize it, he swears by himself!

Isn't it good to know there is only one God! Hopefully you know him. If not, you may be convinced by now that you need to know him. This is a great time to call out to him and be saved. In the midst of his anger and vengeance, there are three very comforting truths for those who obey him:

- **He has the power of resurrection.** The power of life and death is in his hand. God brings to life! Are you feeling dead? Has your marriage died? Your dreams? God brings to life – but first you may have to die to self, crucifying what is left of your life, just as Jesus died on his cross.

- **He has the power to heal.** He does wound, and those wounds hurt, but they are always with a purpose. Where he wounds he will also heal. Have you been wounded? Maybe by God, the devil, or other people? Let God heal those wounds!

- **No one can deliver out of his hand.** No one can stand up to him. When you are in his hand no one can snatch you out of it.

Have you noticed how Moses moved from talking *about* God at the beginning of the song to these very clear prophetic statements? I often see that happening in prophecy. At first the person mixes in some of his own thoughts, but, as the Spirit moves him, it comes straight from God's heart.

Now, as he concludes the song, Moses responds to what God has given him, and calls the people to rejoice in what God will do.

## REJOICE!

*⁴³ Rejoice, you nations, with his people,*
  *for he will avenge the blood of his servants;*
*he will take vengeance on his enemies*
  *and make atonement for his land and people.*

The rejoicing is now; the rest is all future tense. The rejoicing is based on what we believe by faith God will do in the future, not on what we are experiencing now. He has also reminded them of God's past works. They can rejoice about them as well. Do you include both in your worship?

Moses points to three things God will do:

- **Avenge the blood of his servants.** Martyrs are precious to God, and he will surely avenge the blood of each one.

- **Take vengeance on his enemies.** They will pay for all they have done against his kingdom. They may smugly think they are getting away with it now, but a day of judgment and reckoning is coming.

- **Make atonement for his land and people.** The sacrifice of his own Son on the cross provided atonement for his people. The land will be cleansed of its idolatry, and his people restored.

The invitation to the nations to join the rejoicing is particularly impressive. This is good news for everyone! Moses may have prophetically seen the inclusion of the gentiles, maybe even glimpsing that great gathering of people from every nation and tongue in God's kingdom.

*⁴⁴ Moses came with Joshua son of Nun and spoke all the words of this song in the hearing of the people. ⁴⁵ When Moses finished reciting all these words to all Israel, ⁴⁶ he said to them, "Take to heart all the words I have solemnly declared to you this day, so that you may command your children to obey carefully all the words of this law. ⁴⁷ They are not just idle words for you—they are your life. By them you will live long in the land you are crossing the Jordan to possess."*

The annual repetition of this song has been a reminder throughout the generations of what it means to serve the living God. Although there are ominous words of apostasy and judgment, they still have the opportunity to possess the land and enjoy a long life in it. God has given them his Word – and his Word is life. There is no idle word (AMP: *empty and worthless trifle*) in the Bible. Learn to draw life from the Scriptures.

## ANOTHER SONG OF MOSES

We will have the amazing opportunity to hear (and sing) another song of Moses – actually a duet by Moses and Jesus, the Lamb, as recorded in Revelation 15:2-4. What an amazing tribute to the place Moses holds in the Kingdom of God!

> *And I saw what looked like a sea of glass glowing with fire and, standing beside the sea, those who had been victorious over the beast and its image and over the number of its name. They held harps given them by God and sang the song of God's servant Moses and of the Lamb:*
>
> *"Great and marvelous are your deeds,*
> *Lord God Almighty.*
> *Just and true are your ways,*
> *King of the nations.*
> *Who will not fear you, Lord,*
> *and bring glory to your name?*
> *For you alone are holy.*
> *All nations will come*

*and worship before you,*
*for your righteous acts have been revealed."*

# 46

# MOSES' DEATH
## *DEUTERONOMY 34*

It is time for Moses to leave this world. He has had an amazing life:

- The circumstances surrounding his birth and childhood.
- The burning bush.
- An unparalleled string of miracles in Egypt and the wilderness.
- Speaking with God face to face.

Now God tells him when he will die. Moses doesn't protest death. What still troubles him is dying without stepping foot in the land he has been leading God's people to for forty years. At least he could see it from afar, but as he began his final messages to Israel, he tries one last time to change God's mind.

## GOD DENIES MOSES' PLEA (DEUTERONOMY 3:23-29)

Yes, he was a great man of faith whose prayers had repeatedly stayed God's hand of judgment. But when it came to Moses' simple request to see the land, God said no.

*²³ At that time I pleaded with the Lord: ²⁴ "Sovereign Lord, you have begun to show to your servant your greatness and your strong hand. For what god is there in heaven or on earth who can do the deeds and mighty works you do? ²⁵ Let me go over and see* the good land beyond the Jordan—that fine hill country and Lebanon."

It is interesting that Moses feels he was only "beginning" to see God's greatness and strong hand, after witnessing the deliverance in Egypt and the opening of the Red Sea. He longs for much more! Now, as he has done so many times, he reminds God of his power and commitment to his people, and he throws in the word "servant" to remind God of the outstanding service he has faithfully given. He's not asking for a lot! After all, on numerous occasions his prayers had caused God to relent, but that wasn't to be the case for Moses.

*26 But because of you the Lord was angry with me and would not listen to me. "That is enough," the Lord said. "Do not speak to me anymore about this matter. 27 Go up to the top of Pisgah and look west and north and south and east. Look at the land with your own eyes, since you are not going to cross this Jordan. 28 But commission Joshua, and encourage and strengthen him, for he will lead this people across and will cause them to inherit the land that you will see." 29 So we stayed in the valley near Beth Peor.*

It still is hard for Moses to accept responsibility for his actions. With a hint of resentment, he tells Israel that God is angry with him *"because of you."* Moses could look, but not touch. He could see how beautiful the land was, but God was determined he would never cross the Jordan. And if he had rebelliously attempted to, God would probably have struck him dead. Moses' task was to prepare the man who would lead them into the land:

- Commission him
- Encourage him
- Strengthen him

That can be bitter sweet: You pour your life into a young man to prepare him for leadership, and he gets to experience what you desperately longed for. And you have to encourage and strengthen him – as you get ready to die.

We are usually admonished to be persistent in prayer. Jesus encouraged it in several parables (Luke 11:1-13; 18:1-8). But if God is angry with us for some reason, or if it simply is not his will, there may be times we experience what Moses did. God wouldn't listen to him, and even rebuked him: *"That is enough. Don't speak to me anymore about this matter."* At that point we have little choice but to accept God's decision.

Moses delivered his final messages and shared the song God gave him. That same day, after blessing the tribes (chapter 33), he was to climb the mountain one last time – to die.

## FINAL INSTRUCTIONS (DEUTERONOMY 32:48-52)

*48 On that same day the Lord told Moses, 49 "Go up into the Abarim Range to Mount Nebo in Moab, across from Jericho, and view Canaan, the land I am giving the Israelites as their own possession. 50 There on the mountain that you have climbed you will die and be gathered to your people, just as your brother Aaron died on Mount Hor and was gathered to his people. 51 This is because both of you broke faith with me in the presence of the Israelites at the waters of Meribah Kadesh in the Desert of Zin and because you did not uphold my holiness among the Israelites. 52 Therefore, you will see the land only from a distance; you will not enter the land I am giving to the people of Israel."*

There's nothing like reminding someone of their failures on the day they die! God doesn't seem very compassionate with Moses. That act of disobedience was very serious to him!

- Moses (and Aaron) broke faith with God in the presence of the Israelites. By disobeying God's command, they *betrayed* him (NLT). It's one thing to disobey in private, but when it is in front of the whole congregation, it is much more serious.

- They failed to uphold God's holiness among the Israelites by letting anger take the upper hand, and hitting the rock instead of speaking to it. The way they handled the incident didn't reflect God's love and gracious provision for his people.

Moses was one of the greatest men who ever lived. For forty years he provided exemplary leadership to Israel. We would be hard pressed to find a leader in the church today who compares to him. Yet for that one failure he is punished severely. We too may face painful consequences of our actions. I have seen one foolish mistake destroy men who faithfully served God for many years.

## Moses' Death (Deuteronomy 34:1-8)

*[1] Then Moses climbed Mount Nebo from the plains of Moab to the top of Pisgah, across from Jericho. There the Lord showed him the whole land—from Gilead to Dan, [2] all of Naphtali, the territory of Ephraim and Manasseh, all the land of Judah as far as the Mediterranean Sea, [3] the Negev and the whole region from the Valley of Jericho, the City of Palms, as far as Zoar. [4] Then the Lord said to him, "This is the land I promised on oath to Abraham, Isaac and Jacob when I said, 'I will give it to your descendants.' I have let you see it with your eyes, but you will not crossover into it."*

Moses spent many days with God on Mount Sinai. He was privileged to hear more from the mouth of God than any other man. Now, once again, it is just him and God on the mountaintop.

Was Israel watching as Moses climbed the 2,643 feet (805 meters) to the summit of Mount Nebo?

These are God's final words to him:

- This is the land I promised Abraham, Isaac, and Jacob.
- I will give it to their descendants.
- I have let you see it with your eyes.
- But you won't cross over into it.

As Moses took in the sight, he died. Jews traditionally believe God took him with a kiss.

*⁵ And Moses the servant of the Lord died there in Moab, as the Lord had said. ⁶ He buried him in Moab, in the valley opposite Beth Peor, but to this day no one knows where his grave is. ⁷ Moses was a hundred and twenty years old when he died, yet his eyes were not weak nor his strength gone. ⁸ The Israelites grieved for Moses in the plains of Moab thirty days, until the time of weeping and mourning was over.*

Who buried him? Apparently God. And God took his life, since he was still healthy. At 120 years he climbed that mountain, and his eyes were strong enough to see the whole Promised Land!

There is an intriguing New Testament reference to Moses' death: *But even the archangel Michael, when he was disputing with the devil about the body of Moses, did not himself dare to condemn him for slander but said, "The Lord rebuke you!"* (Jude 9) We don't know what that means, but Moses' body would probably have been a prize for the devil! Maybe Satan was attempting to keep Moses from God's presence, citing his sin in striking the rock and killing the Egyptian.

## Moses' legacy

*⁹Now Joshua son of Nun was filled with the spirit of wisdom because Moses had laid his hands on him. So the Israelites listened to him and did what the Lord had commanded Moses.*

Perhaps "spirit" should be capitalized. Surely it was the Holy Spirit who was imparted to Joshua as Moses laid hands on him – the first time hands were laid on someone to anoint a new leader.

*¹⁰Since then, no prophet has risen in Israel like Moses, whom the Lord knew face to face, ¹¹who did all those signs and wonders the Lord sent him to do in Egypt—to Pharaoh and to all his officials and to his whole land.¹²For no one has ever shown the mighty power or performed the awesome deeds that Moses did in the sight of all Israel.*

Moses knew the Lord face to face. No one came close to Moses' relationship with God, until Jesus led a sinless life, fully revealing the Father, and initiating a New Covenant.

What do you find most inspiring about Moses' life? Can you imagine knowing the Lord face to face? Is there anything that would keep you from entering the Promised Land? What will people say about you when you die?

# 47

## MOSES IN THE REST OF THE BIBLE

Moses is mentioned 803 times in the Bible. Not surprisingly, 603 of those are in the books he wrote, the first five books of the Bible. Another 51 are in Joshua. He obviously remained a huge presence in Israel's life for many years. But there are also 85 New Testament references! Some 1300 years after his death! I would call that an enduring influence! So what perspective does the rest of the Bible give us on Moses? Many of those scriptures refer back to the events of Moses' life and the exodus, or the books he wrote and the law he gave.

### MOSES' DESCENDANTS

The Bible never says much about his family. His descendants didn't play any leadership role in Israel, but we do know that they made it into the Promised Land:

*The sons of Moses the man of God were counted as part of the tribe of Levi. The sons of Moses: Gershom and Eliezer. The descendants of Gershom: Shubael was the first. The descendants of Eliezer: Rehabiah was the first. Eliezer had no other sons, but the sons of Rehabiah were very numerous.* (1 Chronicles 23:14-17)

That's it! Kind of unusual for a man of Moses' stature, but then God never said anything about him having a dynasty, as David had. God never even gave him any promises about his descendants, as were given to Abraham. In every respect, Moses' family life was unusual.

## PSALM 90: A PRAYER OF MOSES THE MAN OF GOD

This is the only scripture written by Moses outside his five books, and is likely the oldest of all the Psalms.

*¹ Lord, you have been our dwelling place* (NLT: *home*)
  *throughout all generations.*
*² Before the mountains were born*
  *or you brought forth the whole world,*
    *from everlasting to everlasting* (NLT: *from beginning to end*)
*you are God.*

God is creator. He never changes. The real estate crash of 2008 showed how fragile our earthly homes can be. God is the only secure dwelling place. I have known many people who desperately long for "home" and never find it. God is your home. The word can also be translated refuge. How wonderful to know that God provides that place of rest and safety for us. That Moses would know God as his dwelling place or home is especially relevant, since he was brought up in a foreigner's palace, fled as a fugitive to another foreign land, and spent the last forty years of his life wandering around homeless in the wilderness, only to be denied entry into the Promised Land! In all the insecurity and transitions of this life, Moses had found that God was the one sure refuge.

God will never let you down, he won't die, and you can't lose him. From beginning to end - of your life, of your marriage, and of history – he is God.

*³ You turn people back to dust,*
  *saying, "Return to dust, you mortals."*
*⁴ A thousand years in your sight*

> are like a day that has just gone by,
> or like a watch in the night.
> ⁵ Yet you sweep people away in the sleep of death—
> they are like the new grass of the morning:
> ⁶ In the morning it springs up new,
> but by evening it is dry and withered.

A wasting disease or the death of a loved one quickly remind us how transitory this life is. In the scope of God's eternity your entire life is one millisecond. God sounds a little harsh "sweeping us away" and telling us mere mortals to return to the dust, but that gives some perspective on our overly inflated self-importance. Yes, God loves you and you are of great value to him, but I'm sorry to inform you that you're just not all that important. Moses had seen God sweep thousands of people away in a moment of judgment. God cut his life short because of his sin, yet he was also humbled by unprecedented glimpses of God's splendor.

Perhaps, as he dragged through year after year of seemingly endless wilderness wanderings, God impressed on him that what seemed like an eternity was nothing in God's timeframe. Does God seem to be taking too long to change something in your life? Do you wonder when Jesus will ever come back? Remember, for God, a thousand years are like an evening gone.

> ⁷ We are consumed by your anger
> and terrified by your indignation.
> ⁸ You have set our iniquities before you,
> our secret sins in the light of your presence.
> ⁹ All our days pass away under your wrath;
> we finish our years with a moan.
> ¹⁰ Our days may come to seventy years,
> or eighty, if our strength endures;

> *yet the best of them are but trouble and sorrow,*
>   *for they quickly pass, and we fly away.*
> *¹¹ If only we knew the power of your anger!*
>   *Your wrath is as great as the fear that is your due.*
> *¹² Teach us to number our days,*
>   *that we may gain a heart of wisdom.*

Does life seem a drudgery? Do you search for something to fill empty days? Or are they so full you find yourself constantly missing out on special moments with your wife or children? Does God get pushed to the bottom of your priority list? The *Message* simply paraphrases it: *Teach us to live well!* Today is God's gift to you. May he grant you wisdom to make the most of every single day. Don't waste your life away on pointless and endless internet postings or TV shows. Don't get caught up in the pursuit of worldly wealth and pleasure. Invest in things of eternal value: your family, relationships, and the Kingdom of God. What does God want you doing? How should that impact the use of your time, which God has given you as a steward?

Though Moses' days came to 120 years, he was aware of how quickly they pass. As you age, you become increasingly aware of that. Indeed, when I was in my twenties life seemed to stretch out almost endlessly. Now I am very aware of how it is racing to a close. Maybe Moses had seen enough of God's wrath that he was mindful of it every day. That is part of God's nature, but I am grateful to Jesus for bearing the brunt of that wrath on the cross. Now I am freed to worship and serve him out of a thankful heart – accompanied by an appropriate fear and reverence for him.

For many years I held onto the widely accepted myth that life is basically good. Americans have become experts at isolating themselves from the harsher realities of life, but the truth, for the vast majority of the world, is that life is very hard. There is nothing wrong with the optimism of youth, and we certainly want to see life's difficulties through the eyes of faith. But the very popular message that God wants to make your life as nice and pain-free as possible simply is not the whole truth. Americans may deal with trouble sooner than they think – and find themselves much more poorly equipped to do so than those accustomed to the challenges of daily life.

And sin? That seems taboo in many circles. Do you ever ask the Spirit of God to reveal sin or darkness in your heart? How do you feel about God setting your sin before you (verse 8)? Are there secret sins that you somehow think you can hide from God? Did you know that he shines his light on them to expose them? Jesus said they would be shouted from the rooftops! Are you aware of the depth of your sin nature? Moses had seen it vividly played out day after day on the exodus.

> [13] Relent, Lord! How long will it be?
> Have compassion on your servants.
> [14] Satisfy us in the morning with your unfailing love,
> that we may sing for joy and be glad all our days.
> [15] Make us glad for as many days as you have afflicted us,
> for as many years as we have seen trouble.
> [16] May your deeds be shown to your servants,
> your splendor to their children.

Wait a minute! I thought he was just saying how hard this life is, and how angry God is with our sin! Yet just as surely as sin is judged and we feel its impact every day, God's compassion and love is there to surround us and help us through.

Yes, even Moses, who just acknowledged that what seems endless to us is nothing to God, has to ask how long the trials will continue. Are you in a place where you cry out: "Relent, Lord! I can't take much more!" God is compassionate! Where there is sickness, God can heal. Where there is darkness, he can shine his light. Where there is sin, he can forgive.

Do you go to the Lord the first thing in the morning to receive his love? I often wake up with troubled thoughts and desperately need that daily filling of his love to face the certain difficulties of this life. As he lifts the heaviness, start singing for joy to him, as you reflect on his splendor and mighty deeds.

If it seems you have only seen trouble all your life, God wants to fill you with his love and joy. He may not change all the painful circumstances, but he will give you a song in your heart, and an inexplicable joy in the midst of the trials. God wants to satisfy you with his love and presence.

*17 May the favor of the Lord our God rest on us;*
*establish the work of our hands for us—*
*yes, establish the work of our hands.* (NLT: *Make our efforts successful!*)

There is so much wasted labor done outside of God's will and without his favor. Yet with God, our work can yield lasting results. Work is good. He gave us hands to use! And when he is in the middle of it, our efforts will be successful. Have you experienced the frustration of expending great effort on something that was not of God, only to see it fall apart? May God establish the work of your hands!

## MOSES AND JESUS

Jesus frequently referred to Moses as the author of the Pentateuch, and affirmed its importance. For Jews in Jesus' day, Moses was seen as the "gold standard" to which Jesus was compared: *We know that God spoke to Moses, but as for this fellow, we don't even know where he comes from"* (John 9:29).

## Moses in the Rest of the Bible

Perhaps the most striking tribute to Moses' enduring importance is his inclusion (along with Elijah) at the Transfiguration:

*About eight days after Jesus said this, he took Peter, John and James with him and went up onto a mountain to pray. As he was praying, the appearance of his face changed, and his clothes became as bright as a flash of lightning. Two men, Moses and Elijah, appeared in glorious splendor, talking with Jesus. They spoke about his departure, which he was about to bring to fulfillment at Jerusalem* (Luke 9:28-31).

Moses spent significant time in God's presence on Mount Sinai. God took him home atop Mount Nebo. And now he is on a mountain top again – with someone he obviously knew before he came to earth: The Son of God. Moses knew about the greatest miracle of history: the salvation available through Jesus' death on the cross. And Moses appears in glorious splendor! It sounds like Elijah had become his close buddy!

Jesus was quick to link himself with Moses, and point to the many places Moses wrote about him:

*If you believed Moses, you would believe me, for he wrote about me* (John 5:46).

Moses was part of the conversation the day of Jesus' resurrection, as they walked on the road to Emmaus, and Jesus explained what Moses had written:

*And beginning with Moses and all the Prophets, he explained to them what was said in all the Scriptures concerning himself. He said to them, "This is what I told you while I was still with you: Everything must be fulfilled that is written about me in the Law of Moses, the Prophets and the Psalms"* (Luke 24: 27, 44).

I would love to know Jesus' insights into the books of Moses!

## MOSES IN THE BOOK OF HEBREWS

Great as Moses was, the author of Hebrews makes a point of saying how infinitely greater Jesus was:

*[Jesus] was faithful to the one who appointed him, just as Moses was faithful in all God's house. Jesus has been found worthy of greater honor than Moses, just as the builder of a house has greater honor than the house itself* (Hebrews 3:2-3).

Only Abraham receives more space in the great faith "Hall of Fame," in Hebrews 11:23-29:

*By faith Moses' parents hid him for three months after he was born, because they saw he was no ordinary child, and they were not afraid of the king's edict.*

*By faith Moses, when he had grown up, refused to be known as the son of Pharaoh's daughter. He chose to be mistreated along with the people of God rather than to enjoy the fleeting pleasures of sin. He regarded disgrace for the sake of Christ as of greater value than the treasures of Egypt, because he was looking ahead to his reward. By faith he left Egypt, not fearing the king's anger; he persevered because he saw him who is invisible. By faith he kept the Passover and the application of blood, so that the destroyer of the firstborn would not touch the firstborn of Israel.*

*By faith the people passed through the Red Sea as on dry land; but when the Egyptians tried to do so, they were drowned.*

Moses is commended as a great hero of faith. With all the mighty deeds of faith he had performed, it is interesting that these are the ones noted:

- A decision he made as an adult to essentially renounce his adoption and distance himself from Pharaoh's daughter.

- The choice to identify with fellow Israelites and suffer with them, rejecting the sinful pleasures of the palace.
- Confidence that an eternal reward was worth more than temporary success.
- Moving on, leaving Egypt behind and not fearing Pharaoh's anger, as his faith cast out fear.
- Persevering through many trials because of his deep trust in God.
- He observed, and led all Israel in obeying, God's directions for the Passover, protecting their firstborn from the angel of death.

The final reference to Moses is in Revelation 15:2. We already looked at the song written there which he will sing with Jesus. Yes, Moses will be right there with Jesus when we get to heaven!

www.ingramcontent.com/pod-product-compliance
Lightning Source LLC
Chambersburg PA
CBHW070116100426
42744CB00010B/1846